RAISE YOUR
GLASS

HERBERT PRESS
Bloomsbury Publishing Plc
50 Bedford Square, London, WC1B 3DP, UK
Bloomsbury Publishing Ireland Limited
29 Earlsfort Terrace, Dublin 2, D02 AY28, Ireland

BLOOMSBURY, HERBERT PRESS and the Herbert Press logo
are trademarks of Bloomsbury Publishing Plc

First published in Great Britain in 2026

Copyright © Neile Cooper, 2026

Neile Cooper has asserted her right under the Copyright, Designs
and Patents Act, 1988, to be identified as Author of this work

All rights reserved. No part of this publication may be: i) reproduced or transmitted in any form, electronic or mechanical, including photocopying, recording or by means of any information storage or retrieval system without prior permission in writing from the publishers; or ii) used or reproduced in any way for the training, development or operation of artificial intelligence (AI) technologies, including generative AI technologies. The rights holders expressly reserve this publication from the text and data mining exception as per Article 4(3) of the Digital Single Market Directive (EU) 2019/790

Bloomsbury Publishing Plc does not have any control over, or responsibility for, any third-party websites referred to or in this book. All internet addresses given in this book were correct at the time of going to press. The author and publisher regret any inconvenience caused if addresses have changed or sites have ceased to exist, but can accept no responsibility for any such changes

A catalogue record for this book is available from the British Library
Library of Congress Cataloguing-in-Publication data has been applied for

ISBN: 978-1-78994-370-2; eBook: 978-1-78994-369-6

2 4 6 8 10 9 7 5 3 1

Typeset and designed by Tina Hobson
Printed and bound in China by C&C Offset Printing Co., Ltd.

To find out more about our authors and books visit
www.bloomsbury.com and sign up for our newsletters
For product safety related questions contact **productsafety@bloomsbury.com**

RAISE YOUR GLASS

28 Stained Glass Projects, Patterns, and Tutorials

NEILE COOPER

with Robert Giaquinta

Herbert Press
LONDON · OXFORD · NEW YORK · NEW DELHI · SYDNEY

CONTENTS

Introduction	6
A Guide to Using This Book	11
Workshop, Tools, and Supplies	15
Glass	19
Using Patterns	20
The Complete Stained Glass Process	22
MACKINTOSH ROSE SUNCATCHER	23
Using patterns and templates	23
Cutting glass	26
Grozing, grinding, and final glass preparation	32
Foiling and burnishing	35
Layout	39
Soldering	40
Edge finishing	46
Attaching hanging loops	50
Finishing up: Clean, patina, and polish	52
Painting glass	55
Carolyne Heppenstall	58
Charm Bracelet Suncatchers	60
HIGH FIVE	62
CHARM BRACELET SUNCATCHER VARIATIONS	70
BUDDIES	
FIREFLY	
LA LUNA	
EVENTIDE	
NILLA SKY	
SERPENTIS	
LUCKY CLOVER	
Chevonne Ariss	72
Time Capsules	74
Layout frames	75
RAY OF LIGHT	76
OCULUS	82
PALOMA	82
Masako Ozaki	84

4   RAISE YOUR GLASS

Designing from a Photo	85
RUSSIAN LAKE	88
EAST BAY	88
Laure Forêt	92
Mirror Glass	94
Working with Mirror Glass	95
WOODLAND MIRROR	98
MEADOW MIRROR	101
Window Toppers	104
ARCHIMEDES OWL	106
BIRDWING BUTTERFLY	111
HAVISHAM BAT	112
FOREST TREASURES MINI SHELVES	118
Poets Society Desk Set	126
PENCIL BOX	128
MOLESKINE SLIPCASE	133
Rebekah Marxen	138
Pendant Lights	140
HÉLÈNE	143
ST. JUDIE	148
MARA	151
Gertrude Dufeudedieu	154
Propagation Stations	156
ROOT DOWN	157
FRIENDSHIP	161
Building on a 3D Form	165
WEEPING WILLOW LAMPSHADE	170
Patterns	177
Glossary	202
Resources & Suppliers	206
Photo Credits	208

INTRODUCTION

Cheers to all who love to be surrounded by stained glass!

Whether found in a grand hotel foyer or in your local glass shop, stained glass fills interior spaces with magic. We bask in it when visiting museums and cathedrals. We're charmed when we discover it in an old drugstore or tavern. And, of course, we treasure it in our own homes and studios, which we've adorned with glass crafted by our favorite artists and our own hands.

I've got my go-to favorite glass places. I can hop on a train to Manhattan and head to The Metropolitan Museum of Art to revisit the "Autumn Landscape" waterfall window by Agnes Northrop and Tiffany Studios – a piece that's been there longer than I can remember – or experience "Garden Landscape," a brand-new installation from the same iconic artists. I'll day-trip to the Union Church of Pocantico to see the unique windows by Matisse and Chagall. I look forward to being surrounded by ALL the glass when

▲ My cabin
▼ Garden Landscape, Tiffany Studios

INTRODUCTION 7

▲ My cabin
◀ Gran Hotel

I head to Bullseye Glass and the Youghiogheny Glass factory for resupply. And I retreat daily to the sanctuary of my own stained glass cabin and studio.

Stained glass experiences are for sharing, of course, so I'm sure to drag my loved ones to glass destinations while traveling! Our group was absolutely stunned by Cosmovitral, a massive stained glass installation enclosing a botanical garden in Toluca, Mexico. I took the same group to lunch at the Gran Hotel on the Zócalo in Ciudad de México, just to see the lobby's lovely glass ceiling and ride the stained glass elevator. I'm the glass geek who seeks out these locations, but no one is ever disappointed by an amazing stained glass experience.

So I'm sure I'll find co-conspirators to join me on completing my bucket list: a trip to see Gaudi's masterpieces in Barcelona, or a venture to Glasgow for the lovely work of Charles Rennie Mackintosh and Margaret Macdonald Mackintosh (whose famous rose motif inspired the first project in this book). Maybe a visit to the l'Abbaye Royale de Fontevraud in France to see Pensées by Laure Forêt, one of this book's featured

▲ Cosmovitral by Leopoldo Flores
▶ Cosmovitral
◀ Pensées by Laure Forêt

artists (see pages 92–93). And, of course, my list includes more esoteric destinations, such as Ragland Park at the Kokomo Opalescent Glass factory, where you can pick through literal hills of glass for the perfect piece.

I'm proud to be part of a visit-worthy stained glass experience myself – Margie's Vestibule at the Maker's Mark Distillery in Loretto, Kentucky – which includes two floor-to-ceiling walls of my stained glass. Here, the glass isn't way above your head (as in a cathedral), it's right within reach, immersing you in vivid color. The room is a cozy space dedicated to Margie Samuels, the co-founder of the brand, and it houses Margie's exquisite pewter collection, as well as a portrait of her by Honora Jacob. I'm so honored to have my work featured at a destination that other glass lovers might seek out!

Every time I admire and enjoy stained glass artwork, I think of the artists who put so much time and care into their creations. I'm endlessly inspired by their, and your, work – those utterly unique pieces that could only be made by your hands, your hearts, and your minds.

So, here's a special toast to all of you artists and crafters who inhabit this world of glass! I hope your love for glass links you to a community of like-minded individuals – whether at your local glass shop, craft school, or online. I hope it always inspires you to seek out glass, near and far. Humbly, I hope that the projects, tutorials, and photos in this book will enable you to surround yourself with glass too!

Raise your glass!

◀ (top) Margie's Vestibule
◀ (bottom) Ragland Park

A GUIDE TO USING THIS BOOK

This book is intended for any stained glass crafter interested in the copper foil technique. The twenty-eight projects progress from the simplest (with the most detailed step-by-step instructions) to the more advanced, finishing with the Weeping Willow Lampshade – a three-dimensional lampshade of over 200 glass pieces.

At the back of the book, you'll find clear patterns for the projects (pages 177–201), a glossary of key terms used in the context of this book (pages 202–204), and some useful suppliers and resources (pages 206–207).

Scattered throughout, you'll find the glass and words of several featured artists, each of whom inspires me with their unique and masterful style. I hope they inspire you to continue exploring stained glass too!

▶ Firefly

Absolute newbie project

If you're new to stained glass, you can create the **Mackintosh Rose Suncatcher** (see page 23) as you read through The Complete Stained Glass Process chapter (pages 22–57). Each step for this simple project is discussed and illustrated in complete detail, alongside tips and troubleshooting.

Look for this rose icon to find the specific steps for the project within the more general information. All of the projects in this book follow this format, so once you've completed the Mackintosh Rose, you'll be ready to try the others!

> Begin on page 23

Breaking in
beginner projects

These basic projects have detailed tutorials and can be completed in an afternoon (or two): **High Five Suncatcher** (page 62) and **Ray of Light Capsule** (page 76).

Charm Bracelet Suncatcher Variations (page 70) – These projects contain some more difficult cuts but are small enough to help you practice technique before moving on to more complicated projects.

Oculus (page 82) and **Paloma** (page 82) – These contain more pieces and are edge finished with lead came.

▲ (left) Paloma
▲ (right) Ray of Light

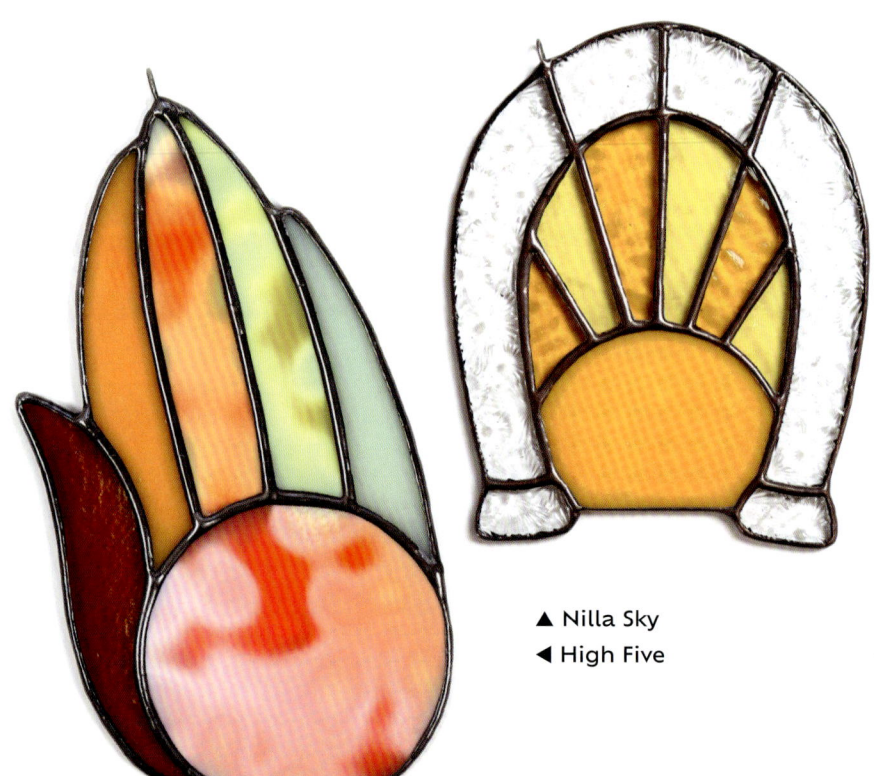

▲ Nilla Sky
◀ High Five

I have some experience, but how can I learn more about a specific skill?

If you already have some experience with the copper foil technique but would like some input on a particular part of the process, then you can brush up in The Complete Stained Glass Process chapter:

- Using patterns and templates (page 20)
- Cutting glass (page 26)
- Grozing, grinding, and final glass preparation (page 32)
- Foiling and burnishing (page 35)
- Laying out (page 39)
- Soldering (page 40)
- Edge finishing (page 46)
- Attaching hanging loops (page 50)
- Cleaning, patina, and polishing (page 52)
- Painting glass (page 55)

Cutting loose
advanced projects

These projects have step-by-step tutorials that focus on a particular more advanced skill, technique, or application:

Designing from a photo: **Russian Lake** (page 88)

Using mirror glass: **Woodland Mirror** (page 98)

Painting glass: **Meadow Mirror** (page 101)

Making a hinged box: **Poets Society Pencil Box** (page 128)

Pendant lights: **Hélène** (page 143), **St. Judie** (page 148), **Mara** (page 151)

Propagation stations: **Root Down** (page 157), **Friendship** (page 161)

Building on a 3D form: **Weeping Willow Lampshade** (page 170)

▲ (left) Russian Lake
▲ (right) Meadow Mirror
◀ Woodland Mirror

> How are "edge" and "perimeter" two different things?
>
> I use common words like **piece**, **project**, and **perimeter** in fairly precise ways, along with more specific jargon, such as **edge bead** and **butting up**. I've highlighted these words in bold in beginner projects, and they (and others) are defined in the glossary at the back of the book (see pages 202–204).

◀ (left) Weeping Willow Lampshade
◀ (right) Mara

A GUIDE TO USING THIS BOOK 13

Further techniques

I hope you'll check out my first book, *Kicking Glass*, which contains more detailed instruction on skills and provides tutorials for some techniques that aren't directly covered here:

- **Working with reclaimed windows**
- **Incorporating non-glass elements** (e.g. stones, shells, pressed flowers, and wings)
- **Jewelry techniques**
- **Making a stained glass hanging lamp** using a pre-made lampshade
- **Creating three-dimensional sculpture** by assembling flat panels
- **Designing patterns**

Am I going to get locked up for photocopying patterns or selling my creations?

You'll need a few copies of each pattern in order to create your projects, so I've included licensing information on page 177 so you won't have any issues asking a print shop employee to copy a page from a copyrighted book.

You are free to use the patterns in this book to create stained glass pieces for personal use, or for sale, with design credit given to Neile Cooper.

WORKSHOP, TOOLS, AND SUPPLIES

Stained glass requires a few specialized tools as well as a variety of more common household items. Here's a list of what you'll need for a complete workshop.

Basic workshop

Crafting stained glass is best when you work in a comfy, inspiring spot. Of course a dedicated workroom is ideal, but you can definitely use a shared space as long as it's easy to clean thoroughly (solder, lead, flux, and patina contain toxins).

Workspace

A suitable stained glass workspace is easy to create. You'll need these essentials:

- Sturdy and level table and chair at a comfortable height
- Multiple light sources: Space these apart to prevent shadows as you lean over your work
- Electrical outlets for the soldering iron and grinder
- Dedicated safe and sturdy glass storage area
- Chemical storage in closed containers away from kids and pets
- Fire-resistant work surface that can be pinned to (such as Homasote)

Safety essentials

Stained glass crafting is generally safe, but some safety considerations are required. Always have each of these items within reach in your workspace.

- Fire extinguisher
- Good ventilation, a fume extractor, and/or personal respiratory protection
- Eye protection
- Rubber gloves
- A soap designed specifically for lead removal (e.g. D-Lead)
- First aid kit, including adhesive bandages, burn cream, antiseptic wipes, antibacterial cream, and an emergency plan

Stained glass tools

Specialized stained glass tools are relatively inexpensive, durable, and easy to store. The grinder is the largest and most expensive tool, but it's essential.

- Pattern shears
- Craft knife
- Glass cutter: Pencil, pistol, or T-grip
- Running pliers
- Breaking/grozing pliers
- Electric glass grinder
- Fid
- Soldering iron (100 watt): I use the Hakko FX-601 with temperature control
- Rheostat temperature controller (if your iron lacks temperature control)
- Soldering iron stand with location for cleaning sponge

Consumable supplies

Each of the consumables that we'll use on these projects will be easy to find at any stained glass supplier.

- Stained glass
- Rubber cement
- Cutter oil
- Copper foil: A variety of widths and backing colors
- Solder: 60/40, 50/50, and lead-free
- Flux: I use liquid flux, but paste and gel varieties are available
- Chemical brush
- Mirror edge sealant
- Patina: Black and copper are most common
- Polish
- 10 gauge copper wire
- 16–20 gauge tinned copper wire for loops, hanging, and reinforcement
- U-channel lead came (3/16" or 5 mm size is a good all-purpose option)
- U-channel zinc came (we use 1/4" or 6 mm size in this book)

Cleaning supplies

Every step of stained glass requires attention to cleanliness: glass can be scratched by a neglected work surface, and solder and patina don't like dirty surfaces. Equip yourself properly to make that glass sparkle!

- Rags, paper towels, and sponges
- #0000 very fine steel wool
- Glass cleaner
- Dish soap or flux remover (e.g. Kwik-Clean)
- Bench brush and dustpan
- Sal ammoniac (or "tip tinner" soldering iron cleaner)

Hardware supplies

These supplies will all be easy to find at your local hardware store, if they're not already in your toolkit.

- Hanging supplies: Chain, cord, hooks, o-rings, and screws
- Pushpins
- Layout strips and layout frames
- Hammer
- Scissors
- Wire cutters
- Pliers
- Metal file
- Straightedges, rulers, and drafting triangles

Dream workshop upgrades

Once you've gathered all of the basic supplies, you'll be fully capable of making all of the projects in this book. Here are some less essential items that might make your crafting a bit easier, more efficient, or more ambitious!

- Silberschnitt running pliers: Great for difficult cuts
- Foil holder
- Fan out lead dykes
- Small chop saw: To easily cut zinc came
- Ring saw: A power saw that cuts glass
- Third hand tool: An adjustable clamp to hold items in place while soldering
- Light box
- Tablet for digital pattern design
- Large-format printer/scanner/copier
- Craft cutting machine for patterns (i.e. Cricut, Silhouette, ScanNCut)
- Adjustable-height workbench
- Slop sink
- Full room exhaust system
- Fancy mouth-blown glass: Lamberts, Fremont, Monarch, and English Antique Glass (treat yourself!)

WORKSHOP, TOOLS, AND SUPPLIES

GLASS

There are no rules for choosing glass. Use what you like and play with mixing and matching different types to create your own personal style. I've noted when a project calls for a specific type of glass; otherwise, use the glass that inspires you.

If possible, buy glass in person so you can see the quality, the details, and how different types might work together. Choose glass using lighting similar to that of the place where your project will live: with sunlight if for a window, with a bulb if for a lampshade, or front-lit if for an object such as a box or mirror. When examining a sheet of glass in the light, avoid holding it up over your face (or any other body part) in case it breaks!

Store your glass vertically, like books on a bookshelf, rather than stacked like plates. The weight of the stacked glass could cause the bottom pieces to crack.

Primary types

Primary types of glass include:

- **Cathedral:** Transparent glass, in a variety of colors and textures. Some textures obscure the view through the glass.
- **Opalescent:** Glass in varying opacity, from milky to completely opaque. These generally let some light through, but you cannot see through them clearly.
- **Streaky:** A mix of cathedral and opalescent, with areas of transparency and opacity, often with a "grain."
- **Antique:** Mouth-blown glass, beautiful and expensive, available in a variety of styles.

USING PATTERNS

Purchasing patterns is a great way to get started in stained glass. Good patterns from experienced designers will allow you to create long-lasting projects. You can find an extensive selection of *my own* well-designed patterns on neile.etsy.com.

Well-designed patterns:

- Are specifically constructed to work well in the medium of stained glass
- Only use cuts that are possible to make, even if they might require honed cutting skills
- Avoid creating stress spots that will crack over time
- Avoid "hinge points" – straight, unbroken lines extending across the design, which are structurally very weak (see illustrations)
- Have consistent line weights that are intended to be cut using pattern shears
- Use techniques and tricks that blend intricate designs with structural elements that ensure integrity and longevity
- Include instructions and locations for reinforcement materials, where necessary
- Include methods for hanging/installing the finished project that consider its weight and dimensions
- Provide images that show a finished version executed in glass, proving that the project has been tested (some patterns are even shown in multiple colorways that can provide inspiration)
- Are unique and do not violate the intellectual property and/or copyright of others
- Are created by an experienced human – AI-generated patterns will not necessarily consider proper design and construction principles

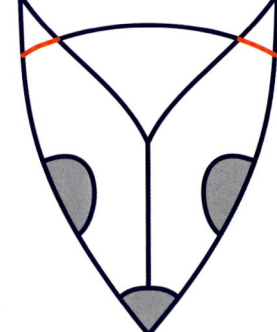
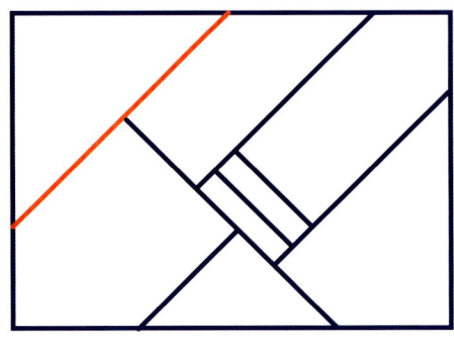

▶ Hinge points (highlighted in red) should be avoided

20 RAISE YOUR GLASS

Warning: altering patterns!

You can alter patterns (add/remove elements, enlarge/reduce, change overall shape or dimensions), but you must consider good design principles:

- If shrinking, some pieces may become too small to cut, or they may just get lost in solder.
- If enlarging, you must consider reinforcement and weight issues. You may also need to subdivide larger glass pieces into multiple shapes for strength.
- If altering size in either direction, you must consider that the line weight of the pattern will change and will no longer be matched to the width of your pattern shears.
- If changing elements, you must be sure that the piece will remain structurally sound (avoiding hinge points, for example).
- If cropping or otherwise altering overall dimensions, you need to consider overall design balance as well as structural integrity.

1
THE COMPLETE STAINED GLASS PROCESS

A detailed description of every step of the stained glass copper foil technique.

Using patterns and templates

Once you've chosen a beautiful, well-designed **pattern**, you're ready to begin constructing your stained glass **project**. Be sure that you have a few copies of your pattern: one will be cut into **templates** (individual shapes used to guide the **cutting** and **grinding** of glass pieces), another will be used for laying out the cut glass into position, and extras can be used for fixing mistakes.

Supplies

- Colored pencils or markers
- Regular scissors
- Craft knife
- Straightedge
- Pattern shears
- Rubber cement

Instructions

1 Before cutting the **pattern**, you might want to use colored pencils to provide information (i.e. color, **grain** direction) that will help you to position **templates** on glass (a).

MACKINTOSH ROSE SUNCATCHER

Difficulty: Beginner Tutorial

Supplies

- Basic tools listed in the Workshop, Tools, and Supplies section on pages 15–17
- 10" (25 cm) square sheet of glass for the main color and 2" (5 cm) square piece of glass for the secondary color. The two roses here use Wissmach Amber and White Iridized glass and Wissmach English Muffle Rose Red (a great beginner glass because it cuts so nicely)
- Copper foil, 7/32" size
- Flux
- 60/40 solder
- 20 gauge wire
- U-channel lead came, 3/16" size (optional)
- Patina (optional)
- Polish

Pattern

- Make 3 copies of the Mackintosh Rose Suncatcher **pattern** on page 177

> Next step: Templates (page 25)

THE COMPLETE STAINED GLASS PROCESS

2 Cut curved **perimeter** lines of the pattern with regular scissors. For long, straight perimeter lengths, cut using a craft knife and straightedge.

3 Cut **interior lines** of the pattern into templates using **pattern shears** (b), which are special scissors that remove a strip of paper that compensates for the copper foil thickness (c) between glass pieces in stained glass construction.

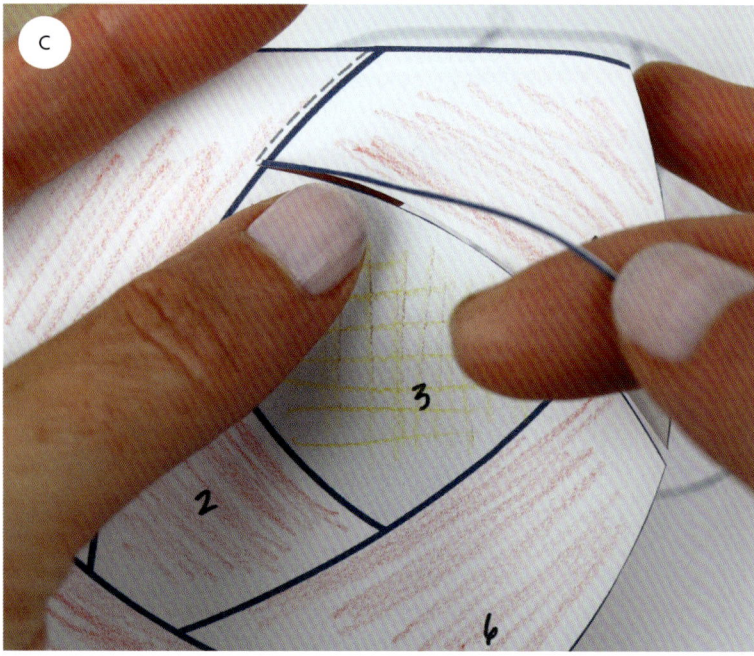

4 Position the cut templates on your carefully chosen glass sheets (d). You can cut down full-size glass sheets first, so that they're easier to work on.

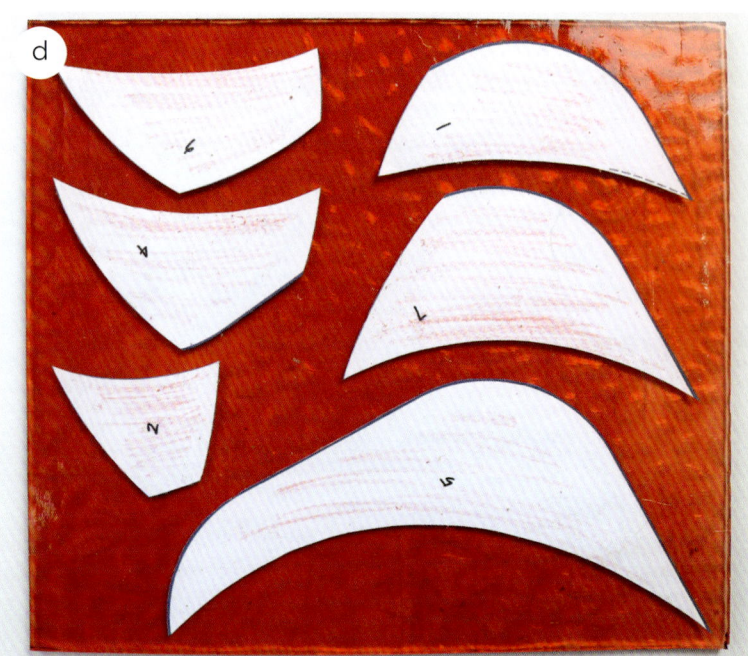

5 Glue your templates to the smooth side of clean glass using rubber cement (e). If you want the textured side on the **front** of the finished project, glue the template number-side down.

Considerations for template placement

Place all templates on the smoother side of the glass (the side that you will **score**). If you desire the texture to be on the front side of the project, place the template with its numbered side down (facing the smooth glass).

Consider how the grain of the glass should be oriented in your design. Do you want all grain to run horizontally, or maybe radially for a sunburst effect? Now is the time to position your templates properly.

When placing multiple templates on the same glass sheet, visualize how your cuts will run (you can even draw them in marker on the glass). You can't stop a score in the middle of a sheet, or make a sharp turn, so be sure that none of your cuts will force you to run through the center of another template to get to an edge.

Consider efficiency as your cutting skills progress. At first, you'll want more space between templates – maybe start with about 1/2" (1 cm) between them. Eventually you can conserve glass by moving them closer together.

 Templates
Mackintosh Rose

1 Cut paper **templates** from one **pattern**. Use regular scissors for the **perimeter** and **pattern shears** to cut the **interior lines**. If you're just starting out and don't yet own pattern shears, you can use regular scissors for smaller projects like this.

2 Select your glass and glue the templates to the glass.

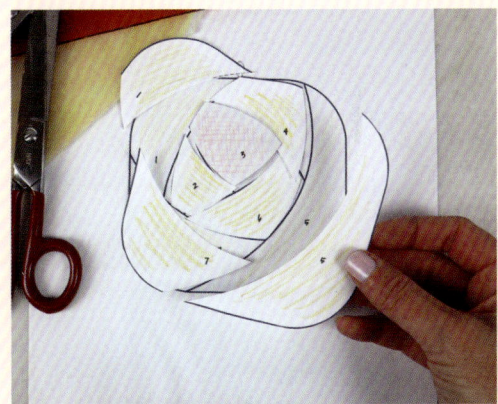

> Next step: Cutting (page 31)

Fussy cuts

Once, while making glass selections with a class, a student commented that in the quilting world when you find a perfect pattern on a piece of fabric, you "fussy cut" it, cutting into the interior of the fabric to isolate it. You'll want to "fussy cut" glass if the perfect color or a beautiful swirl deep is located in the interior of a sheet. Just cut the sheet down into multiple pieces so that you can access that element.

THE COMPLETE STAINED GLASS PROCESS   25

Cutting glass

Supplies

- Glass cutter (and cutter oil)
- Straightedge, about 1/8" (3 mm) thick, to guide glass cutter head
- Running pliers
- Grozing pliers
- Bench brush

Safety

Use eye protection

Terms

Scoring – using a glass cutter to create a scratch, or score, on the glass surface
Breaking – running the score so that the glass separates into two pieces
Cutting – the combined process of scoring and breaking the glass

Preparation

- Clean your work surface with a bench brush to avoid scratches to the glass surface.
- Apply templates to the smoother side of the glass (or draw outlines on the glass using a marker).

Tip

If you're new to stained glass, practice cutting a variety of shapes on cheap glass. Start with straight strips then progress to gentle curves and waves, and eventually try some geometric, multi-cut shapes.

Scoring dos and don'ts

Do:
- Understand that glass likes to break in a straight line, so use several cuts to create tighter curves.
- Take your time but keep the cutter moving.
- Listen and look – you should hear a zipping sound and see a consistent, faint white line on the glass.
- Be sure that you're aligning the cutter *wheel*, not the side of cutter *head*, with the template.

Don't:
- Roll the cutter back and forth.
- Rescore over a line.
- Start or stop a score anywhere but at a glass edge.
- Lift your cutter until the end of your score.
- Try to make an angle or super-tight curve in one cut.

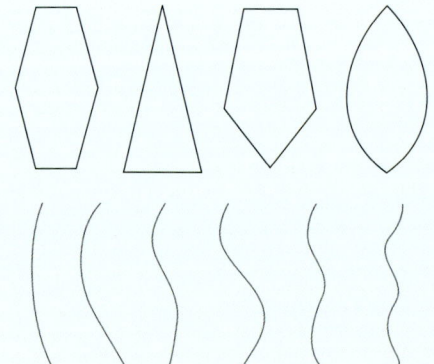

26 RAISE YOUR GLASS

BODY POSITION

- Scoring glass is easiest if you are standing.
- Position the glass at a height where you can apply some bodyweight in order to apply pressure, rather than using sheer muscle power.
- Rotate the glass so the score will be easy to reach from start to end, and so that you can keep your upper body over the entirety of the score.
- Visualize the whole score. You will push the cutter in the direction away from your body. Reposition yourself and the glass, if necessary.
- Hold the cutter in your dominant hand, using your preferred grip (a). Try out a few types of cutters and grips if you're just starting out.

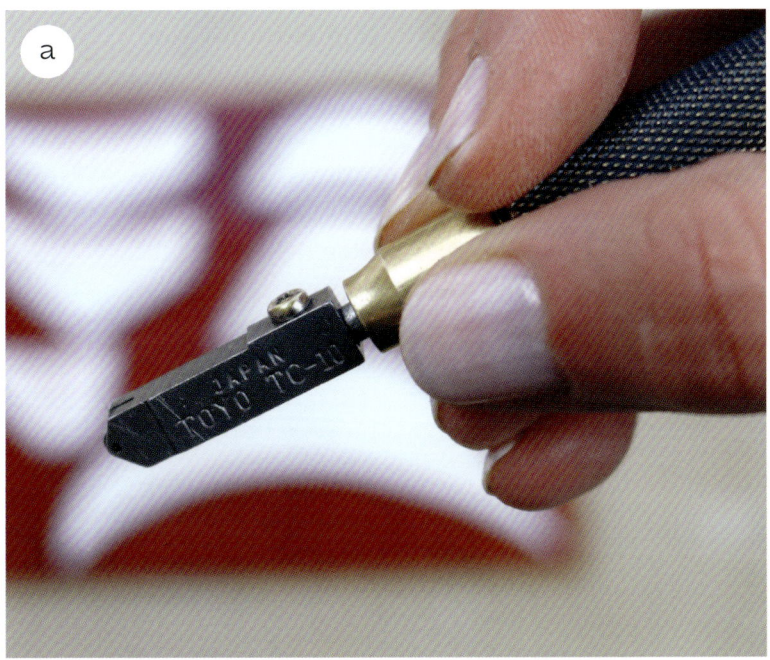

- Keep your elbow close to your torso and keep your upper body over the cutter as you move along, providing a constant pressure.
- If you need extra pressure, you can use your non-dominant hand to assist.
- Hold the cutter perpendicular to the glass surface (not leaning left or right) for the entire score.

EXECUTING THE SCORE

- Be sure that you are scoring the less textured side of the glass (b).
- Begin your score at the edge of the glass closest to your body. Do not start a score in the interior of a glass sheet.
- Continue your score to an edge. Never stop in the middle of a sheet. Stop just before the cutter would roll off the glass onto the work surface.

- Maintain constant, moderate pressure and speed through the score. You should hear a bit of a "zip." If there's no sound, press more firmly; if there's a crunch, press more lightly.

Cutter oil

Most glass cutters have a reservoir that automatically dispenses cutter oil. I find that using this dispenser usually creates a mess. Instead, I pour a small amount of cutting oil into a jar with a piece of fabric at the bottom. As I work I roll the cutter wheel on this oiled fabric every few cuts. When not in use, my cutters live in this jar.

Breaking glass

USING YOUR HANDS

The advantage of using your hands to **break** glass is that it is efficient because it doesn't require you to pick up a tool. The disadvantage is that it is less useful for smaller pieces of glass.

- Hold the glass horizontally, slightly above your work surface.
- Position your hands as if you were holding ski poles. Grip the glass so that the bottom face rests upon your coiled pointer fingers, with your thumbs on the top face, close together, just on opposite sides of the score line.
- Rotate your wrists so that your thumbs move away from each other and slightly downward. Your index fingers provide a slight upward pressure.
- The glass should break smoothly along your score. If it doesn't, try another method (see opposite).

TAPPING

An efficient method for running a score is tapping with the ball end of the glass cutter that's already in your hand. It works best on larger sections of glass.

- Gently tap the underside of the glass, directly under the end of the score line.
- Continue this light, repetitive tap until you hear or see the break begin to run, then follow the run with your tapping motion.
- Be careful with the unsupported side of the glass sheet – the break might quickly run along the score, and the glass will drop to your work surface.

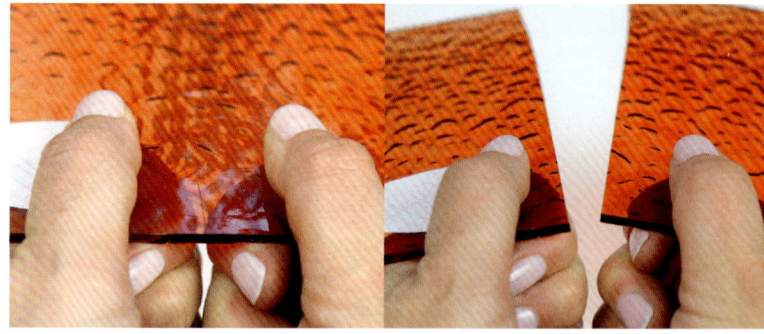

▲ Hand position for running score. Turn your wrists so that your thumbs rotate outward

USING RUNNING PLIERS

Using running pliers is best for longer, straighter runs on larger sheets of glass. The disadvantages are that it involves lots of picking up and putting down, and it is less useful on smaller glass pieces.

- Hold the pliers in your dominant hand, with the guide line on the jaw facing up.
- Use your other hand to hold the glass slightly above your work surface.
- Place the glass in the jaw so that the score aligns with the guide line on the pliers.
- Give a few gentle squeezes until you hear a "tick" that indicates the start of the running break, then give another few squeezes to continue the run (c).
- For a long score on a larger sheet of glass, you can use the pliers on the other end of the score so that the breaks meet up in the middle of the score.
- Keep the glass low to your work surface so that you're not depending on the pliers to hold the glass from dropping.

USING BREAKING/GROZING PLIERS

Using breaking/grozing pliers is efficient because you can run and **groze** without swapping tools. This is especially useful on harder cuts that require some cleanup. The disadvantage is that they are harder to use with larger sheets of glass.

- Hold the glass in your non-dominant hand, near the score line, with your thumb on the top face of the glass.
- Hold the pliers in your dominant hand with the flat-sided jaw on top.
- Grab the glass just beside the score line with the tip of the pliers (d).

- Gently pull outward and downward until you hear the "tick" that indicates the start of the running break.
- Continue to gently pull until the score runs completely.

Cutting Considerations

CUTTING STRAIGHT LINES

When a project contains straight lines (such as the Ray of Light capsule on page 76 and the Poets Society Desk Set on page 126), it's important to cut your glass perfectly straight. Three-dimensional constructions, hinged projects, and zinc came edge finishing usually require some precise straight cuts. The straighter your cuts, the easier the rest of the project will come together.

- Cut your **template** with a straightedge and craft knife, rather than scissors, or use a thin marker and straightedge to mark the line on the glass.
- Score glass using an appropriate straightedge. You'll need something at least 1/8" (3 mm) thick, tall enough that the cutter *head* – not the cutter *wheel* – runs flush along the straightedge (e). Apply some rubbery tape or cork to the back of the straightedge to prevent slippage.

▲ Use a straightedge tall enough to guide the head of the cutter

THE COMPLETE STAINED GLASS PROCESS 29

First, place the cutter wheel into position onto the glass on the line that you will score, then slide the straightedge so that it butts up against the cutter head. Finally, align the straightedge parallel lengthwise to the line that you will score, hold firmly in place, and make your score.

▲ Straightedge aligned to cutter head

▲ Straightedge parallel to cut line

CUTTING CURVES

Glass likes to break in straight lines and gentle curves, so in order to create tighter curves, you must coax it in a series of steps. Don't try forcing it to make a tight curve in one cut. Visualize (or draw) difficult shapes as a series of cuts, slowly progressing toward the final shape. Practice complex cuts on scrap glass to get a feel for how to coax out the shapes below.

Convex cuts

A long convex curve, such as the circumference of a semi-circle, can be broken up into several steps, so that each cut deals only with a portion of the circumference, and your glass cutter doesn't need to turn too much on any single cut (h). You'll often be left with small bumps of glass where your cuts intersected; nip and scrape these away with the curved side of your grozing pliers.

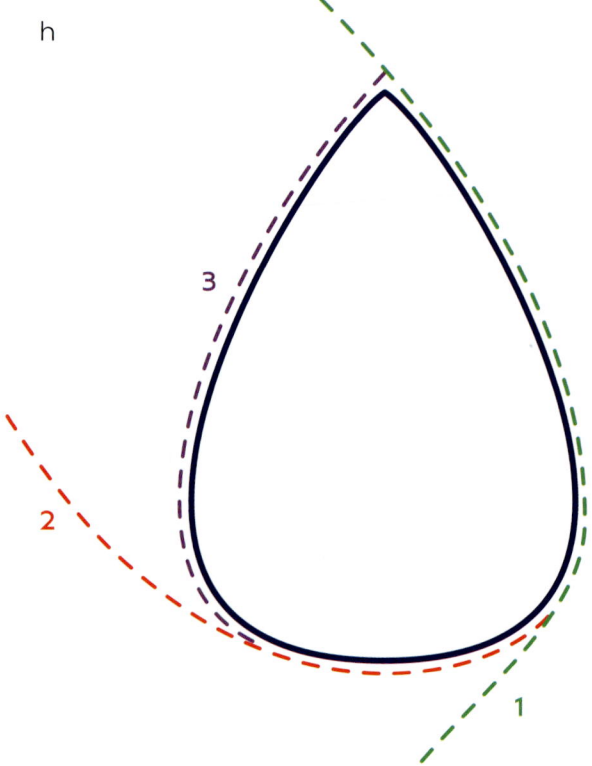

▲ Use a series of cuts for convex curves

30 RAISE YOUR GLASS

Concave cuts

Concave curves – such as the inside of a crescent – tend to be more difficult than convex curves. Start these shapes with a shallow cut across the ridges, then remove glass in the curved interior with a series of small, shallow cuts (alternating between scoring and breaking each time) (i).

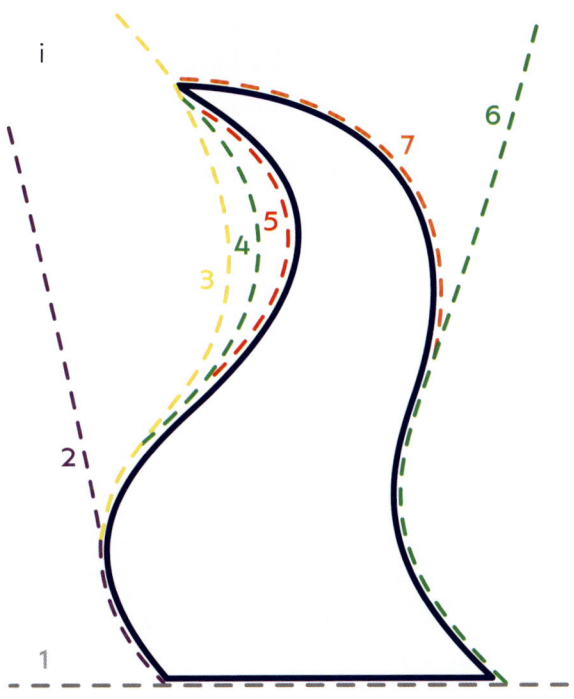

▲ Use a series of cuts for concave curves. For cut 7, run the break from the bottom edge, away from the narrow point

Cutting
Mackintosh Rose

3 Cut all glass **pieces**. If you make any mistakes, cut new templates from your extra patterns, and recut the glass!

> Next step: Grinding (page 33)

Troubleshooting cutting problems

- Make sure the glass is clean. Dust and debris can interfere with making a good score line.
- Reapply cutter oil to the cutter wheel.
- Try a lighter touch; pressing too hard can cause a "chippy" score line that will run haywire.
- Try warming up the glass, either under an incandescent light or with a heating pad.
- Check that the cutter wheel is not seized and is able to roll freely.

Grozing, grinding, and final glass preparation

To prepare the cut glass for foiling, you'll need to create smooth, flat edges by grozing and grinding. Careful glass cutting will reduce, but not eliminate, time spent at the grinder.

Tools

- Electric glass grinder
- Grozing pliers

Safety

Always use eye protection for these steps

USING GROZING PLIERS

Use grozing pliers to:
- Pinch away small bits of glass that don't conform to your template
- Remove little triangles of glass between scores when creating a convex curve
- Scrape jagged, non-perpendicular breaks with the curved jaw of the pliers
- Save time, effort, and grinder bit longevity by cleaning up edges before moving to the grinder

USING A GRINDER

Use a grinder to create a clean, lightly textured surface that's flush with the template.

- Be sure that your grinder tray contains water to lubricate the bit and prevent glass dust, and that the grinder bit is free to spin.
- Turn on the grinder power.
- Practice your touch with scrap glass to be sure that you can get a good grind.
- Place a glass piece on the grinder tray and use the fingertips of both hands to hold it securely, while gently pushing it up to the grinder bit.
- Work at a speed that gives the grinder time to dull the glass edge and conform it to the template, without creating a divot that digs into the glass.
- If the glass piece bounces off the bit, press more firmly.
- Work around the full perimeter of the piece so the entire edge is smooth.
- Wipe off the piece with a rag and check that the edge is fully ground.

▲ Good grind on left side, no grind on right

Signs of a good grind

- The edge of the ground piece looks textured, dull, and slightly sand-blasted (not shiny).
- The edge is perfectly perpendicular to the glass face.
- The edge of the paper template perfectly matches the edge of the glass.

Why am I working so hard?

- If you have good cuts but still use lots of effort, your grinder bit might be dull.
- If you always need to do a lot of grinding, you may need to work on your cutting skills so that you're creating nice cuts that mirror the template shape.

Grinding
Mackintosh Rose

4 Grind, clean, dry, and number all pieces.

> Next step: Foiling (page 37)

Final glass preparation

The final prep involves removing templates, checking for fit and fine-tuning.

Supplies

- Glass cleaner
- Towels and rags

Instructions

- Lay out the uncut copy of the pattern upon a work surface that can be pinned into. If there are any straight edges on the perimeter, tack down layout strips upon those lines.
- Pick up a ground piece, mentally take note of the number and orientation of the paper template, then peel it off.

THE COMPLETE STAINED GLASS PROCESS

- Use a rag and glass cleaner to remove all glue and grinder sludge, then dry the piece completely.
- Place the piece in its position on the pattern and write the number on it with a marker (a).

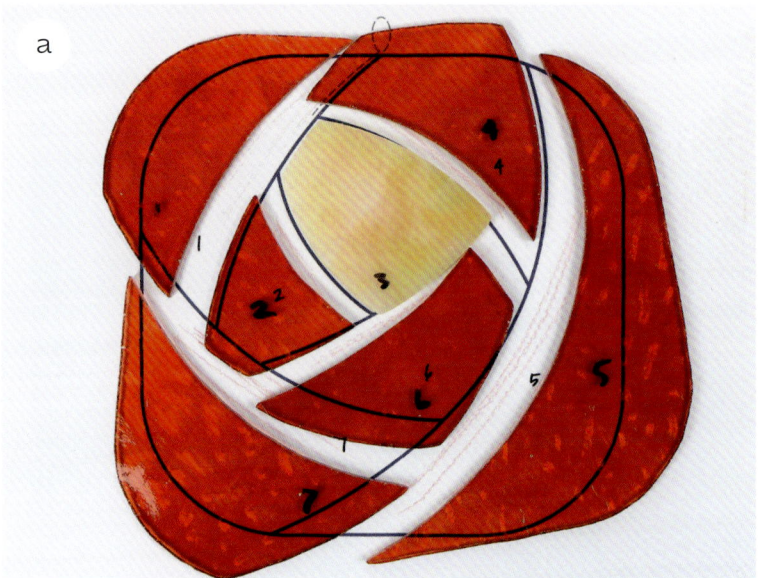

a

- Check the piece for proper fit on the pattern. Adjacent pieces should touch each other loosely all along their common edges. Foil will fill in the slight gap.
- If a piece has a bump that resists proper fit, bring it back to the grinder for fine-tuning, then clean and dry it again (b).

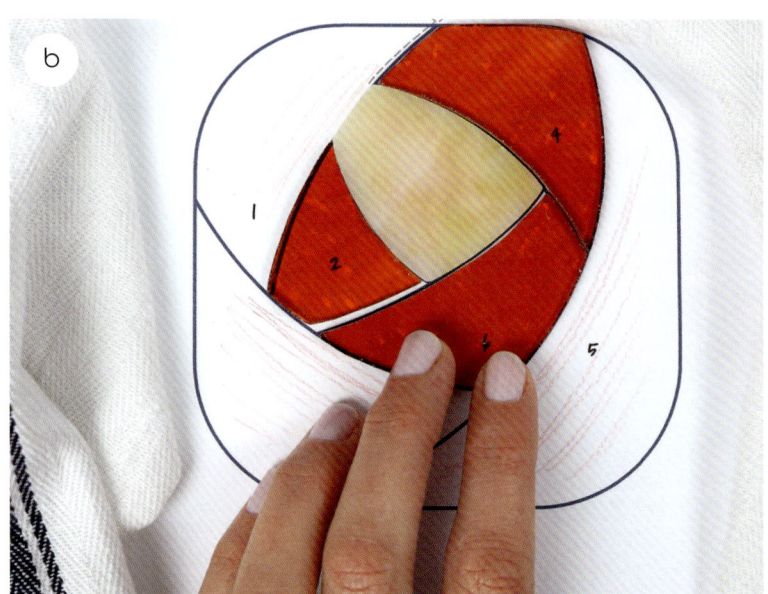

b

- Repeat this until all pieces are neatly laid out upon the pattern. The overall dimensions might shrink slightly (especially for a larger piece), but the foil will bring it back to proper size.
- Any fit problems now will be very difficult to correct later, so don't move forward until you work them out.
- Double-check that all of your pieces are numbered and get ready to foil!

Foiling

Copper foil, a thin strip of copper with an adhesive backing, will be wrapped around each glass piece. The copper facilitates the flow of solder to create a strong channel that holds the glass pieces in place. The solder does not stick to the glass, nor does the foil adhesive contribute to holding the final project together.

Foil is available in a variety of widths (5/32", 3/16", 7/32", 1/4"). Have several widths on hand if you plan to use thicker, heavily textured, or thinner glass. You'll most frequently use 7/32", especially if you're new to the craft.

You can purchase copper foil with a choice of three **backing colors** – copper, black, or silver – that match your final **patina** options. Be sure to match the foil backing with your vision for the finished piece. This step is unnecessary with opaque glass, but with any transparent glass a color mismatch will be glaring!

Once unspooled and handled, copper foil will begin to **oxidize** and tarnish, so do not foil unless you will be able to solder within a few days. Foil is also super finicky about sticking to dirty glass, so remember to include time for cleaning and drying all pieces between your grinding and foiling steps.

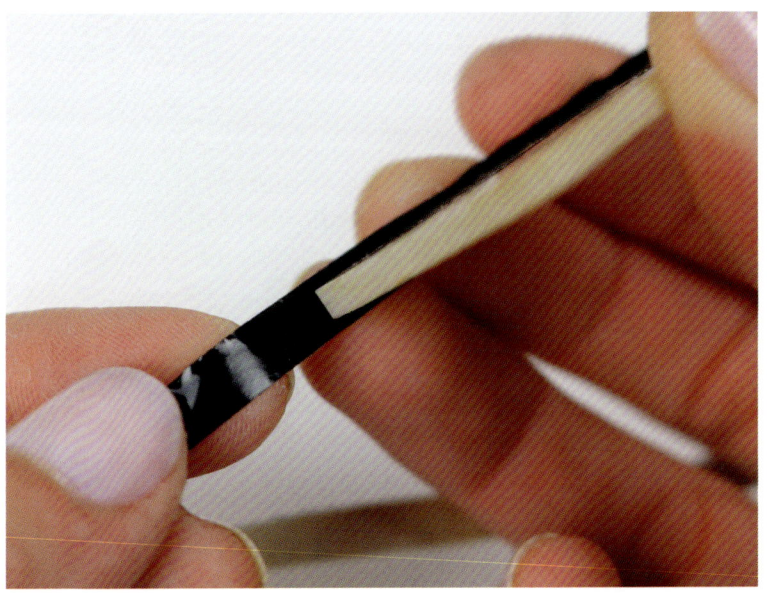

▲ Foil with black backing

THE COMPLETE STAINED GLASS PROCESS **35**

▲ Copper-backed foil is visible before copper patina is applied

Tools

- Copper foil: 7/32" (5.5 mm) and other widths
- Fid
- Scissors

Applying foil

- Unroll about an arm's length of foil from the spool. Set the spool on your work surface or use a foil dispenser.
- Peel back an inch or two (a few centimeters) of the protective backing from the end of the foil, exposing the sticky side.
- Pick up a glass piece and consider whether any part of it will be exposed on the **perimeter** of the project. If so, be sure to apply the **leading end** of the foil in a spot that will not be on the perimeter. If the piece is an **interior piece**, you can start the foil anywhere.
- Apply the adhesive side of the foil to the ground **edge** of the glass piece. Be sure that the foil is centered so that the same width of foil will fold over onto each **face** of the glass. Press the end of the foil firmly to the glass (a).

a

- Continue centering the foil along the edge of the glass and firmly pressing it to the edge, an inch or so (2–3 cm) at a time (b).

b

- When you complete the trip around the edge, overlap about 1/4" (6 mm) past the leading end of the foil and neatly cut with scissors.
- Carefully press the trailing end of the foil so that it overlaps the leading end; the overhangs of each end should align perfectly, creating one smooth foil line.
- Burnish the foil to the edge by rubbing with a fid, so that the foil adheres to all contours of the glass piece (c).

⊗ Fold the foil overhangs over onto the glass faces, pinching them carefully with your fingers (d). At sharp angles where the foil folds onto itself, visualize wrapping a gift or creating a "hospital corner" on a bedsheet, and carefully make the folds so that only the copper side (not the adhesive side) is exposed.

⊗ Burnish the overhanging foil onto both glass faces so that it conforms to the texture of the glass (e).

⊗ If the edges of the foil tear when applying to tight concave curves, patch the tear with a small piece of foil applied perpendicularly and cut with a craft knife (f, g).

Foiling
Mackintosh Rose

5 Foil the glass, matching the foil backing with your intended **patina** color. **Burnish** all pieces.

> Next step: Layout (page 39)

THE COMPLETE STAINED GLASS PROCESS 37

Where to start the foil

On a suncatcher where you'll finish the **perimeter** with an **edge bead**, you'll want to avoid having foil overlaps on that outside edge. Be sure that the overlaps on perimeter pieces are positioned in an interior line.

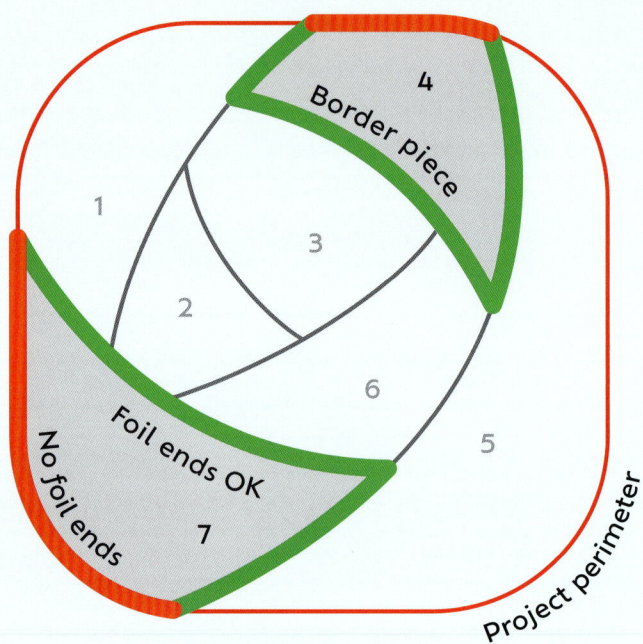

For a three-dimensional project, such as the Pencil Box (see page 128), be sure to position overlaps in less noticeable locations as well. For the lid of the box, position the overlaps on the **hinge** edge rather than the front edge. For the walls, hide the overlaps on the bottom edges of the pieces, not on the top edges where the lid will rest, because you'll want a smooth, perfect edge bead in those visible spots.

Best practice for foiling

- Keep a variety of foil widths at hand so that you can match the foil to the glass thickness, keeping the foil overhang consistent across all your pieces.
- Experiment with the different foil widths. You can control the weight of the final solder lines by controlling foil width. In my Archimedes Owl topper (see page 106), I use narrower foil for the pieces that make up the face, providing a delicate contrast to the heavier lines that outline the wings.
- It's OK to pull misaligned foil off an edge and recenter it. The adhesive may not stick as well on the second try, but once you burnish the piece, the foil should stay in place long enough to solder it.
- Watch for breaks and tears in the foil overhangs as you burnish. Solder will not span these breaks, and will in fact make the break even more noticeable. Refoil or patch that spot.
- If the overlapping foil ends are not perfectly aligned, trim neatly with a craft knife.

A sloppy overhang

Trim the overhang with a craft knife

Layout

When the glass pieces have been cut and foiled, you'll lay them out upon the pattern to prepare for soldering. You can purchase layout frames in a variety of geometric shapes to make this stage easier – they are used in several projects in this book (see Ray of Light, page 76, Oculus, page 82, and Paloma, page 82).

Tools

- Pushpins, horseshoe nails, or masking tape
- Straightedges or layout strips
- Layout frames

Instructions

- Lay the foiled glass pieces in position on top of the paper pattern.
- Hold the pieces snugly in place with pushpins, or use pieces of masking tape to hold them together.
- For straight perimeters, tack down straightedges such as Morton layout strips.
- For a round or oval perimeter, you can use a layout frame.
- Use whatever combination of methods works best for the project.

▲ Layout frames and Morton layout strips

Layout
Mackintosh Rose

6 Lay out the pieces upon the pattern and pin in place.

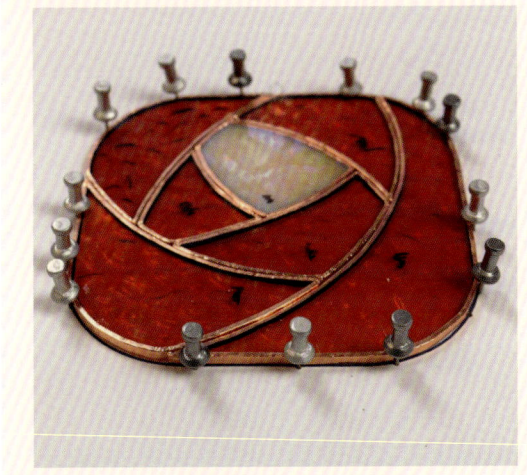

> Next step: Soldering (page 43)

THE COMPLETE STAINED GLASS PROCESS 39

Soldering

There are three types of solder that you might use for your stained glass projects:

60/40 solder will probably be your go-to solder, as it flows easily and has a nice shiny appearance. It melts at a lower temperature (375°F/190°C) than 50/50 and lead-free solder.

50/50 solder is useful for a first coat when working on three-dimensional constructions (such as the pendant lights (see pages 140–153), and Weeping Willow Lampshade (see page 170). It melts at a higher temperature (418°F/214°C) than 60/40, so it won't melt and drip through when you use 60/40 at a lower temperature to create your final neat bead.

Lead-free solder also requires a higher temperature to melt (422°F/217°C). You must use lead-free when crafting items that will be handled, such as the Poets Society Desk Set (see page 126), and for jewelry or wearable items. Consider using this for any item that might be kept within reach of children.

Tools

- Soldering iron
- 60/40 solder
- Flux: This cleans and prepares copper foil to accept solder
- Flux brush: You can create a perfect flux brush by trimming the bristles of a chemical brush to about 1/2" (1 cm) so that it doesn't carry too much flux
- Soldering stand
- Damp sponge for cleaning
- Sal ammoniac block

Safety

The soldering iron and soldering process are safe when handled properly but are among the more hazardous aspects of stained glass, so always pay proper attention to safety:

◇ Use an exhaust ventilation system or a respirator to protect from fumes released by soldering.
◇ Wear gloves to protect your hands from chemicals in flux and lead in solder.
◇ Wear protective clothing that covers your skin, including footwear.
◇ Never leave your soldering iron unattended, even when preheating.
◇ Be conscious of the soldering iron power cord. Be sure that it can move freely without knocking into your flux bottle or other work surface items.
◇ Solder only on a fire-resistant surface, such as Homasote fiberboard.
◇ Don't blindly reach for your soldering iron in a hurry. You never want to touch any part of the iron other than the insulated grip.

How to apply solder

① First, use a flux brush to apply flux to the exposed copper foil on the top surface of your laid-out project (a). All copper must have a light coat of flux, but you don't need more than that.
① Heat your iron to 410°F/210°C. Adjust this temperature as you solder – if you solder slowly, you may want to lower it; if you move quickly, you can raise it.
① Hold the solder spool in your non-dominant hand, and straighten out about 8" (20 cm) of solder.
① Hold the soldering iron in your dominant hand.
① Place the soldering iron tip to the fluxed copper foil, then feed the solder wire where the soldering iron meets the copper (b, c).

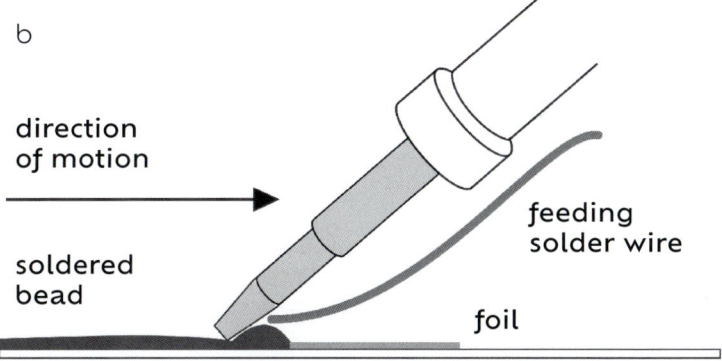
b

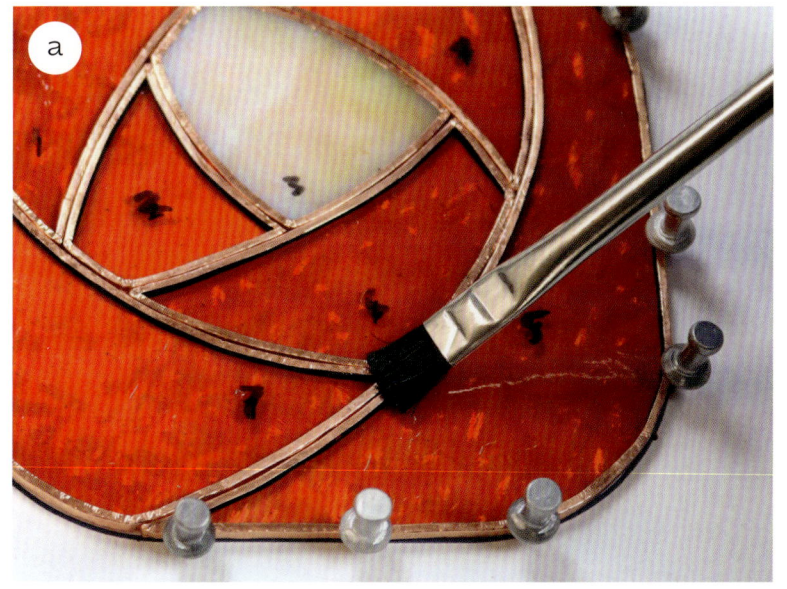

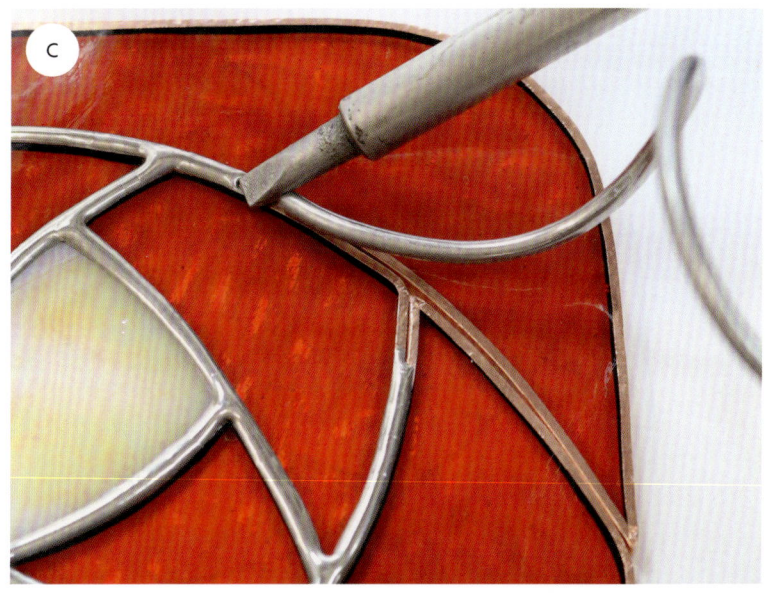

- As the solder melts and forms a bead, move the soldering iron and solder along the copper foil, slowly feeding more solder toward the tip as it melts, leaving behind a continuous line of solder.
- Wipe your soldering iron tip on your damp cleaning sponge every few lines. The tip should always have a thin coating of clean, shiny solder.
- Use enough solder to create a symmetrical, curved bead above the **face** of the glass (d, e).

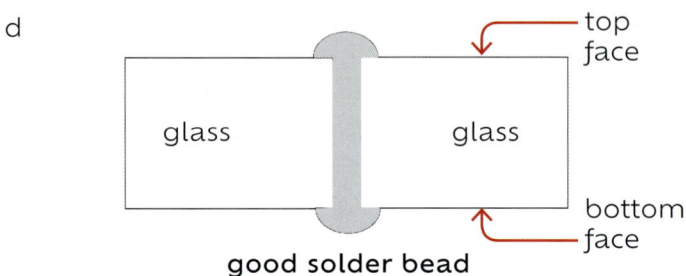

good solder bead

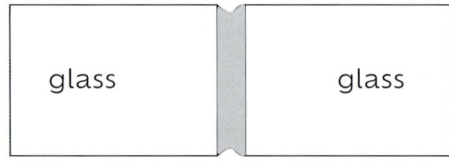

too little solder

Cross-section of solder joints
(gap between pieces is exaggerated)

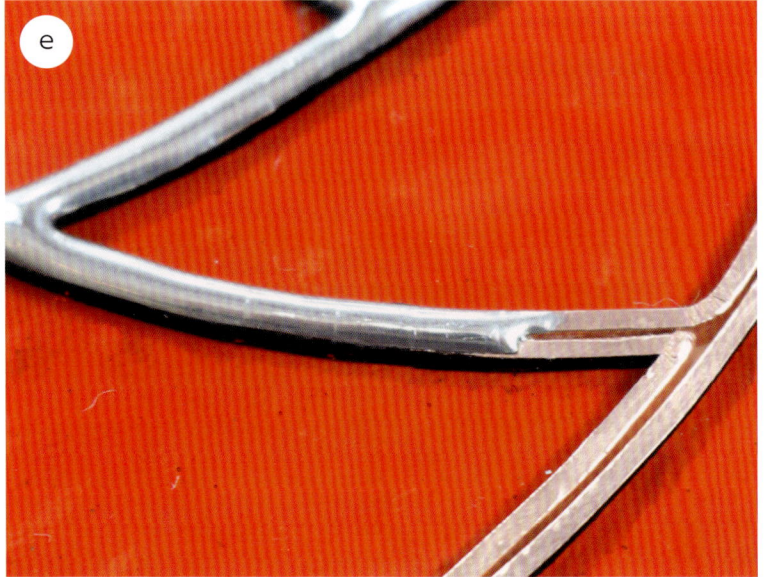

- When you reach a junction of multiple lines, continue soldering smoothly in one of the directions for an inch or two (a few centimeters). Then return to the junction and start soldering along the other line, blending the new solder into the previous line.

Soldering troubleshooting

If your soldering is less than perfect, here are a few things that might be causing you trouble:

- You might be using the wrong solder. Never use plumbing solder (acid-core or flux-core).
- You may have applied too much flux if you're getting sputtering, bubbling, and pitted solder lines. Wipe off any excess.
- Solder may seep down through the gap between glass pieces if that portion of the project has become too hot. Allow it to cool a little before continuing to work in that area.
- Your iron temperature might be wrong. Raising the temperature can help the solder to flow better, while lowering the temperature can prevent **drip-through**.
- Your soldering iron tip might be dirty. Remember to wipe it on the damp sponge occasionally as you work. Keep your soldering iron in top shape by rubbing the hot tip on a sal ammoniac block at the start and end of a soldering day.
- Glass can crack from excessive heat, so don't focus for too long on one spot before letting it cool down.

The path to perfection

It takes a ton of practice to create beautiful solder lines! Don't let it get you down if you're sloppy at first. With practice, you'll develop instincts with the materials and your solder lines will shine.

- If there are any ripples, indentations, bumps, or other irregularities, you can use the iron to re-melt that section, adding or removing solder, if necessary.
- You can remove excess solder by using your soldering iron tip to draw molten solder away from the line and allowing it to drop onto your work surface.

 **Soldering**
Mackintosh Rose

7 Flux the front of the project.

8 Tack solder (connect all pieces using little dabs of solder) the entire front so that all pieces are connected.

9 Remove pushpins or layout strips so that you can move the project around freely.

10 Run a nice **bead** of solder on the interior solder lines. Leave the project's **perimeter** unsoldered until later. If you plan on finishing with **lead came**, end your **interior lines** just short of the perimeter of the project so that the came will fit.

11 For locations where you will embed hanging loops (indicated on the pattern by dashed lines), leave about 1/2" (1 cm) unsoldered.

12 Flip the project, flux, then solder the back interior lines, taking care not to linger too long in any one area, which could overheat the solder and create **drip-through**.

> Next step: Edge soldering (page 47)

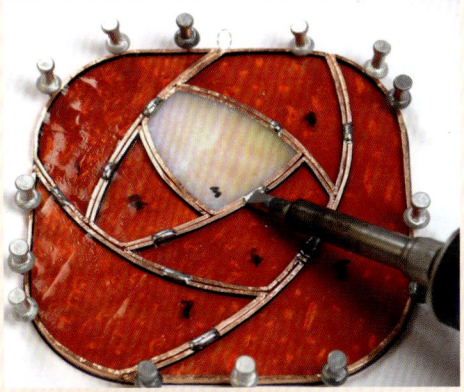
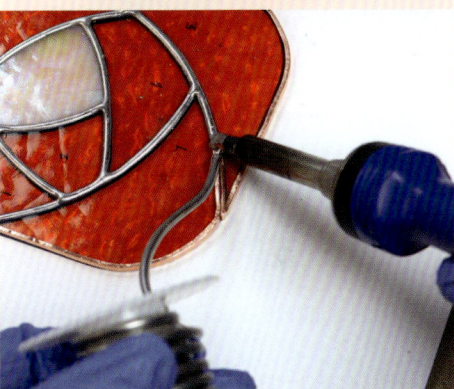
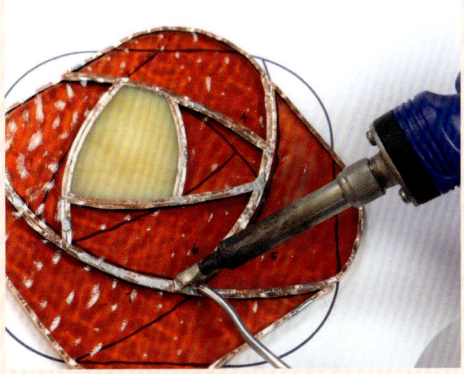

THE COMPLETE STAINED GLASS PROCESS

Edge finishing

There are three common options for finishing the **perimeter** of a project:

- **Edge beading with solder on foil:** The perimeter is foiled and soldered like the interior lines, but a strong, raised solder bead is formed. This is appropriate for small- and medium-sized suncatchers, panels, and complex edge design profiles. This will accept all patina colors and is used in the Charm Bracelet suncatcher variations (page 70) and the Poets Society Desk Set (page 126), for example.

- **U-channel lead came:** Flexible lead is cut and pressed along the perimeter, then soldered to the interior lines. Lead came is available in many sizes; for our projects we will use 3/16". This is appropriate for small and medium sized suncatchers, panels with a more uniform profile (like the capsule projects), and projects that will not be handled (as lead is toxic). It will accept black patina but will not accept copper patina. It is used in the following projects: Ray of Light (page 76), Oculus (page 82), Paloma (page 82), and Havisham Bat (page 112).

- **Rigid U-channel zinc came:** Zinc is cut into lengths and anchored with solder to interior lines. It comes in many sizes. Copper and brass came options are available as well. This is appropriate for straight perimeters and for larger projects that need added strength. Zinc came doesn't love patina, though you can achieve a black appearance by using copper patina on zinc came. Substitute copper came if using copper patina on a project. Zinc came is used in the window toppers: Archimedes, Birdwing, and Havisham (pages 104–117).

EDGE BEAD SOLDERING

Safety

Put on protective gloves and clothing. You'll be holding the project as you solder, and it's possible that solder may drip toward your hands and body.

Instructions

- Flux all foil on the **perimeter**, including the **edge** and the foil overhangs on the front and back.
- Preheat your iron to 375°F/190°C (a little cooler than regular soldering).
- **Tin** all of the foil on the front and back faces: apply just a thin layer of solder to the foil so that it becomes silver colored. You don't need to create a raised **bead** and can move quickly.

Tinning the overhangs

46 RAISE YOUR GLASS

- Position the project perpendicular to your work surface, supporting it near the top with your non-dominant hand and resting the bottom on your work surface. The key here is applying solder to the edge that is facing upward and rotating the project as you go – always soldering the edge that is horizontally level.
- Unspool and position a length of solder so that it is near the top edge of your project.
- Hold your soldering iron in your dominant hand and melt about 1/2" (1 cm) of solder onto the edge. This dab of solder should form a raised, rounded **bead** atop the foil, and it should wrap around on to the foil overhangs, creating a smooth cap.
- Let this bead solidify for a second or two, then melt another dab of solder onto the edge, and apply heat so that it melts into the previous dab.
- Reposition the project as you move along, rotating it as necessary to keep the working area level.
- When you arrive at a junction where an interior line meets the perimeter, blend the edge bead into the interior solder line neatly. Don't allow these areas to get too hot – your solder might run off if you do.
- Reposition the project and repeat this process around the entire perimeter, adding and connecting dabs of solder to form a smooth bead. Skip over any areas where hanging loops will be attached.

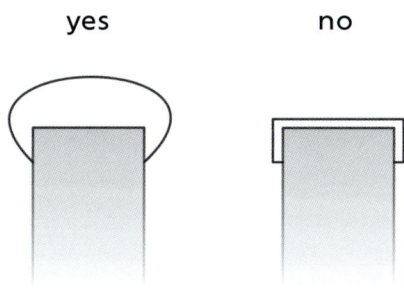

Proper edge bead profile

Tips for edge soldering

- If your edge bead solder tends to drip off the edge, turn down the heat on your iron a little.
- Edge beads do not provide much strength, so do not depend on them to bear weight. Do not attach hanging loops or ornamentation to an edge bead alone – be sure to provide strength by embedding these into an interior line.
- Edge beads can be rather delicate, so be careful when cleaning, polishing, and handling the perimeter of a finished project.

Edge soldering
Mackintosh Rose

13 Finish the **perimeter** of the project with a neat, strong **edge bead**. If you plan on finishing with **U-channel lead came**, skip this step.

> Next step: Lead came finish (page 49)

THE COMPLETE STAINED GLASS PROCESS 47

U-CHANNEL LEAD CAME

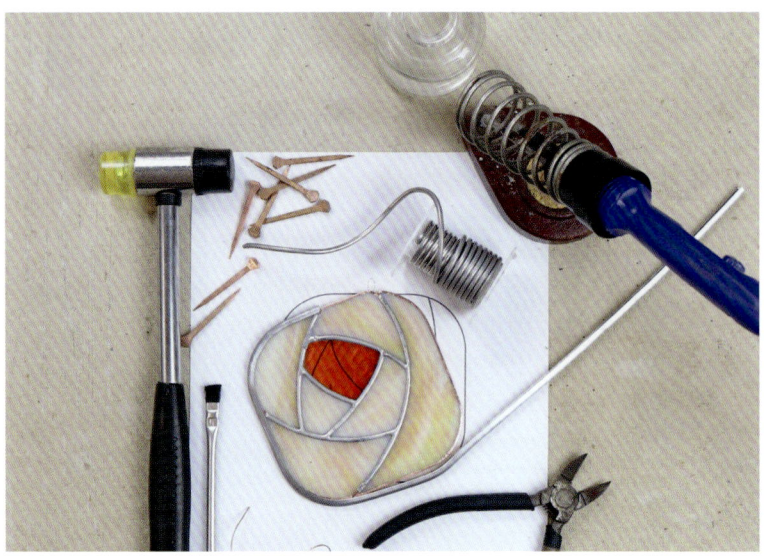

Lead melts at a lower temperature than solder, so you'll need to turn down your iron heat. You can test your temperature first on a scrap piece of lead came.

Tools

- U-channel lead came, 3/16" size
- Lead stretching vise (or other vise)
- Pliers
- Wire cutters or lead dykes
- Horseshoe nails

Safety

Put on protective gloves and clothing. You'll be holding the project as you solder, and it's possible that solder may drip toward your hands and body.

Instructions

- Stretch the lead came to straighten and "harden" it. Clamp one end of the came in a vise (a) attached to a stable surface. Hold the free end with pliers and pull the came firmly away from the vise until you feel the length stretch a bit. Once it begins to resist more firmly, you're done. Use wire cutters or lead dykes to cut off the ends of the came that were crushed by the vise and pliers.

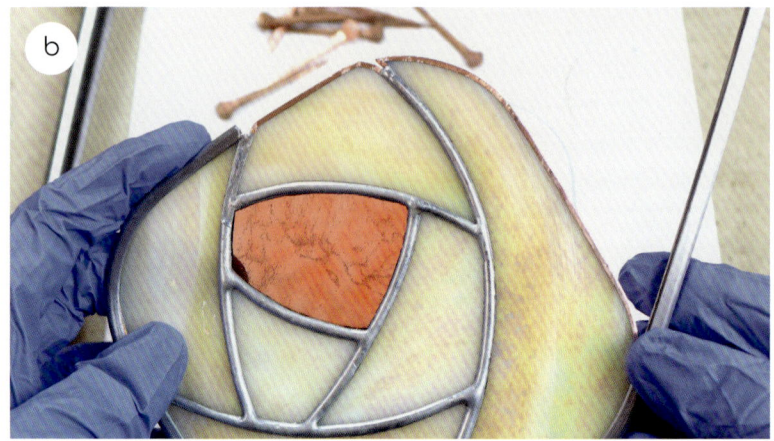

- Take an approximate measure of the perimeter of your project using a piece of string. Use wire cutters to cut a length of stretched lead came slightly longer than that measurement.
- Press the lead came on to the perimeter of the project, aligning the leading end of the came to a spot where an interior solder line intersects with the perimeter (b). Continue to apply the lead came along the perimeter, firmly pressing the glass into the lead channel. Tack the lead came in place using horseshoe nails – their flat faces will not mar the soft lead (c).

48 RAISE YOUR GLASS

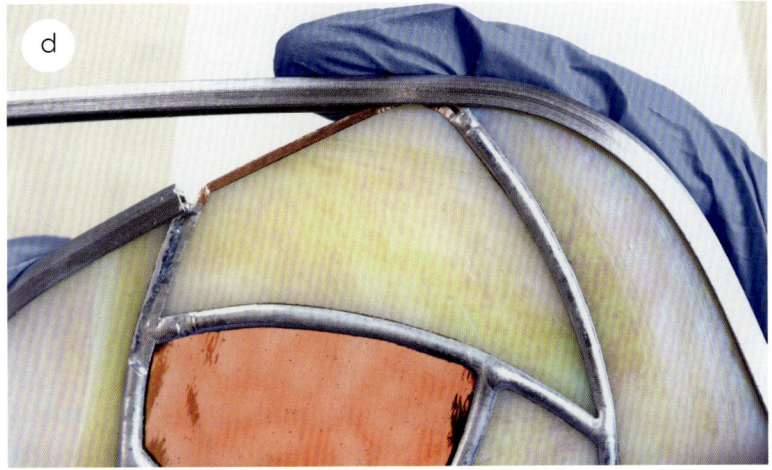

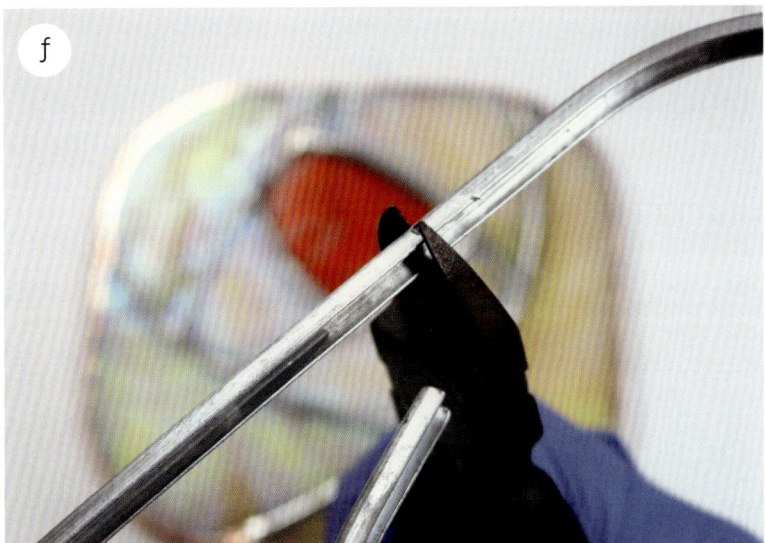

- ⓥ If you see any foil peeking out from under the came, trim it off with a craft knife.
- ⓥ Apply flux at each point where the lead came intersects with an interior solder line, and where any ends of lead came meet up.
- ⓥ Preheat your iron to 375°F/190°C (a little cooler than regular soldering).
- ⓥ Tack solder each of these intersection points by applying a bit of solder to connect the lead to the interior solder line.
- ⓥ Remove the horseshoe nails, flip the piece, and tack solder the intersections on the back.
- ⓥ Solder the junctions of the cut ends of lead.
- ⓥ Clean flux away with flux remover to prevent corrosion.

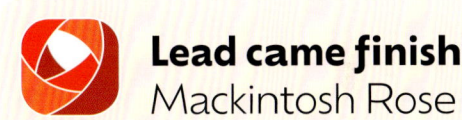

Lead came finish
Mackintosh Rose

14 Apply stretched **lead came** to the **perimeter** of the project and pin it in place. Flux and solder the lead came at every intersection with an **interior solder line** on both sides of the project. Use a bit of solder to close the gap between the ends of the lead.

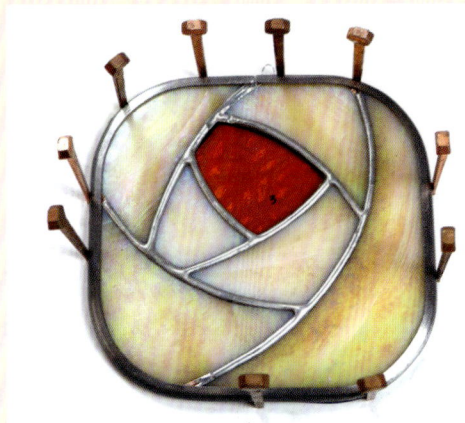

> Next step: Hanging loops (page 51)

- ⓥ If you have a sharp point or indentation where the lead cannot curve smoothly, you can cut the lead at that point to make application easier.
- ⓥ When you have gone fully around the perimeter (d), make a mark to show where to cut the came (e), and cut to size with wire cutters (f). The leading and tailing ends of the lead came should meet nicely.

THE COMPLETE STAINED GLASS PROCESS

Attaching hanging loops

We'll create simple, unobtrusive hanging loops suitable for the weight of small suncatchers. You can add additional loops for stability or for heavier projects.

Tools

- ☮ 16–20 gauge copper wire
- ☮ Wire cutters

Instructions

- ☮ Use wire cutters to cut a 2" (5 cm) length of wire, and leave it straight.
- ☮ Solder the wire into proper position (indicated by a dashed line on the pattern) in the interior line on the front of the project (a).

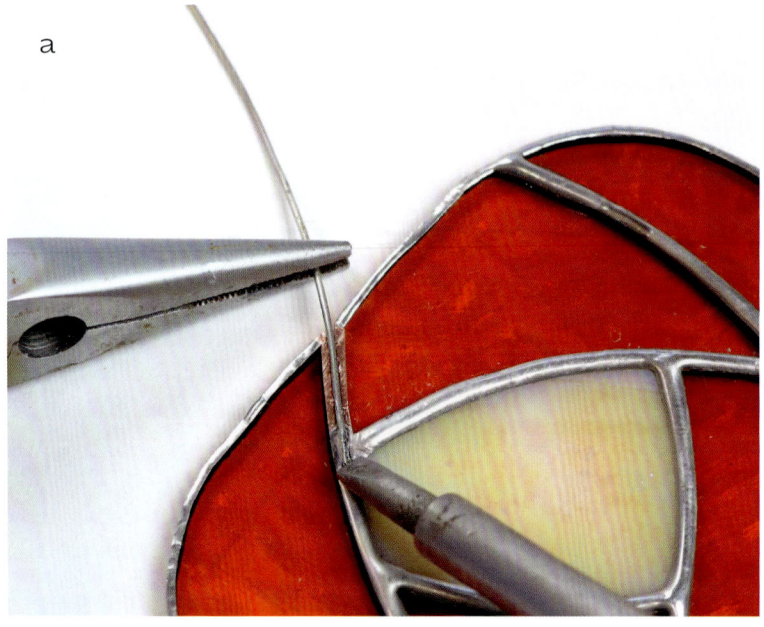

a

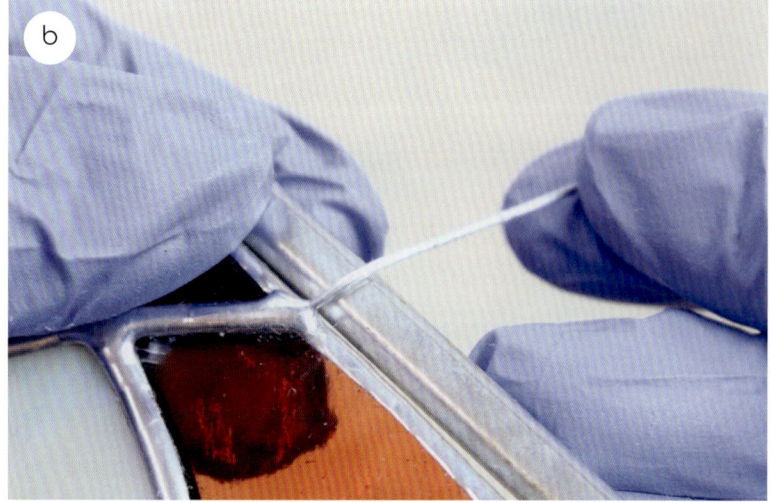

b

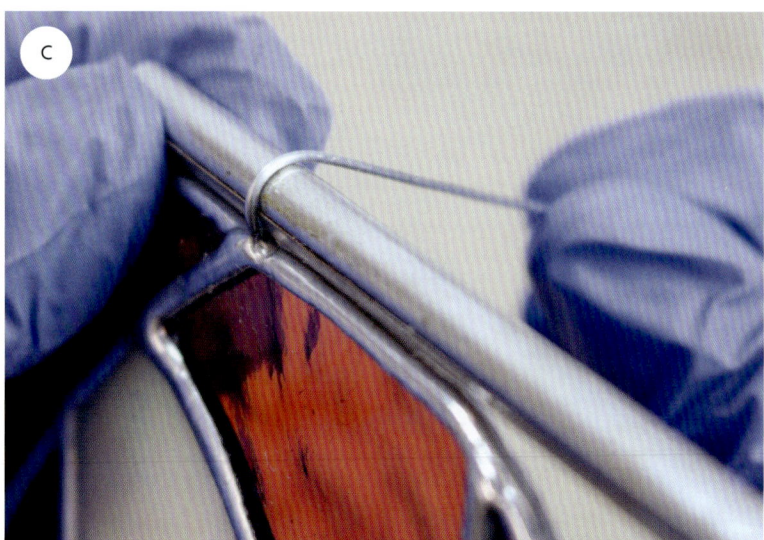

c

- ☮ Bend the wire around a pen or flux brush toward the back (b) so that it forms a loop (c).

50 RAISE YOUR GLASS

▲ Hanging loop with edge bead

◉ Trim the wire to the proper length and solder it into position on the back (d).

Tips for hanging loops

- ⓥ Always anchor hanging loops in an interior solder line to provide strength. Never anchor solely to the edge bead or lead came of the project's perimeter, or you'll risk having the edge finishing pull away from the glass over time.
- ⓥ If you've finished the perimeter with an edge bead, blend the hanging loop into the surrounding solder.
- ⓥ Attach hanging loops after lead or zinc came is soldered in place.

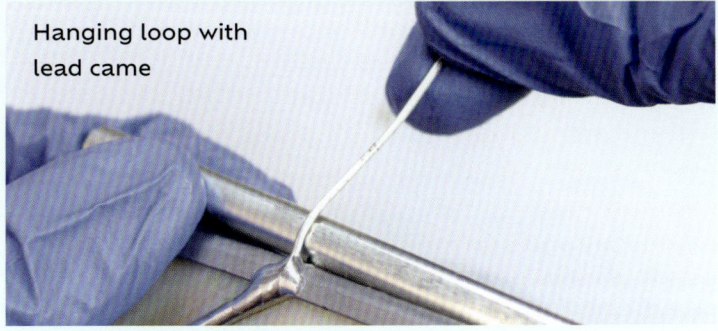

Hanging loop with lead came

- ⓥ For heavier projects, be sure that the hanging loop wire extends to a junction of interior lines for strength, but for little suncatchers just be sure that the wire extends 1/2" (1 cm) or so into the line.

Hanging loops
Mackintosh Rose

15 Apply a hanging loop where indicated on the pattern, soldering wire into the **interior line** on the front and back.

> Next step: Finishing up (page 54)

THE COMPLETE STAINED GLASS PROCESS

Finishing up: Clean, patina, and polish

Many of the supplies used for this finishing stage are common household items (rags, sponges, brushes, etc). Be sure that once you use them for stained glass, they become dedicated to that task only and are not used for other purposes. You don't want lead, flux, patina, and polish to move outside your studio. Note that different types of patina and polish require different procedures. Manufacturers' recommendations should be followed where they differ from the steps below.

Supplies

Cleaning and drying
- Lots of clean rags and absorbent towels
- Flux remover (Kwik-Clean) or dish soap
- Dish sponge
- Soft bristled brush

Patina
- Very fine (#0000) steel wool
- Applicator: A sponge cut into small cubes and other shapes (safely discard after use)
- Patina: Use a fresh bottle of black or copper patina
- Disposable plastic cup that can hold a few tablespoons of patina and is wide enough to dip your sponge in without it spilling over
- Disposable rubber gloves
- Apron
- Newspaper, rags, or paper towel to cover your workspace and clean up

Polishing
- Polish: A stained glass finishing compound
- Soft-bristled application brush
- Soft towels

Cleaning

Clean immediately after soldering to prevent **oxidation**.

- ◇ Apply flux remover or regular dish soap to a (dedicated) sponge and brush, and clean your project with warm water. Be sure that cleaner gets into all corners and crevices.
- ◇ Rinse and repeat several times until all flux is removed and the project is completely clean. Any remaining flux will damage your beautiful new solder lines, making it difficult to achieve a shiny, bright patina and eventually causing "white mold."
- ◇ Use an absorbent towel to dry completely.

Patina

You can patina your project to change your silver solder lines to rich copper or black. Skip the patina if you want your lines to remain silver.

Patina is a liquid that chemically reacts with solder. It is toxic, so you must take care to protect your skin, and be sure to clean up properly to protect kids, pets, and other living things.

Patina is temperamental, and good handling techniques must be practiced to create a consistent patina. Apply patina only when your solder lines are perfectly clean and free of oxidation, water, cleaners, and fingerprints. Patina is finicky with minerals in water; if you have hard water, do a final cleanup of your project with distilled water or denatured alcohol. Pour out just a little patina into a small cup for use – nothing (a brush, leftover patina) should ever go into a patina storage container or it will become contaminated.

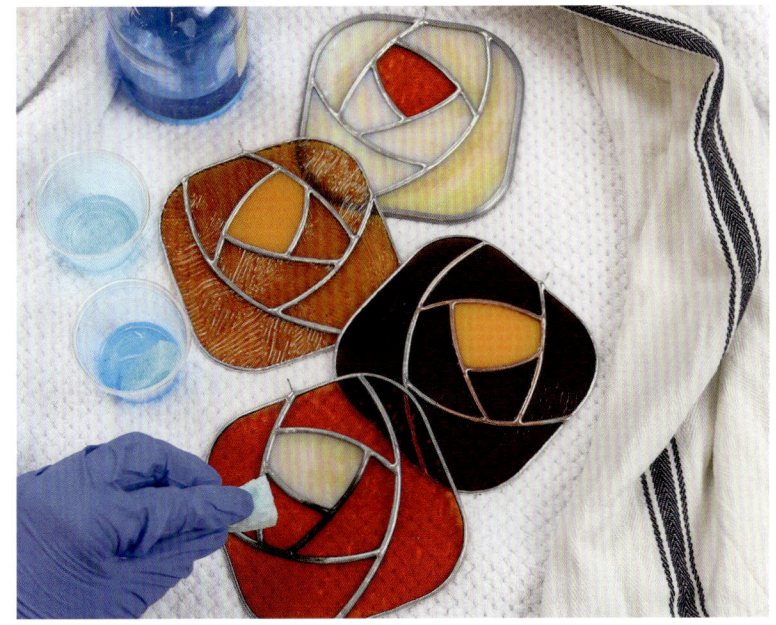

- ⓥ Apply patina as soon as possible after soldering and cleaning so that the solder does not have time to oxidize.
- ⓥ Rub all solder lines with #0000 steel wool, so that the solder is even-colored, bright, and shiny. Brush away the dust.
- ⓥ Put on work clothes and disposable gloves. Cover your work surface with a disposable material such as newspaper, rags, or old towels.
- ⓥ Pour a small amount of patina from the storage container into your plastic cup.

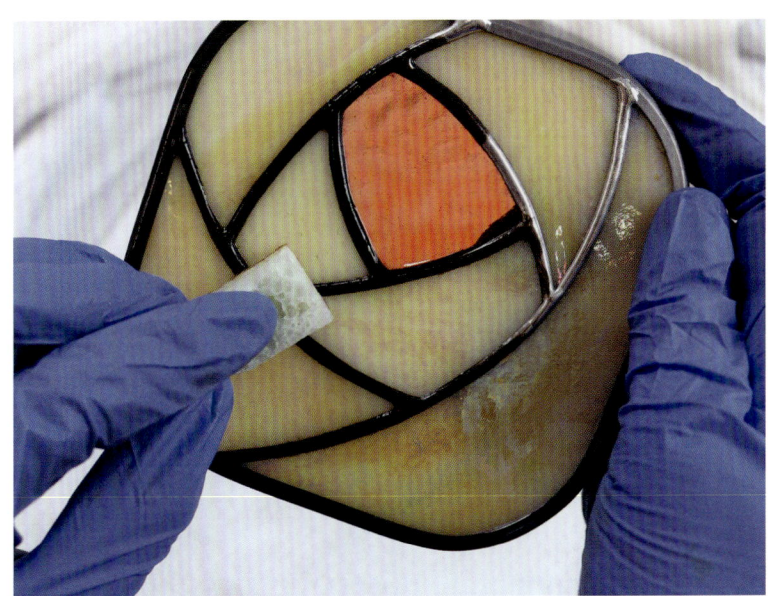

THE COMPLETE STAINED GLASS PROCESS

- Dip your applicator into the plastic cup, squeeze out excess liquid, and rub the patina onto all of the solder until you have a bright, even color.
- Wipe off excess patina with a paper towel.

Polishing

You'll need to polish your project to create a beautiful luster on your solder and glass. Polish contains a wax that will coat the solder and the glass, resisting oxidation and ensuring that your project will shine. Apply polish as soon as possible after soldering (and applying patina), while first taking the time to thoroughly clean and dry the project. Polishing requires some pressure and rubbing, so be careful when polishing near delicate foil overlay, edge beading, and hanging loops.

- Apply a light coat of polish to the entire project, using a brush to get into all the nooks and crannies.
- Allow the polish to dry to a haze (a).
- Use a soft towel and soft-bristled brush to wipe the polish off of the project.
- Use clean towels to continue to buff to a beautiful shine. Hold the project up to the light to look for any remaining smudges and keep buffing until it looks perfect.

a

Finishing up
Mackintosh Rose

16 Clean and dry thoroughly.

17 **Patina**, if you like.

18 Polish. Hang in the perfect sunlit spot, or give to a special person!

Congratulations! You've finished the basic tutorial. For your next project, consider High Five (see page 62) or Ray of Light (see page 76) – both are small projects with step-by-step instructions.

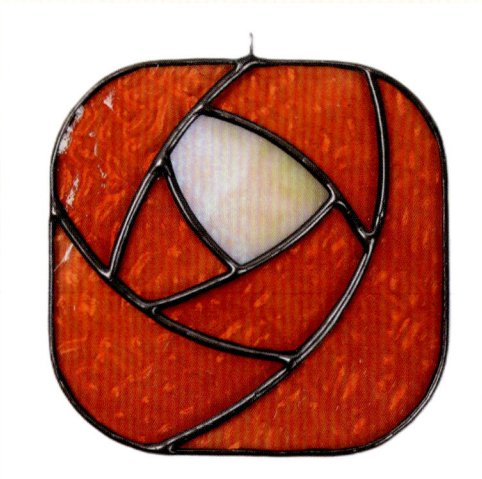

PAINTING GLASS

Traditional kiln-fired glass painting is a specialized technique that takes years to master. Here, we will explore an easier method using a paint that can be fired in a kitchen oven.

I'm happy with the Pébéo brand Vitrea 160 paint line, which is water-based and nontoxic. It can be **oven cured** at 325°F/160°C to create a permanent bond that resists scratching and fading. You can find it at the big chain art and craft supply stores. Pébéo makes a wide range of glass paint in many colors (transparent, opaque, and pearl) and in a variety of dispensers (in a jar that is applied with a paintbrush, a paint marker, and a small, tipped outliner tube). If you can, get yourself one of each and play around to see what works best for your task.

If you're an experienced painter who has worked on canvas or paper with watercolor, acrylic, or oil paints, take note: applying this paint onto glass is quite different from using those other media! Take some time to experiment. You'll get different results on variously textured glass surfaces. Colors might spread or flow in different ways. If you are familiar with piping a royal icing design onto cookies, or applying glaze to pottery, this might feel similar. Borrow some techniques from those crafts, and experiment with others:

- Create a marbled effect: Make dots of alternating colors and drag a toothpick through, causing one to streak into the other.
- Use a stencil and a sponge to apply some lettering.
- Play with "scraffito" technique: apply a thin coat of paint, let it dry, then scratch away, removing paint to create your design.
- Outline a shape, let the outline dry, then flood the interior of the outlined area.
- Practice your signature so that you can sign your larger creations.

Fortunately, unlike cookie icing, this paint allows you to easily erase your "failures" and start over. While the paint is still wet, you can wipe it off with a wet rag. If the paint is dry but you have not yet cured it, you can wash it off with a scrubby sponge or scrape it off with a razor blade.

In these photos, you can see my experimentation on these Day of the Dead styled monarch wing glass pieces. I enjoyed using both the brush and the marker to make some dotted details. I feel the most successful results came when I acted with strong, decisive strokes – the paint doesn't respond as well to reworking and multiple overlapping strokes. It can be frustrating at first, so give yourself time to get to know the product. Overall, this type of paint is best suited for adding details that are too small or oddly shaped to represent with solder lines – a sparkle in the eye of your portrait subject, the dotted pattern on a moth wing, the gills of a mushroom.

Get creative and push the boundaries, but if the nature of this paint limits your ability to create the shading and more intricate detailing that you desire, you might want to look further into traditional glass painting techniques and paints that use kiln firing.

Try it out

The following projects include some optional painting:
- Havisham Bat (see page 112)
- Meadow Mirror (see page 101)

Instructions

Note: these are relevant for Pébéo Vitrea 160 paint. Other paint brands are available; make sure you follow the instructions for your specific product.

☮ Cut and grind glass pieces to be painted, but don't foil yet.

☮ Prepare your materials (a). Shake the bottle well, then let it sit for a while to remove air bubbles.
☮ Clean your glass pieces very well, and dry completely.
☮ Apply the paint (b).
☮ Allow the paint to cure for 24 hours at room temperature.
☮ Place the painted glass on an oven-safe tray (c).
☮ Follow the manufacturer's instructions for curing the paint. I have good results baking at 350°F/177°C for 45 minutes.
☮ Turn the oven off and let the glass pieces cool completely in oven (this can take a few hours).

Paint Tips

◊ Paint colors can be mixed.
◊ Paint can be layered, but it must dry between applications.
◊ If you're getting streaks that you don't want, let the paint dry and then reapply another layer.
◊ Thick paint layers can be used to create a little texture, but if you go too thick, the paint may discolor and appear cakey after firing.
◊ Pébéo Vitrea 160 paint is water-based, so cleanup is easy – just rinse your brushes thoroughly in water.

Workflow Tips

☯ Plan the paintwork in your initial design, drawing it right onto your pattern and template pieces so that you don't confuse what goes where.
☯ Adapt your timeline: you'll cut and grind, then paint (apply, dry, cure, fire, cool), then move on to foiling and soldering. It can take up to two days for the painted glass to be ready for foiling, especially if you need extra drying time when layering colors.

THE COMPLETE STAINED GLASS PROCESS

CAROLYNE HEPPENSTALL

Wirksworth, Derbyshire, UK | lumieglass.com @lumie.glass

Art Deco-inspired shapes and careful selections of color and texture, layered using a confident eye, create the vintage glamour of a Lumie Glass artwork. Carolyne creates these beauties in her Derbyshire studio.

Would you care to share your artistic background?
I have experience as a conservator of historic interior decorative schemes. Working in historic buildings allowed me to immerse myself in the rich traditions and artistic skills of the past. This experience shaped my understanding of design, especially the importance of craftsmanship and detail. In addition to my work as a conservator, I also ran a mid-century furniture and home decor shop. This venture gave me an appreciation for the clean lines, bold forms, and vibrant colors of mid-century modern design. My aesthetic draws from these experiences, bringing historical influences into conversation with contemporary design.

What drives your compositions?
My work is inspired by the intricate and ornamental styles of the Art Nouveau and Art Deco periods, where the interplay of shapes and colors creates a sense of flow. Colors can shift and take on new qualities when placed next to others, completely changing how they're perceived – enhancing or altering their intensity, warmth, or coolness. Also, the overlapping pieces create new hues, even through opaque glass. This interplay is something I always consider in my work, as the

relationships between colors are just as important as the individual hues themselves.

With such complex yet free arrangements, how do you know when a piece is "completed"?
Knowing when a piece is finished is a deeply intuitive process for me. It's a moment when everything feels balanced. I think of it as a story, a journey, or a piece of music. Resisting the urge to add or subtract just one more element is challenging, but it's about trusting that feeling of wholeness. Once I reach that point, I know that any further changes would disrupt the harmony I've worked so hard to achieve.

How do you hope your work exists in the world?
My goal is to create spaces and experiences that foster a sense of joy, serenity, and emotional balance. Using color combinations found in nature, I seek to evoke the soothing and rejuvenating effects of the natural environment and provide a gentle reminder of the importance of well-being. Whether expressed in the tranquil blues of the ocean, the vibrant greens of a forest, or the warm hues of a sunset, my designs are intended to reconnect people with the peace and beauty inherent in the world around us, no matter how chaotic it often feels.

3
CHARM BRACELET SUNCATCHERS

I love charm bracelets – they're collections of little talismans that tell your story with unique flair. These charm suncatchers can similarly serve as symbols of our stained glass journey together. Create the whole set to decorate your studio window with a garland of good luck charms.

The first suncatcher project, High Five, is the simplest to construct, and the instructions will guide you through every step in detail. Follow these same steps as you work through the other charms, which get progressively more challenging as you go. Notably, Eventide (page 70) and Serpentis (page 71) both require a few difficult cuts. Don't worry if you get stuck, just turn back to the cutting glass section on page 26 and look for the advice on convex and concave cuts. Your skills will also progress along the way!

HIGH FIVE

Difficulty: Beginner

Here's a high five for anyone learning a new craft!

Supplies

All standard stained glass tools and supplies (see page 15)

Pattern

3 copies of the High Five pattern on page 178

Instructions

1 Cut paper **templates** from one **pattern**. Use regular scissors to cut the **perimeter** (a), then use pattern shears to cut the **interior lines** (b). If you're just starting out and don't yet own pattern shears, you can use regular scissors for smaller projects like these charm bracelet suncatchers. Save the second pattern to lay out the cut glass, and another as a backup if you make mistakes with the other two.

▲ Pattern shears remove a width of paper

HIGH FIVE

2 Select a nice palette of a few glass types, paying attention to color, texture, **grain**, and **opacity** (c). Glue the paper templates to the smoother side of the glass, carefully considering the grain orientation and leaving enough room to cut the glass easily (d).

3 Cut all glass **pieces** (e, f). If a piece doesn't cut properly, use the extra pattern to make a replacement template, and cut a new glass piece.

4 Grind all glass pieces (g). Gently move the **edge** of the piece against the grinder bit and remove glass until the ground edge is flush with the paper template and the entire edge is ground smooth and **opaque**. Lay each piece in place upon the uncut pattern as you go, and regrind or recut if a piece does not fit the pattern perfectly.

5 Check that all pieces fit well together upon the pattern and fix anything that isn't perfect. One at a time, pick up a piece, mentally note its number and orientation, and remove the paper template. Clean the glass completely using a rag and cleaning solution, dry the piece, then renumber it with a marker, and place back into position on the pattern.

6 Foil each piece (h). Use foil with a backing color that matches your chosen **patina** (silver, black, or copper). Peel off a bit of the strip that covers the adhesive on the foil and press the adhesive to the edge of a glass piece, centering the glass so that there's a small, even foil overhang to each side of the glass edge. Press the adhesive to the glass, holding it in place with your finger. Different thicknesses of glass require different widths of foil, so be sure to switch spools if the overhanging foil doesn't seem consistent with your other foiled pieces. Continue to apply foil along the entire edge of the piece, until you return to the **leading end** of the foil, then cut the foil and overlap the trailing end to create a neat, continuous foil surface.

7 Burnish the foil onto each piece with a **fid** so that the foil is smooth and follows the contours of the glass edge and **faces**.

8 Lay the foiled pieces back upon the pattern and pin them into position with pushpins around the perimeter (i).

9 Flux and solder the **interior lines** on the **front** of the project (j). Do not solder the perimeter, nor the locations where the **hanging loops** will be installed (represented by dashed lines on the pattern).

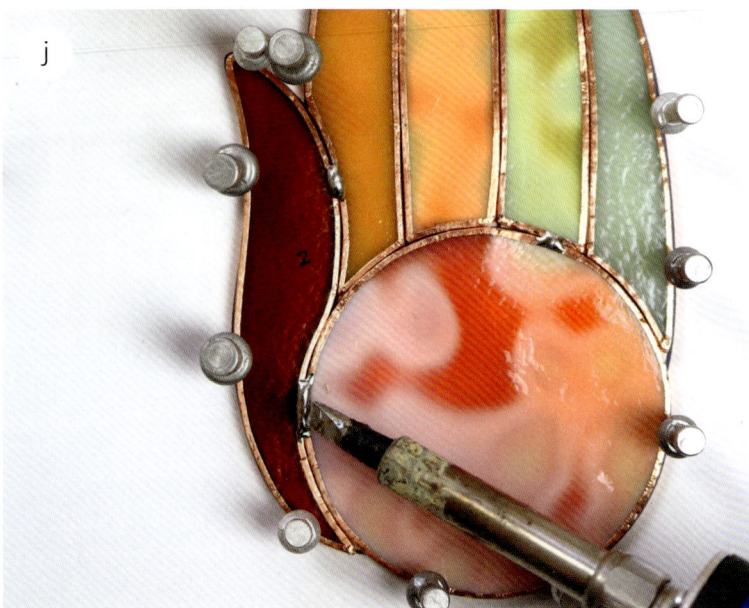

10 Flip and solder the interior lines on the **back** in the same way (k).

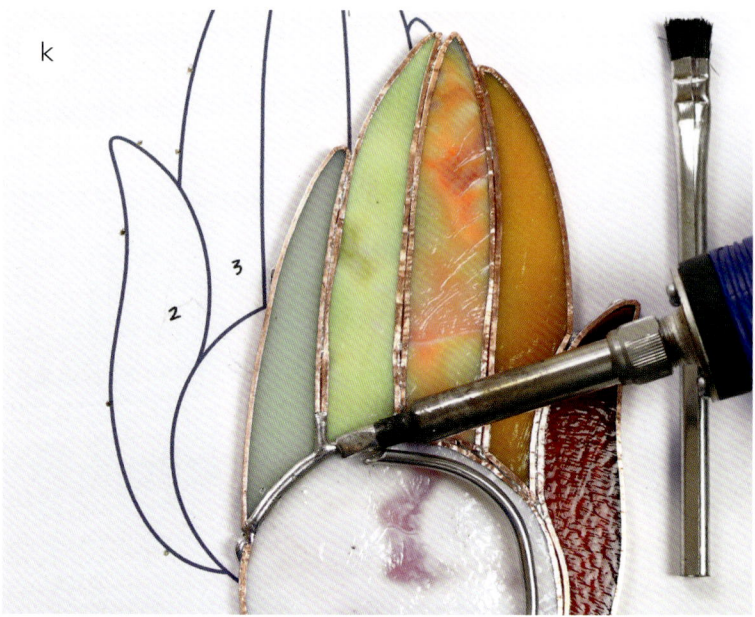

11 Finish the perimeter of the project with a neat, strong **edge bead** (l, m).

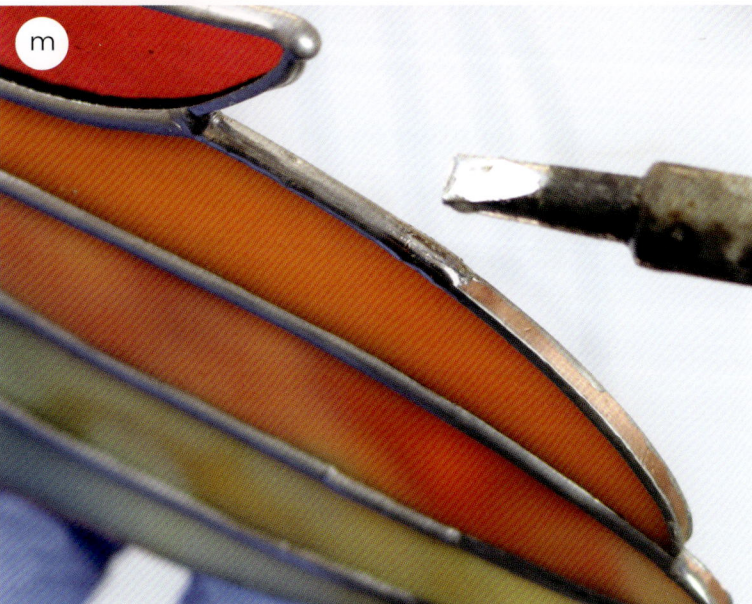

12 Attach hanging loops. Cut a length of wire, about 2" (5 cm), and leave it straight. Solder the wire into proper position in the interior line on the front of the project (indicated by a dashed line on the pattern) (n). Bend the hanging wire around a flux brush (o) or pencil toward the back so that it forms a loop. Trim wire to proper length (p) and solder into position on the back (q).

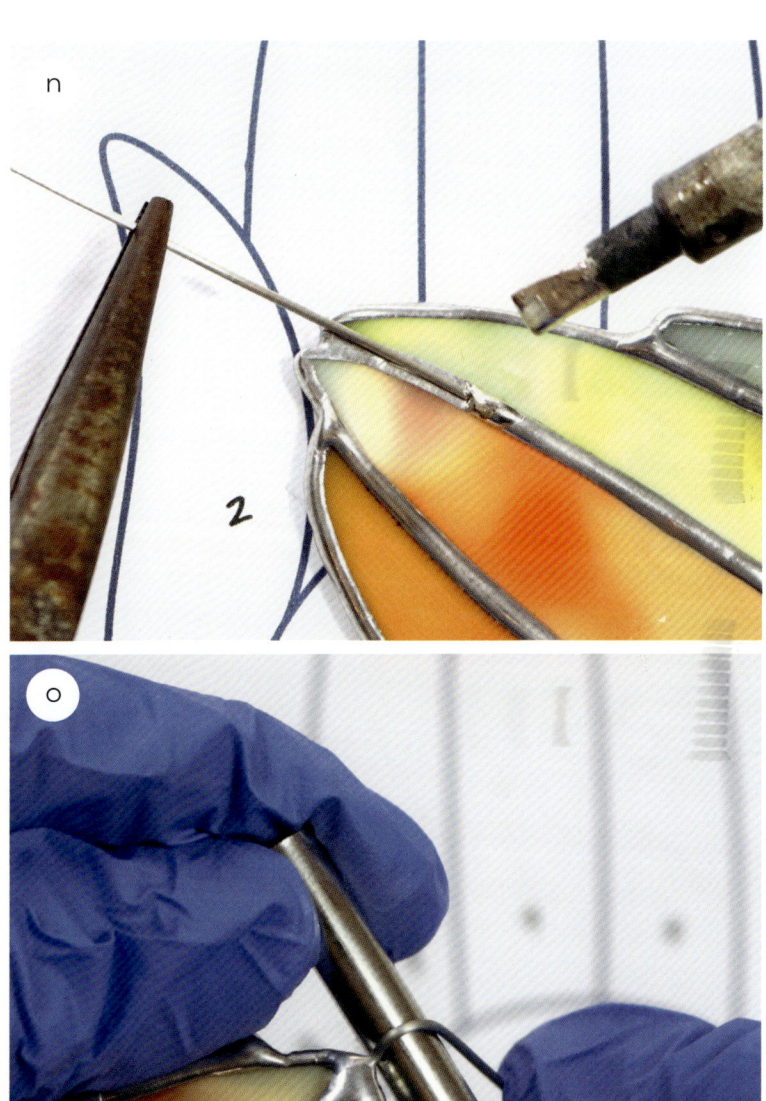

HIGH FIVE 67

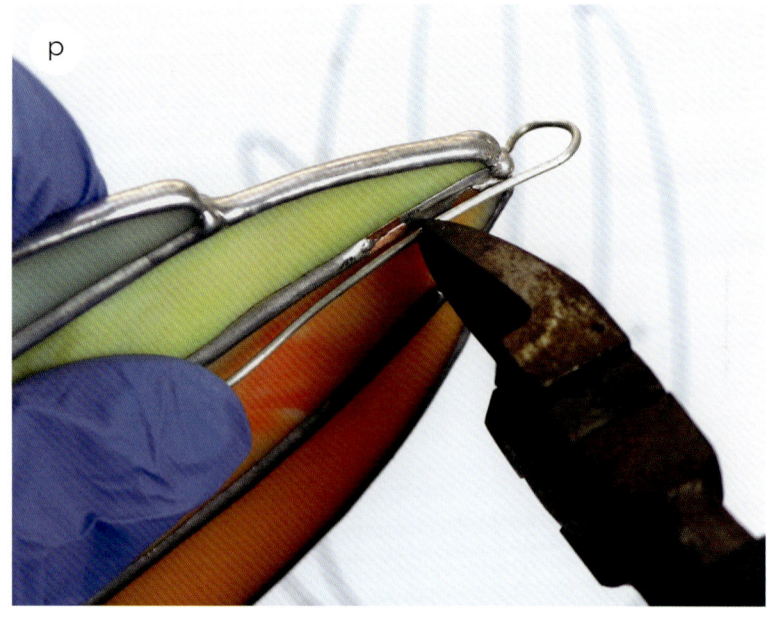

13 Clean the project with flux remover, then **patina** if you desire (r), and finally polish. Do each of these steps immediately after soldering to prevent corrosion and **oxidation**.

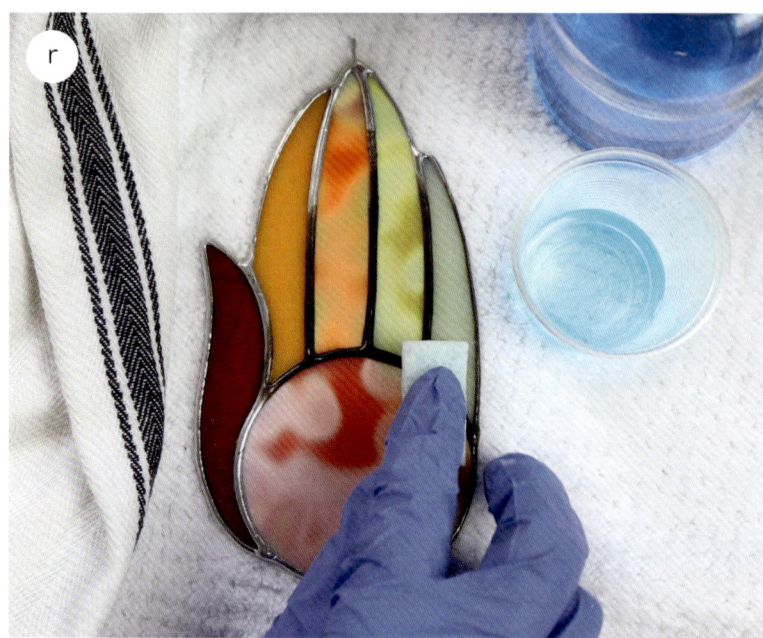

14 String some fishing line or a leather lace through the hanging loop to finish. Hang the suncatcher where it will get lots of light (and attention)!

CHARM BRACELET SUNCATCHER VARIATIONS

Difficulty: Beginner

Fill your window with a bounty of lucky charms! Each of these projects is of similar size and difficulty as High Five, and you can use the instructions from that project to create these.

Lucky Clover

Buddies

Eventide

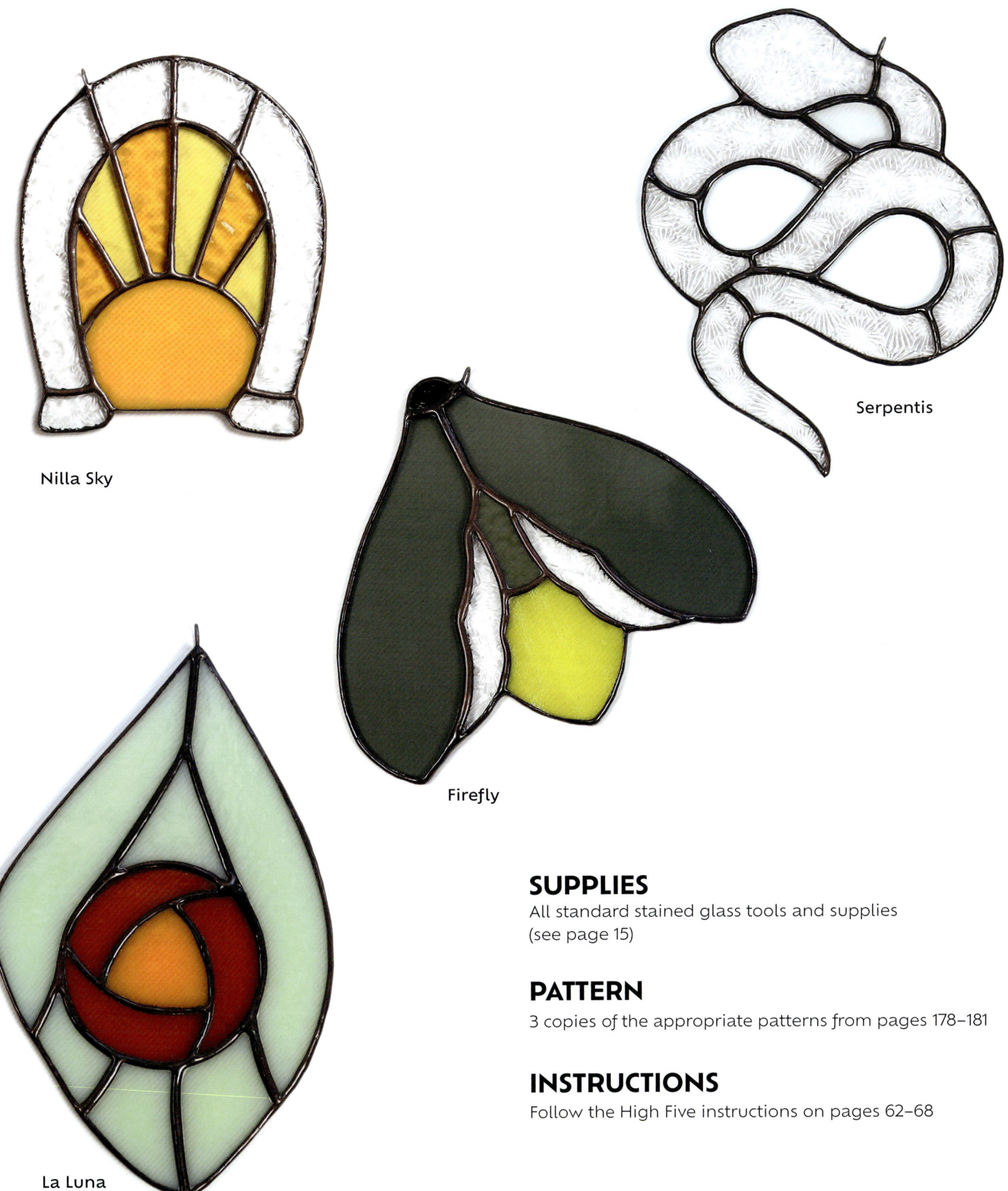

Nilla Sky

Serpentis

Firefly

La Luna

SUPPLIES
All standard stained glass tools and supplies (see page 15)

PATTERN
3 copies of the appropriate patterns from pages 178–181

INSTRUCTIONS
Follow the High Five instructions on pages 62–68

CHARM BRACELET SUNCATCHER VARIATIONS

CHEVONNE ARISS

Portland, Oregon, USA | runaglassworks.com @runaglassworks

Chevonne's personality and unique sense of style shine through in her work, both in her thoughtfully constructed Rüna Glassworks stained glass interiors and in her warm and insightful conversations with her contemporaries on her podcast "Cracked with Chevonne Ariss." The podcast provides a platform for both well-known and emerging artists to discuss their creative processes and inspirations, as well as the challenges they face in their work.

What's your favorite aspect type of glass project?
Stained glass in public spaces is exciting, but creating artwork for someone's home is my favorite type of project. From the first meeting until installation day, I find the experience to be so intimate and rewarding. You're collaborating with someone to bring both beauty and comfort into a space where they feel most themselves. Your art is right there where their personal moments unfold, where their families evolve. In this world of instant gratification, short attention spans, and fast-paced trends, I like to know that my work will be savored over time.

Do you struggle to find a balance between producing the podcast and creating your other artwork?
Yes, sometimes. I am wildly impressed with and inspired by the "Cracked" guests. I love celebrating them, shining a spotlight on them and boosting their visibility, hopefully leading to more opportunities for them and an abundance of whatever it is they seek from their career. But all of that celebrating and boosting takes time and energy. If I hadn't started the podcast, would I be further along in my art? We'll never know! But I do know that I need to be very protective of my artistic growth, so I'm always trying to practice balance.

What role does the podcast have in the stained glass community?
Each episode serves as an archival record. Over time, these recordings will collectively provide a detailed and nuanced history of this moment in stained glass art, offering insights that can be referenced by historians, researchers, preservationists, and enthusiasts. "Cracked" also spreads knowledge of our craft to

a broad audience and hopefully will promote the art form to future generations. Equally important to me is the telling of the personal stories of today's artists, which might otherwise be overlooked in traditional historical records.

Do you worry about running out of people to talk to?
The opposite is true! When I started "Cracked," my sense of the stained glass community was adorably small compared to what it is now. For every new artist I meet, it leads me to twenty more. The talent seems to be endless!

Are there any common themes that keep popping up in your discussions?
Grief. So much grief. It's been astonishing how many of my guests are navigating the death of a loved one. Sometimes the grief is fresh and raw, completely unprocessed. Sometimes the story of their loss is found deeper in their history, but there's still a tangle of pain they can't escape, close to the surface. Regardless of how much time has passed, it's a piece of their narrative prominent enough that it's impossible to not acknowledge it when they share their story. I take it as a reminder that most people are, in some capacity, working through the passing of someone very pivotal in who they are and what they offer the world. It's served as a reminder for me to be gentler with people I don't know.

4
TIME CAPSULES

These three projects use the same capsule-shaped layout frame. Ray of Light (page 76) contains mostly straight cuts and is a great beginner project, while Oculus (page 82) and Paloma (page 82) contain some more challenging concave cuts. I'll provide all instructions for Ray of Light, and you can use the same steps to construct Paloma and Oculus.

LAYOUT FRAMES

Layout frame jigs are used to hold the glass pieces in place while making these projects. During layout, they make it easy to check your pieces for proper fit, and they'll keep things tidy if you need to remove some for more grinding. They also hold the pieces snugly in place as you solder, eliminating the need for tacking with thumbtacks, horseshoe nails, or straightedges. The layout frames that I use, from Erin Glassworks, come in a variety of shapes (from basic geometric polygons and ovals to hearts, crescents, teardrops, and arches) in various sizes up to 12" (30 cm). If you plan on making multiple projects using the same shape, you might want to keep one clean frame for design and initial layout, and use another frame that'll get fluxy during soldering.

Any of these projects can also be constructed without the aid of layout frames; just pin the pieces in position on the pattern before soldering. Additionally, we'll finish the perimeter with U-channel lead came (see pages 48–49) rather than edge beading, but you're free to use whichever technique you prefer.

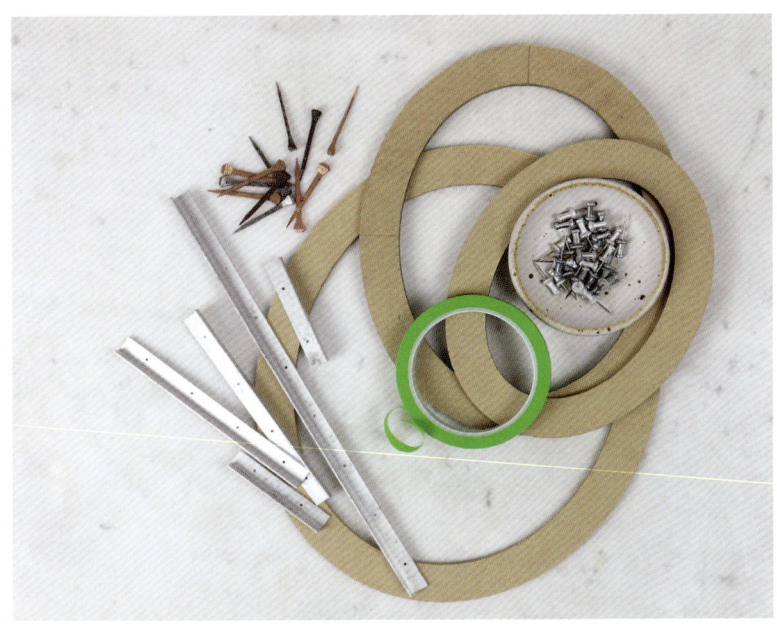

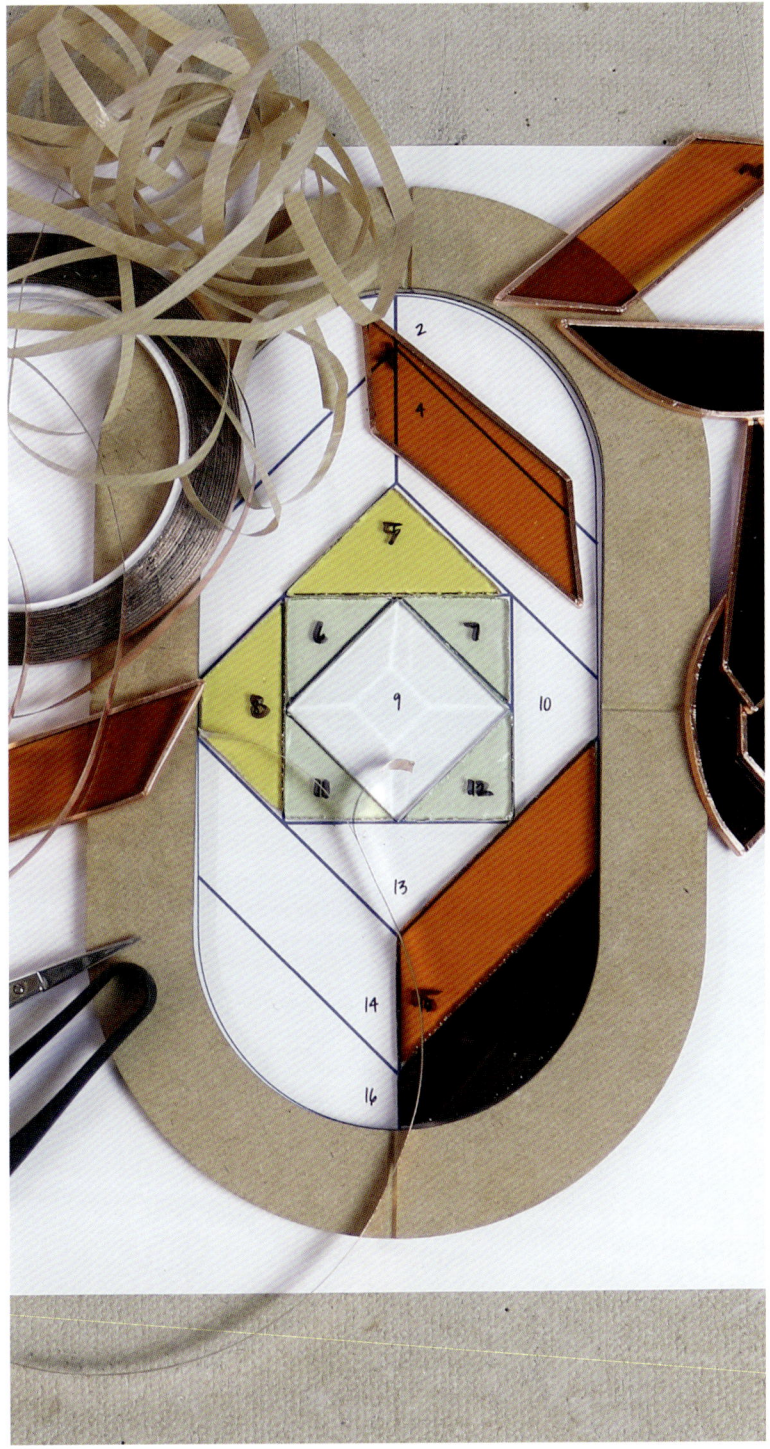

RAY OF LIGHT

Difficulty: Beginner

This simple design is a great place to get familiar with the process of using a layout frame and finishing with lead came. The use of a square bevel for the center piece will cast rainbows across the room, but you can substitute regular glass, if you like.

Supplies

- All standard stained glass tools and supplies (see page 15)
- Square bevel, 1 1/2" (4 cm) (optional, can substitute regular glass)
- Layout frame (optional) – 8" (20 cm) pill-shaped frame from Erin Glassworks (8 x 3 13/16" interior)
- U-channel lead came, 3/16" size – about 24" (60 cm) length
- Horseshoe nails

Pattern

3 copies of the Ray of Light pattern on page 182

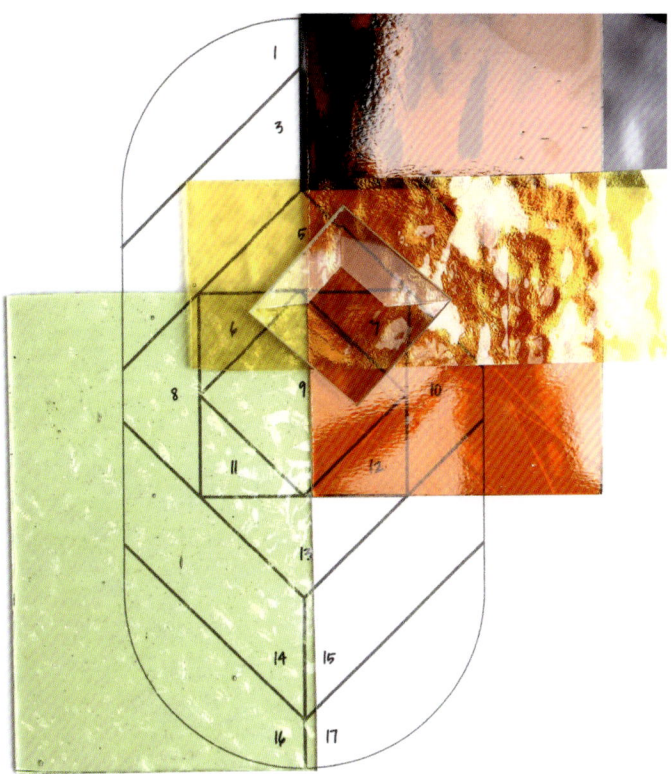

Instructions

1 Cut the paper **templates** from one **pattern**. Use regular scissors to cut the **perimeter**, then use pattern shears to cut the **interior** (a). If you're just starting out and don't yet own pattern shears, you can use regular scissors for smaller projects like this. Save the second pattern to lay out the cut glass, and the third as a backup in case you make mistakes with the other two!

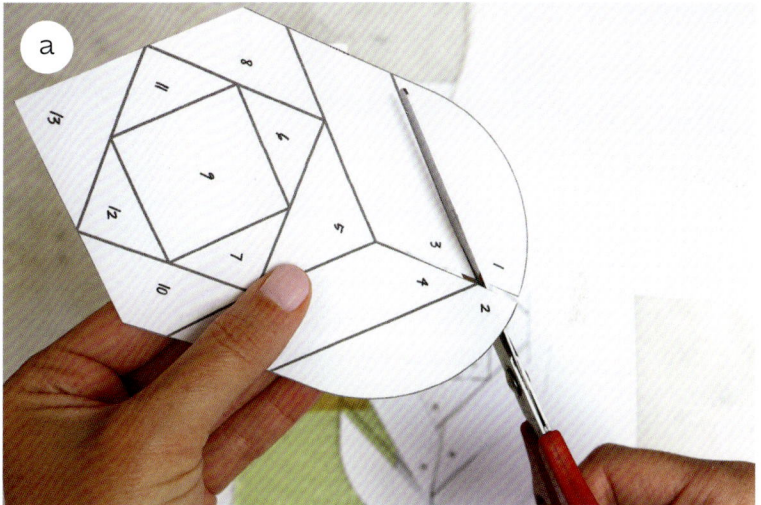

2 Select a nice palette of a few glass types, paying attention to color, texture, **grain**, and **opacity**. Glue paper templates to the smoother side of the glass (b), carefully considering the grain orientation and leaving enough room to cut the glass easily.

3 Cut all glass **pieces** (c). If you opt not to use the square bevel for the middle piece, then cut a piece of glass for that square too. If a piece doesn't break properly, use the extra pattern to make a replacement template, and cut a new glass piece.

4 Grind all glass pieces except the beveled piece (d). Gently move the **edge** of the piece against the grinder bit and remove glass until the ground edge is flush with the paper template and the entire edge is ground smooth and opaque.

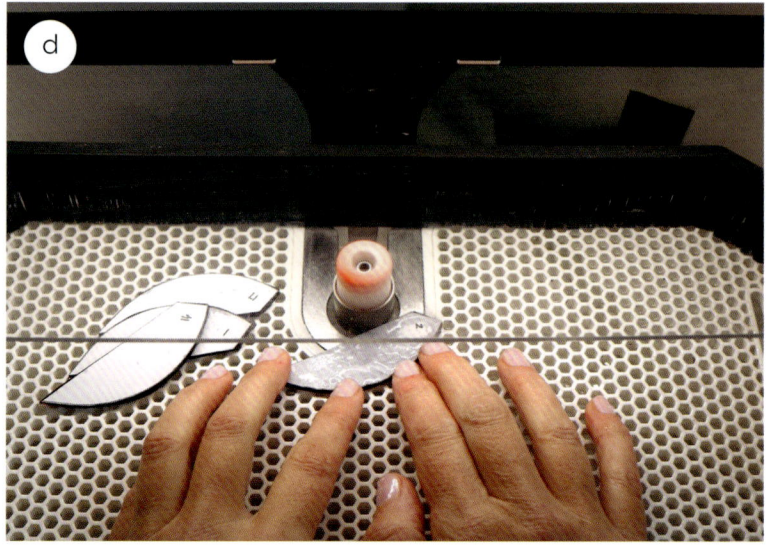

5 Pin the layout frame in place upon the pattern (if using).

6 Lay out the ground pieces inside the layout frame (or on your pattern). They should fit together, gently touching, with no large gaps. If any pieces are too tight, return to the grinder to create a better fit.

7 One at a time, pick up a piece, mentally note its number and orientation, and remove the paper template. Clean the glass completely using a rag and cleaning solution, dry the piece, then renumber it with a marker, and place it back into position on the pattern.

8 Foil each piece, including the beveled piece (e). Use foil with a backing color that matches your chosen **patina** (silver, black, or copper). Peel off a bit of the strip that covers the adhesive on the foil and press the adhesive to the **edge** of a glass piece, centering the glass so that there's a small, even foil overhang to each side of the glass edge. Press the adhesive to the glass, holding it in place with your finger. Different thicknesses of glass require different widths of foil, so be sure to switch spools if the overhanging foil doesn't seem consistent with your other foiled pieces. Continue to apply foil along the entire edge of the piece, until you return to the **leading end** of the foil, then cut and overlap the trailing end to create a neat, continuous foil surface.

9 Burnish the foil onto each piece with a fid so that the foil is smooth and follows the contours of the glass edge and **faces**.

10 Lay out the pieces in the frame (f), or pin them in place upon the pattern (g).

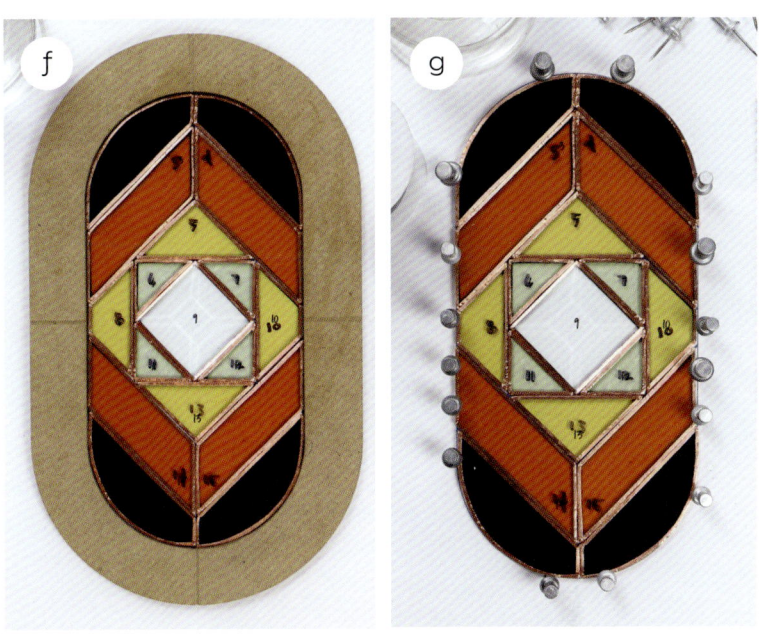

▲ Pin if not using layout frame

11 Flux and **tack solder** all pieces together, then remove the pushpins or frame (h), wiping off any errant flux if you want to reuse the frame.

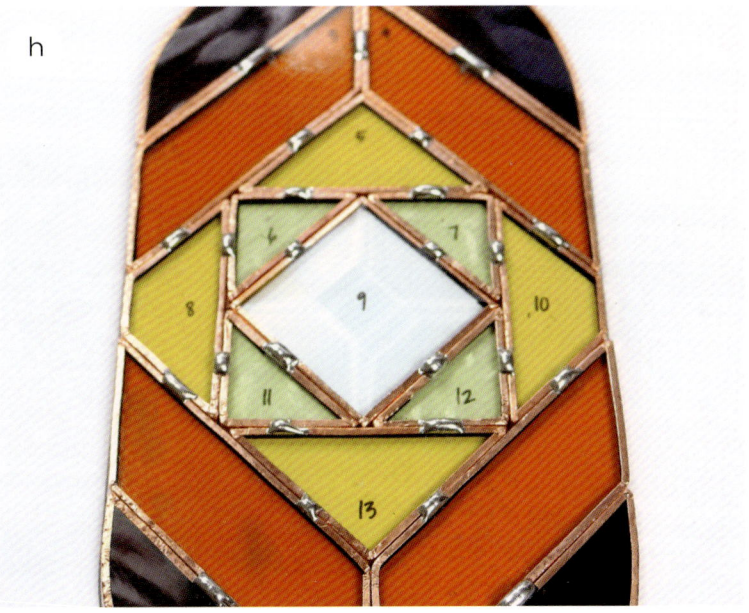

12 Fully solder the **interior lines** on the **front** (i). End interior lines just short of the **perimeter** so that the **lead came** will fit, and don't solder the perimeter (j). Also leave unsoldered the locations where the **hanging loop** will be installed (indicated by dashed lines on the pattern) (k).

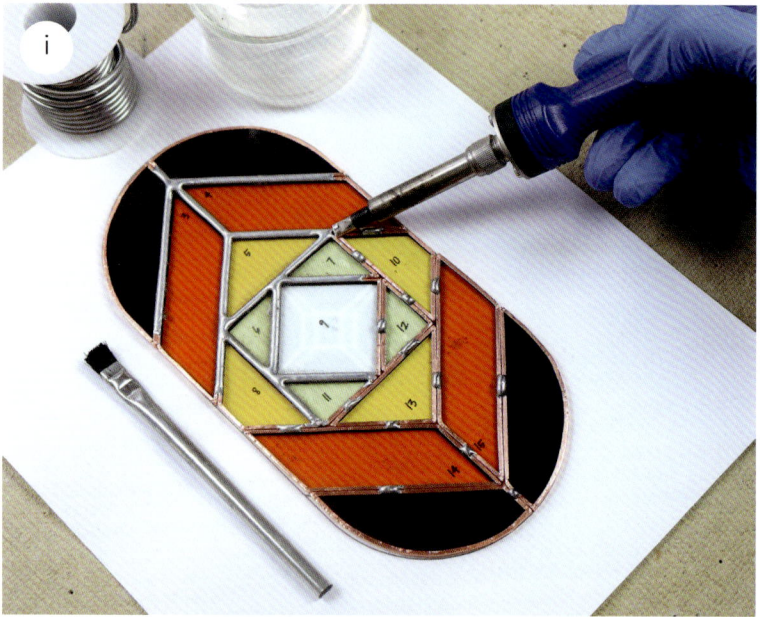

▲ Leave room for the lead came

13 Flip the project and solder the interior lines of the **back**.

14 Stretch the **U-channel lead came** (see page 48), and use wire cutters to clip off the crushed ends.

15 Press the lead firmly onto the perimeter so that the glass fills the U-shaped channel, working around the entire perimeter (l). Then mark and cut the trailing end of the came with wire cutters so that both ends of the came meet neatly.

16 Pin the lead came in place on your work surface using horseshoe nails. If you see any foil peeking out from under the came, trim it off with a craft knife.

17 Extend all interior solder lines so that they connect neatly to the lead came (m). Turn down your heat a bit to avoid melting the lead. Leave the hanging loop location unsoldered.

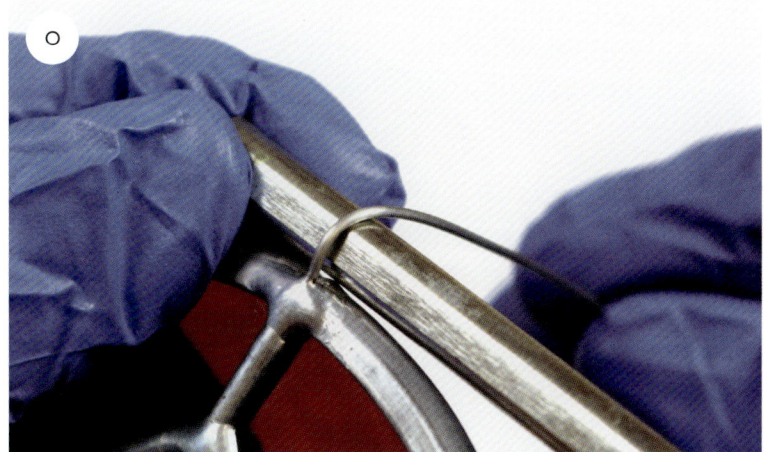

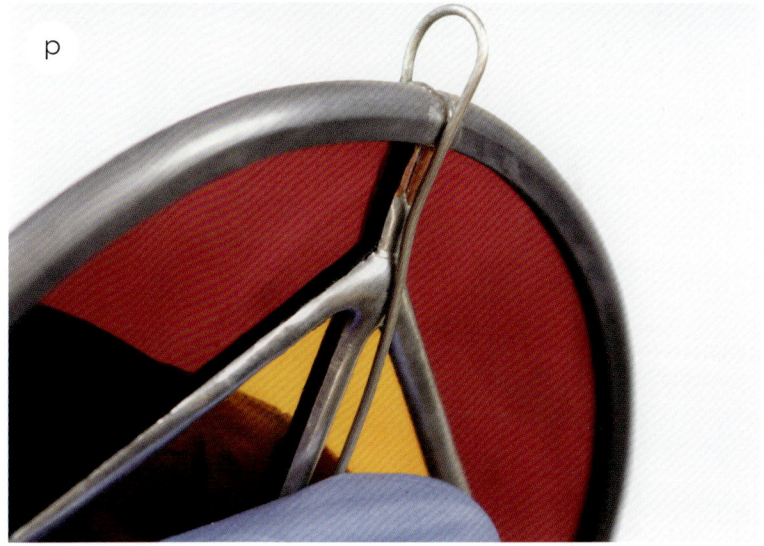

18 Attach the hanging loop. Cut a 2" (5 cm) length of wire and leave it straight. Solder the wire into proper position (indicated by a dashed line on the pattern) in the interior line on the front of the project (n). Bend the hanging wire around a flux brush or pencil toward the back so that it forms a loop (o, p). Trim to the proper length and solder into position on the back.

19 Clean, patina, and polish (q).

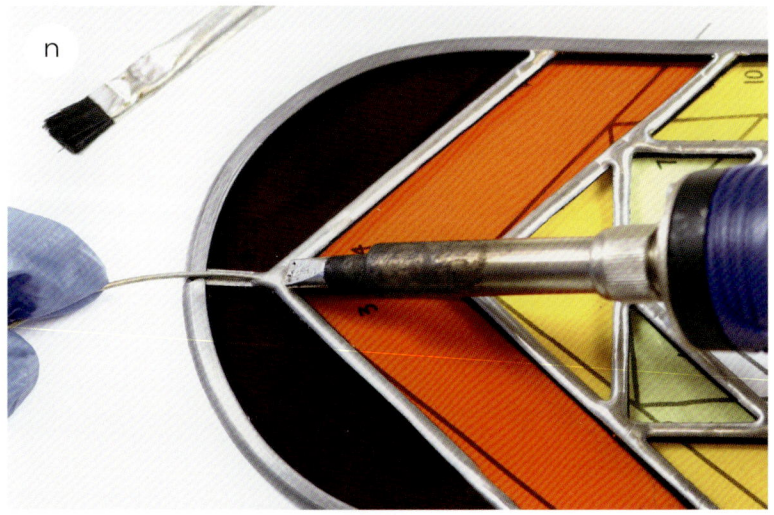

OCULUS & PALOMA

Difficulty: Adventurous Beginner

These suncatchers are beginner projects, but they're exercises in precision because of their symmetry. Any misalignment will be glaringly obvious, so keep an eye on perfect curves, straight lines, and conformity to the patterns.

Supplies

- All standard stained glass tools and supplies (see page 15)
- Layout frame (optional) – 8" (20 cm) pill-shaped frame from Erin Glassworks (8 x 3 13/16" interior)
- U-channel lead came, 3/16" size – about 24" (60 cm) length
- Horseshoe nails

Pattern

3 copies of the Oculus pattern on page 182
3 copies of the Paloma pattern on page 183

Instructions

Note: these are abbreviated steps – for more detail, follow the instructions for Ray of Light on pages 76–81.

1 Cut paper templates from one pattern. Use regular scissors to cut the perimeter, then use pattern shears to cut the interior lines.

2 Select glass, glue the templates to the glass, then cut, grind, clean, and number all the pieces.

3 Foil, using foil with a backing color that matches the color of your chosen patina, and burnish.

4 Tack the layout frame in place upon the pattern (if using).

5 Lay out the pieces in the layout frame, or lay them on the pattern and pin the perimeter in place.

6 Flux the front and tack solder all pieces, then remove the frame or pushpins.

7 Fully solder the interior lines on the front. End interior lines just short of the perimeter so that the lead came will fit, and do not solder the perimeter. Also leave unsoldered the locations where the hanging loop will be installed (indicated by dashed lines on the pattern).

8 Flux and solder the back interior lines in the same manner.

9 Finish the perimeter with stretched U-channel lead came, or with an edge bead.

10 Attach a hanging loop. Cut a 2" (5 cm) length of wire and leave it straight. Solder the wire into proper position in the interior line on the front of the project (indicated by a dashed line on the pattern). Bend the hanging wire around a flux brush or pencil toward the back so that it forms a loop. Trim the wire to the proper length and solder into position on the back.

11 Clean, patina, and polish.

MASAKO OZAKI

Okayama City, Okayama Prefecture, Japan | **Instagram: ozaki___m**

The work of Japanese artist Masako Ozaki is suffused with such elegance and simplicity it feels like poetry. Sculptural stand-alone works, meant to hang on a wall or sit on a tabletop, are finely crafted with a restrained and refined glass palette.

What inspires and informs your artwork?

Transformation in the natural world certainly inspires me – I like to reflect upon the changing of the seasons, the passage of time throughout the day. I hope to express the sense of impermanence with my work. Additionally, the philosophies and symbolism of Japanese Shinto and Zen Buddhism are manifest in my work. For example, in Japan, arrows symbolize protection against evil, and keys symbolize the fulfillment of wishes, so I create them as small talismans to help navigate the uncertainty and anxiety of this world. I hope to deliver peace of mind to those who see my works.

Can you describe your evolution as a glass artist?

My mother is a stained glass artist, and I learned the technique from her. At her atelier, I learned that only traditional technique is not enough to survive, so my sculptures moved beyond that tradition. I started working with three-dimensional forms about twenty years ago, when I created a sculpture of butterbur leaves. I relish in the malleability of techniques that I've developed. For example, when assembling a leaf sculpture, I apply small, flexible dots of solder on lines of the leaf veins, then I place the piece on my palm and gently shape it into a natural form as a whole.

What does working as a glass artist make you feel?

Liberation! I believe in simplicity – as I subtract unnecessary elements from a piece, my spirit is more fully expressed. I feel truly confident when I make a work that I don't even want to sell.

What is the stained glass community like in Japan?

Fellow artists of all types are freely connected in Japan. I have many close stained glass artist friends. The supply shops are few, but I can get material enough.

5
DESIGNING FROM A PHOTO

Let's explore how to use a favorite photo as the inspiration for a design. We'll use the shape of a layout frame to provide a starting point that informs the composition.

For my design subject, I choose a photo containing an interesting arrangement of mushrooms and ferns (a). I took this photo on a hike to Russian Lake in the Adirondacks in New York State, one of my favorite places, with Will and Kate, two of my favorite people. By using a photo with personal significance, I'm primed to create an artwork that's full of heart.

I peruse the photo for my favorite elements, and those that will be intriguing for translation into stained glass. I'm drawn to the top cluster of mushrooms – the way they form a little unit of stacked shapes. I'm also interested in the layering of the fronds in the bottom-left fern. I mentally abstract the mushrooms as circles and the fronds as wedges and visualize them overlapping like playing cards on a table.

To create the sketch, I trace the shape of the layout frame onto a blank sheet of tracing paper. On a separate sheet, I print the photo at a scale where my chosen subject elements will fit nicely into the frame. Using a light pad, I then loosely trace the elements into the outline, focusing on the overall composition and balance, merging the ferns from the bottom of the photo with the mushrooms on the top (b). I'm not making an exact tracing – I'm always considering how to simplify and how the shapes will work in glass, avoiding

tiny pieces and impossible cuts. At some point, I stop tracing from the original photo (though I keep it around as a touchpoint), and I use my innate sense of what will look best.

Now I redraw the sketch, refining the lines, simplifying the shapes, and editing out unnecessary and unwieldy pieces (c). I decide to leave just a few tinies in there for a bit of detail that differentiates foreground from background, creating depth. Sometimes, the sketch is a bit oversimplistic at this point, so I allow my imagination to fill in details and add some magic. After a few redrawings and refinements, I create the actual pattern, neatly tracing the lines with a 1 mm marker (d).

Creating a design in this way is often fruitful beyond the finished stained glass project itself. As this particular fern and mushroom oval evolved, I became enchanted by its lovely, layered shapes. I contemplated expansions on the theme: different textures, more color, new details. This inspired a follow-up project, East Bay (page 88), where I've flipped a couple of mushroom caps to feature their delicate gills. Time and time again, a simple exploration like this leads to a whole new body of work for me – each piece leading to the next, veering from abstraction, to stylization, to exaggeration, and who knows where else. This is the power of simply noticing a little thing that appeals to you, delving into the details you're drawn to, and then putting in the time and having the faith to follow the trail that the work takes you on.

RUSSIAN LAKE & EAST BAY

Difficulty: Intermediate

Here's the final result of my design exploration discussed in the previous pages – two small panels inspired by an Adirondack hike.

Supplies

- All standard stained glass tools and supplies (see page 15)
- Layout frame (optional) – 10" (25 cm) oval frame from Erin Glassworks (about 10 x 8" interior)
- U-channel lead came, 3/16" size – about 36" (1 m) length
- Horseshoe nails

Pattern

3 copies of the Russian Lake pattern on page 184
3 copies of the East Bay pattern on page 185

Instructions

Note: these are abbreviated steps – for more detail, follow the instructions for Ray of Light on page 76.

1 Cut paper templates from one pattern. Use regular scissors to cut the perimeter, then use pattern shears to cut the interior.

2 Select glass, glue the templates to the glass, then cut and grind the pieces.

3 Lay out the ground pieces on your work surface inside the layout frame (a). They should fit together, gently touching, with no large gaps. If any pieces are too tight, return to the grinder to create a better fit.

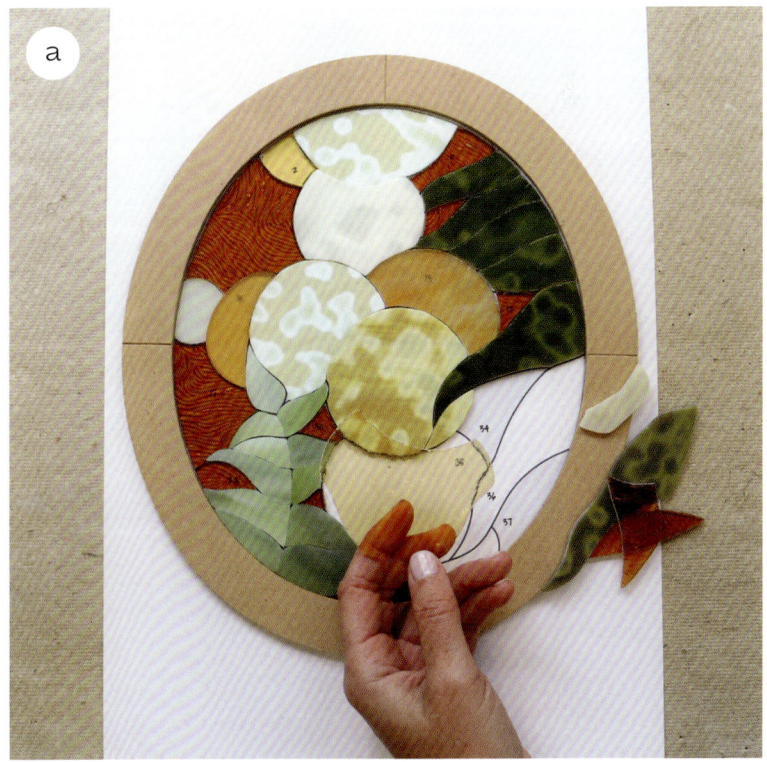

4 Foil (b), using foil with a backing color that matches the color of your chosen patina, and burnish.

5 Return the pieces to the layout frame, or pin in place on the pattern.

6 Solder the front of your project with the pieces held in place in the layout frame. End interior lines just short of the perimeter to leave room for the lead came, and leave the perimeter unsoldered. Also leave unsoldered the locations where hanging loops will be installed (indicated by dashed lines on the pattern).

7 Remove the layout frame, flip the project, and solder the interior lines of the back.

8 Use wire cutters to cut a piece of stretched U-channel lead came to roughly the length of the perimeter of the project.

9 Press the lead firmly onto the perimeter so that the glass fills the U-shaped channel, working around the entire perimeter. Then mark (c) and cut the lead came with wire cutters so that the ends of the came meet neatly.

10 Use horseshoe nails to hold the lead came in place on your work surface (d). If you see any foil around the perimeter after the came is applied, trim it off with a craft knife.

11 Extend all interior solder lines so that they connect neatly to the lead came (e). Turn down your heat a little to avoid melting the lead. Leave the hanging loop locations unsoldered.

12 Attach hanging loops. Cut two lengths of 2" (5 cm) wire and leave straight. Solder the wire into the proper position in the interior line on the front of the project (indicated by a dashed line on the pattern) (f). Bend the wire around a pencil or flux brush so that it forms a loop and can be soldered to the back of the project (g). Trim to the proper length and solder into position on the back. Repeat for the second loop.

13 Clean, patina (h), and polish.

LAURE FORÊT

Antwerp, Belgium | **laureforet.com** @laureforet

The play and experimentation in Laure's work always keep me wondering what she'll create next. The way the materials (often, but not always, glass) are manipulated – assembled in nontraditional ways with traditional stained glass technique – creates a simultaneously visceral and emotional reaction.

What is the role of play in your art?
I would say that play is the root of my creativity. To start creating, I need to be interested in something – maybe a certain piece of glass, or a problem to be solved – that inspires an idea or a form, which in turn causes me to wonder, "Is it possible to make this?" I then begin to experiment, and test, and transform. I believe that play is what makes us human beings: the impulse to play and experiment with our surroundings and create something uniquely "us."

For your sculptural pieces, do you sketch and prototype carefully before beginning to construct?
I should! In reality, I draw mainly to not forget the idea. Drawing also keeps me grounded – sometimes an idea looks great in the blur of my imagination, but it isn't able to be physically represented on paper. For a huge project, I will draw more, mainly to be sure that the piece can be disassembled for transport yet will not fall apart when installed! Part of me approaches a project with all the necessary seriousness and planning, but an even bigger part of me loves the risk of improvisation and evolution. To me, glass is a living material, always shifting in color and transparency, so I want to give it the freedom to transform beyond my first idea. Trusting my process often gives me very good surprises.

What inspires the visceral feel of your work?
My art is, of course, grounded in my personal experience of this world. I have atopic skin, contact allergies, and generally a body that expresses my feelings whether I want it to or not (stress rash, gut issues, anxiety, etc). To cope, I've learned to laugh with myself and my twin (my inside and my outside). I question borders and patterns in our complex connections to our surroundings

(vegetal, animal, mineral...) and the boundaries that we desperately create to protect ourselves. Glass is one representation of this: a border that is porous like skin, which you can see through if you are curious. A material that constantly changes as our identity is constantly changing.

Will you share your inspiration and evolution as a mixed-media artist?
Every artist must find their own inspiration. Some dedicate themselves to a single material, but I can't do this, because moving between materials is what nourishes me and my work. So, I work with both glass and textile. These materials have similarities: both are transparent, fragile, and react with their surroundings.

Also, in France where I was an art student, both were considered to be related to arts and crafts, rather than to fine arts such as painting and drawing. But I've never liked these boundaries.

Glass appeared in my palette only in the past decade, when I luckily met Noor from Glas & Glas in Belgium, who taught me the Tiffany stained glass technique. I fell in love with the whole process. Glass, like all materials, has its own personality and it has allowed me to move into three-dimensional sculpture. Where I'm from, stained glass is strongly associated with sacred art, so I'm also interested in playing with this dimension – creating something sacred, usually untouchable – but bringing it back down to the eyes of the viewer.

6
MIRROR GLASS

Leave your superstitions at the door, because we are about to break some mirror!

Though mirror seems quite magical, it is simply regular clear glass backed by a layer of "silvering" – a metallic compound deposited on one side of the glass, usually covered with a layer of paint to prevent scratches. We can work with it (pretty much) just like any other glass.

Mirror can be incorporated into any project, but it adds a few constraints to your design. Keep in mind that mirror glass is not translucent – no light will shine through it. Additionally, the back of mirror glass is not nice to look at – it is usually a dull gray. Therefore, projects using mirror glass are typically best hung against a wall, rather than in a window where light would shine through and both sides would be visible.

Fortunately, glass crafters are not limited only to the "standard" mirror glass that you use to check your look before heading out of the house. There are some lovely specialty glasses that use a silvering layer. Check out "Van Gogh," a colorful mirrored gluechip glass, available in many colors; "Spectrum Silvercoat," also available in many colors, which has the texture of Spectrum or Oceanside Waterglass; and the lovely vintage mirror effects of ML Walker glass. These specialty glasses must be treated in the same manner as standard mirror glass, as described below.

WORKING WITH MIRROR GLASS

Mirror glass behaves like any other glass (in fact, it's especially easy to cut – like clear float or sheet glass), but it does require that you take some extra, minor precautions. Avoid scratches: damaging the back side will ruin the silvering and will be visible from the front, and even a scratch on the front side will be amplified by its own reflection.

Additionally, you need to seal the mirror so that it is not susceptible to "mirror rot" – black markings that appear when oxidation develops between the backing and the glass, caused by scratches, flux, patina, or even ambient humidity. Sealant is available in various forms: as an aerosol spray, as a liquid to be painted on, or in a bottle with a sponge dauber applicator. If your usual glass supplier does not stock it, you can find it at automotive parts stores.

Keeping the following advice in mind will help your mirror remain flawless for years to come.

▲ Mirror rot

Cutting

- Score the mirror only on the "front" reflective side, not on the painted, silvered "back" side.
- Keep your work surface very clean, using a bench brush to clear away any glass chips every time you make a score and break.
- Do not slide the mirror around on the work surface; instead, lift it up and place it down onto an area that has been brushed clean.

Grinding

- Use a fine grit grinding bit to avoid chipping the silvering.

Too much chipping

- Alternately, you can use an old bit that is too worn down to work efficiently for your normal grinding tasks. Test it on a few scraps of mirror to see that you can create a nice, smooth, chip-free edge, and make that bit your designated "mirror bit."

Nicely ground mirror

- Lay a thin, soft cloth – such as a scrap of flannel – on the grinder bed to discourage any chips from scratching the mirror glass as you move it around on the grinder surface.

▼ Use cloth to prevent scratching

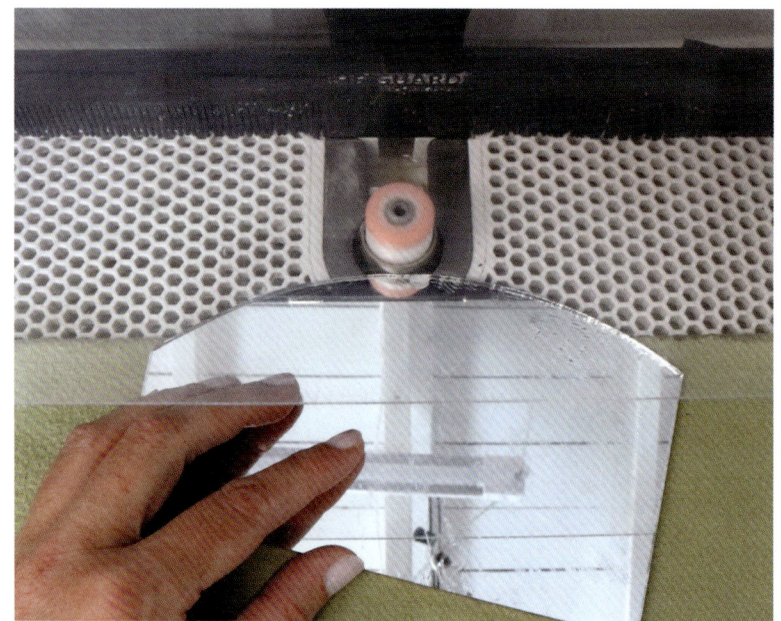

96 RAISE YOUR GLASS

- You might want to grind with the silvered side facing up but remember that scratches on the front of the mirror are also undesirable, so you must still be careful.

Cleaning

- Use water to rinse the ground mirror pieces. Never use glass cleaner that contains ammonia on mirror glass.
- Use extra care when drying to avoid damaging the silvering.

Sealing

- After grinding and cleaning, be sure that the pieces are completely clean and dry.
- Spray, paint, or dab sealant onto the entire silvered side of the mirror as well as the ground edges, but not the front.
- Let dry, then apply an extra coat to the edges, and about 1" (2.5 cm) onto the back.
- If you get any sealant on the front, let it dry and scrape it off using a razor blade flat against the glass.
- Allow the sealant to dry completely before foiling.

Foiling

- As with any other glass, match your foil backing color to the color of the patina with which you plan to finish the solder.
- To provide a little more protection of the silvering, use a wider foil than you usually would: 1/4" is great. To prevent this wider foil from creating a thicker solder line on the front, when applying the foil, don't center it around the glass as usual; instead, leave more of the overhang to be folded over the back of the mirror glass.
- Be sure that the foil on the silvering is burnished flat to prevent flux from seeping in.

Flux, soldering, and patina

- Use flux and patina sparingly and clean them off promptly.
- Do not linger while soldering to avoid damaging the sealant.

Finishing

I like to give my mirrored projects (and the wall on which they hang) a little extra protection by covering the back of the mirror with felt, which will prevent the silver being scratched by the hanging wire and hook.

WOODLAND MIRROR

Difficulty: Intermediate

My favorite motifs – mushrooms and ferns – make a wreath around the mirror in this whimsical design, joined by a bit of honeycomb and a happy little moth. If I lived in my dream house (lakeside, tall pines, moss, and loons) this would be the perfect decor to brighten a dark corner.

Because this project will most likely hang on a wall rather than in a window (where light would shine through the glass), choose opaque or opalescent glass that looks beautiful when lit from the front.

Supplies

- All standard stained glass tools and supplies (see page 15)
- 20 gauge wire to create hanging loops
- Mirror edge sealant
- Felt for the backing
- Picture hanging wire

Pattern

3 copies of the Woodland Mirror pattern on page 186, enlarged to 110%

Instructions

Note: for each of these steps, use special care on the mirror glass pieces (see Working with Mirror Glass on page 95–97).

1 Cut paper templates from one pattern. Use regular scissors to cut the perimeter, then use pattern shears to cut the interior.

2 Select glass and glue the templates to the glass.

3 Cut, grind, clean, and number all glass pieces.

4 Apply **sealant** to the mirror piece before foiling, then let it dry. Apply another coat and let it dry again.

5 Foil and burnish all pieces.

6 Lay out all pieces on the pattern and pin in place.

7 Flux and solder the front and back, then create a nice edge bead along the perimeter.

8 For hanging loops, cut two 1 1/2" (4 cm) lengths of 20 gauge wire. Shape the wire into loops that can accommodate the picture hanging wire, and then angle each loop so that one side will lay flat upon a solder line on the mirror (b).

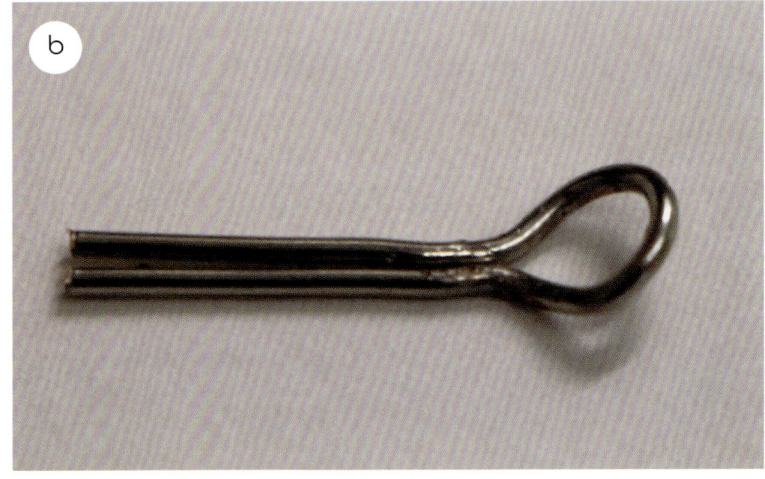

b

WOODLAND MIRROR

9 Embed hanging loops in the solder seams where indicated on the pattern, positioning them so that the loops do not extend over the back of the mirror and are lifted from the surface (c).

10 Clean, patina, and polish.

11 Cut a piece of felt to fit just inside the solder line that borders the mirror, using the pattern template as a guide (d). Apply spray adhesive to one side of the felt, press the felt into position on the back of the mirror (e), and allow to dry.

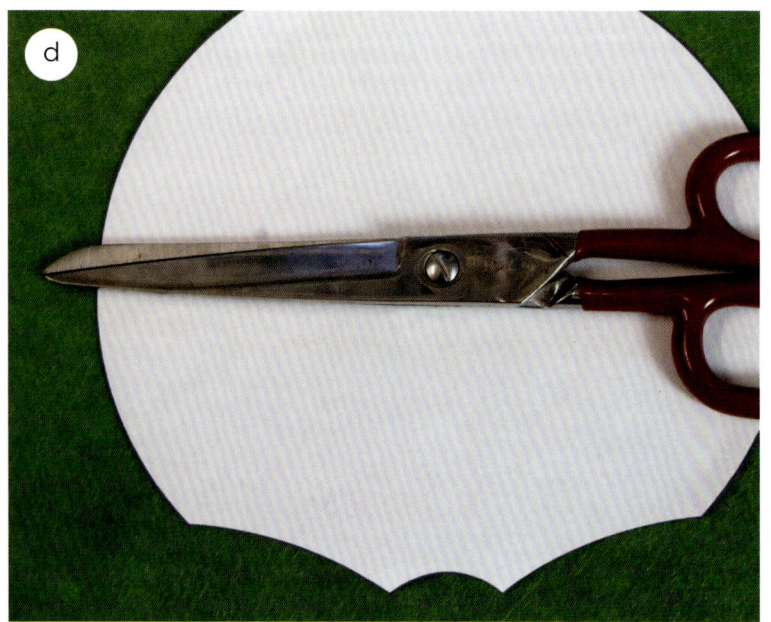

12 Attach picture wire to the hanging loops (f).

MEADOW MIRROR

Difficulty: Intermediate

The simple unpainted version of this mirror will look charming in your favorite glass, but the painted version is even more enchanting. Here the painted folk-art motif is repeated on every wing, creating a pattern and evoking the dream of a swirling cluster of butterflies. I used Bullseye opalescent glass in Petal Pink and Marigold, adding amber and white paint for a "golden hour in the wildflower meadow" vibe.

Because this project will most likely hang on a wall rather than in a window (where light would shine through the glass), choose opaque or opalescent glass that looks beautiful when lit from the front.

Supplies

- All standard stained glass tools and supplies (see page 15)
- Glass paint (see page 55)
- Mirror edge sealant
- 20 gauge wire to create hanging loops
- Felt for the backing
- Picture hanging wire

Pattern

3 copies of the Meadow Mirror pattern on page 187, enlarged to 120%

Instructions

Note: for each of these steps, use special care on the mirror glass pieces (see Working with Mirror Glass on page 95).

1 Cut paper templates from one pattern. Use regular scissors to cut the perimeter, then use pattern shears to cut the interior.

2 Select your glass and glue the templates to the glass.

3 Cut, grind, clean, and number all glass pieces.

4 Paint and bake the butterfly pieces, using the design on page 187 (or your own design, of course!) (a). See the Painting Glass instructions on page 55–57.

5 Before foiling, apply two coats of sealant to the mirror edges, allowing it to dry completely after each coat (b).

6 Foil and burnish all pieces.

7 Lay out all pieces on the pattern and pin in place (c).

8 Flux and solder the front and back, then create a nice edge bead along the perimeter.

9 For the hanging loops, cut two 1 1/2" (4 cm) lengths of 20 gauge wire. Shape the wire into loops that can accommodate the picture hanging wire, and then angle each loop so that one side will lay flat upon a solder line on the mirror (d).

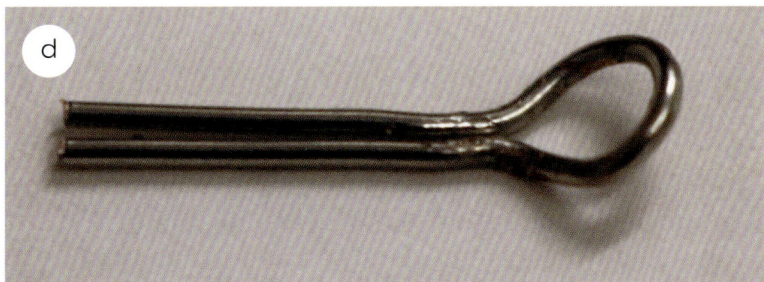

10 Embed the hanging loops in the solder seams, where indicated on the pattern, positioning so that the loop does not extend over the back of the mirror and is lifted from the surface (e).

11 Clean, patina, and polish (f).

12 Cut a piece of felt to fit just inside the solder line that borders the mirror, using the pattern template as a guide (g). Apply spray adhesive to one side of the felt, press into position on the back of the mirror, and allow to dry.

13 Attach picture wire to the hanging loops.

MEADOW MIRROR

7
WINDOW TOPPERS

Rigid U-channel zinc came is used to finish the top straight edge of these projects to provide resistance against stresses across such a wide, narrow span.

For ease and flexibility in hanging, we'll use hanging "rings" here, rather than the "loops" we've used in other projects. The rings, made of heavy gauge wire soldered directly to the zinc, are appropriate for these lightweight projects; heavier pieces would require the solder line anchoring that embedded loops provide. This ring technique creates a great-looking fixture that can hang from two tiny nails or hooks below a rafter, above a doorway, or against a window. If you make all three window toppers, you'll be able to easily swap between them as the season – or your mood – changes.

▲ Hanging ring and U-channel zinc came

ARCHIMEDES OWL

Difficulty: Intermediate

This owl is a great "scrap-buster" project that can be created in an unlimited variety of colorways. I chose a subtle ombré of greys from Bullseye, Youghiogheny, and Wissmach.

Pro tip: For the owl's face, use the narrowest foil possible (I used 3/16" on average-thickness glass). This will result in thinner solder lines, making the face appear finer and more elegant.

Supplies

- All standard stained glass tools and supplies (see page 15)
- Layout strips or straightedges
- Horseshoe nails or pushpins
- U-channel zinc came, 1/4" size – about 15" (40 cm) length
- Chop saw or sharp wire cutters
- Metal file

Pattern

3 copies of the Archimedes Owl pattern on page 188–189, enlarged to 130%

Instructions

1 Cut paper templates from one pattern. For the long straight edge, use a straightedge and craft knife. Cut the curved perimeter lines using regular scissors, then use pattern shears to cut the interior lines.

2 Select your glass and glue the templates to the glass.

3 Cut, grind, clean, and number all the pieces.

4 Foil, using foil with a backing color that matches your chosen patina, and burnish.

5 Pin a straightedge or layout strip at the top edge of the pattern.

6 Lay the foiled pieces on the pattern, making sure that the top edges are perfectly snug against the straightedge. Pin the bottom perimeter in place with horseshoe nails or pushpins (a).

a

7 Flux and solder the front and back interior lines. Leave the perimeter edges unsoldered, as well as any locations within the dotted lines on the pattern, where the zinc will be placed (b).

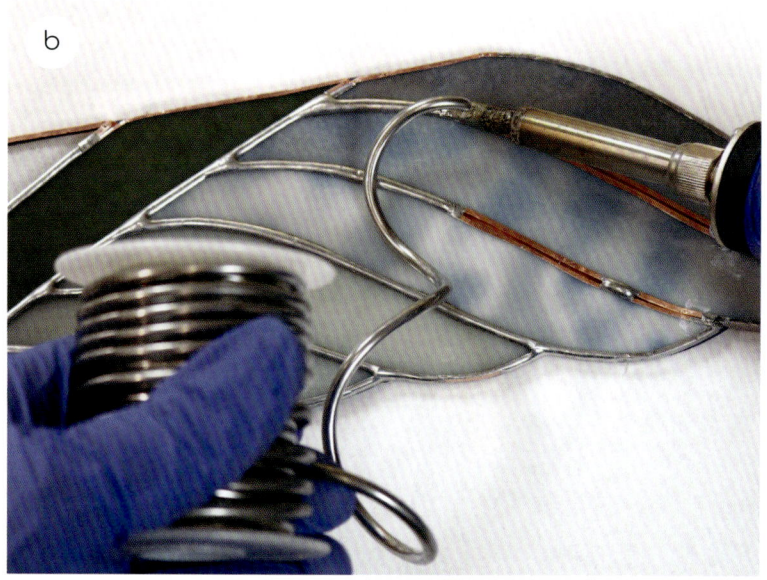

8 Cut the zinc came to the length and angle indicated on the pattern. First, draw the cut line onto the zinc with a marker, then cut with a chop saw or wire cutters (c). To avoid crushing the U-channel with wire cutters, cut through each flange of the U separately (d), then bend a few times so that the back snaps (e). File smooth any burrs or jagged edges (f).

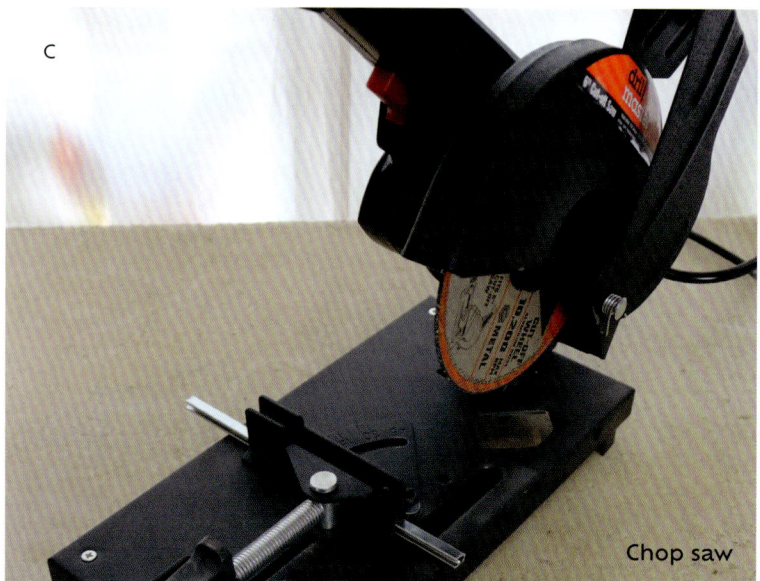

Chop saw

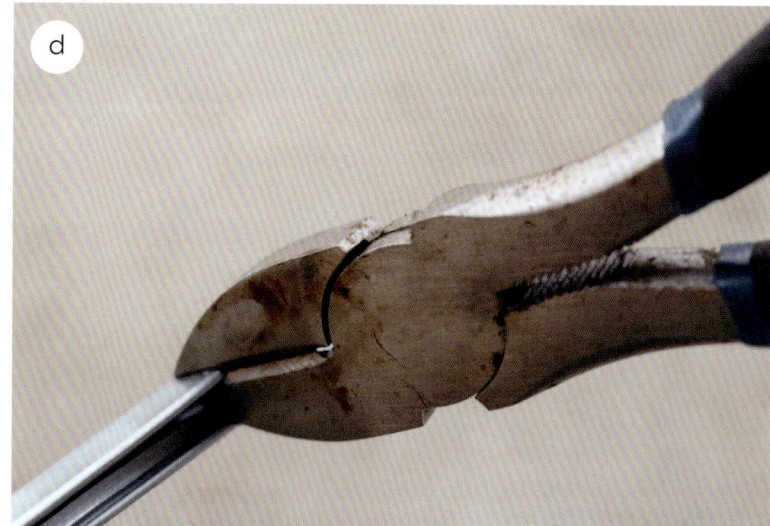

9 Insert the project into the zinc channel and push it up against the layout strip (g).

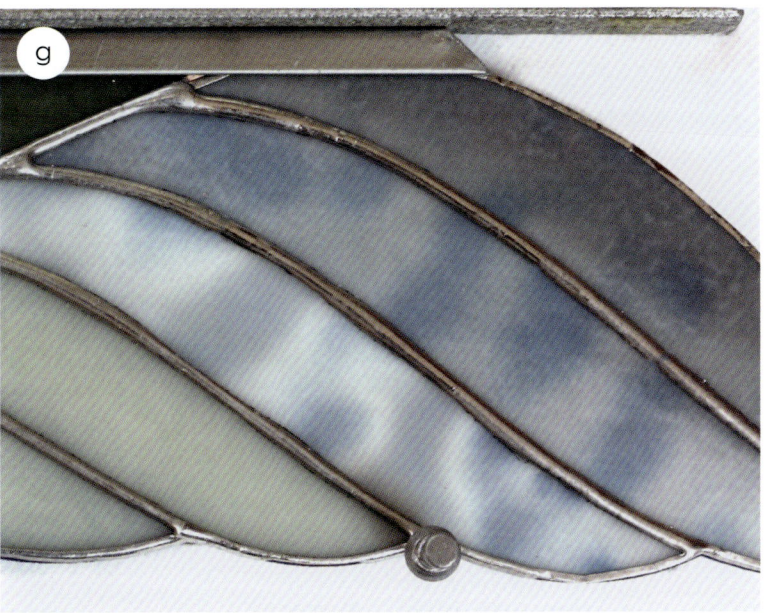

10 Flux and solder at every intersection between zinc and an interior line (h), using just a neat little touch of solder on the zinc.

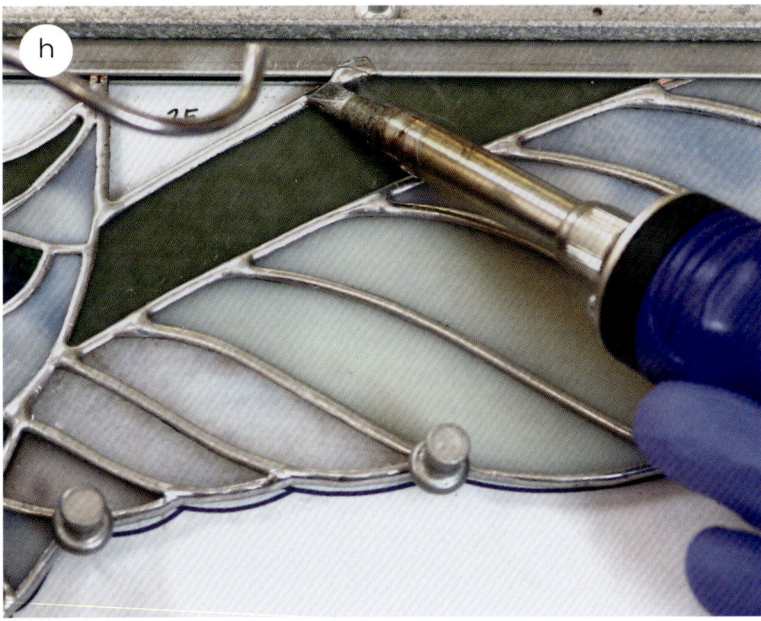

11 Finish the bottom perimeter of the project with a nice edge bead.

12 Fill in the gaps on the cut ends of the zinc with solder, blending into your edge bead (i, j).

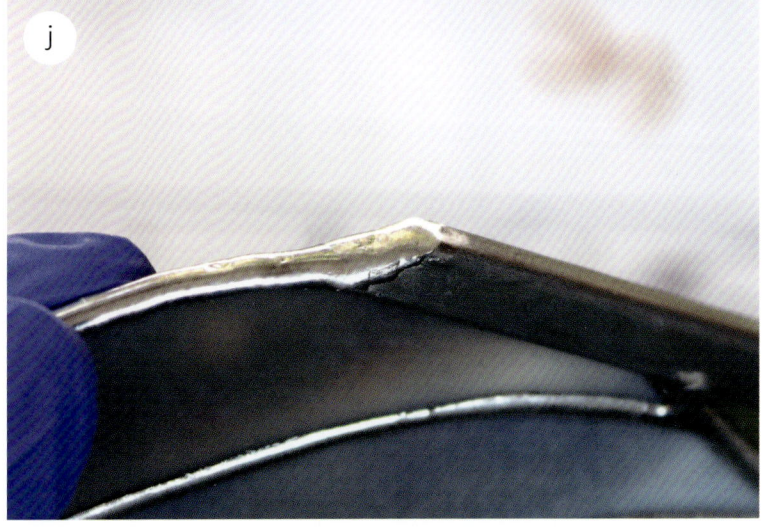

13 Make the hanging rings. Coil 6" (15 cm) of 12 gauge copper wire around the barrel of a felt tip marker so that a little more than two full circles are formed (k). Remove from the marker and cut two "C" shaped rings (about three-quarters of a circle) from the coil using wire cutters (l, m).

14 Solder the rings to the top edge of the zinc. Be sure to hold the rings with pliers – the copper wire will heat up. First, flux and tin each ring with a thin coat of solder so that the copper is entirely covered. Next, flux the top edge of the zinc at the locations indicated on the pattern, hold the ring in place and tack the front (n). Flip the project and solder the other side fully, creating a neat join all around the wire. Let cool, then return to the tacked side of the ring and solder fully. Repeat with the second hanging ring.

15 Clean, patina, and polish.

BIRDWING BUTTERFLY

Difficulty: Intermediate

Like the Archimedes Owl, this project is great for using up scraps and can be created in an unlimited variety of colorways. Why not choose a color combination that's inspired by the hues of your favorite moth or butterfly?

Supplies

- All standard stained glass tools and supplies (see page 15)
- Layout strips or straightedges
- Horseshoe nails or pushpins
- U-channel zinc came, 1/4" size – about 16" (40 cm) length
- Chop saw or sharp wire cutters
- Metal file

Pattern

3 copies of the Birdwing Butterfly pattern on page 190, enlarged to 160%

Instructions

To make the Birdwing Butterfly, follow the instructions for the Archimedes Owl on page 106–110.

HAVISHAM BAT

Difficulty: Intermediate

For this little guy's body, I used Youghiogheny 333HS, an iridescent opaque black glass. For the background, I chose Floreal, a pressed clear lacy glass with an appropriately creepy, vintage Miss Havisham vibe.

Though this is a good "advanced beginner" project, the cuts on pieces 18 and 23 are difficult, so make sure you choose a familiar glass that behaves nicely. Paint is optional on the bat's head and body (pieces 13 and 17) – use the painting template provided on the pattern and refer to the Painting Glass instructions on page 55. For the simple semicircle perimeter, I've used U-channel lead came to create a super-clean edge, but you can also finish with standard edge bead soldering.

Supplies

- All standard stained glass tools and supplies (see page 15)
- Layout strips or straightedges
- Glass paint (see page 55)
- Horseshoe nails or pushpins
- Chop saw or sharp wire cutters
- U-channel lead came, 3/16" size – about 24" (60 cm) length
- U-channel zinc came, 1/4" size – about 12" (30 cm) length
- Metal file

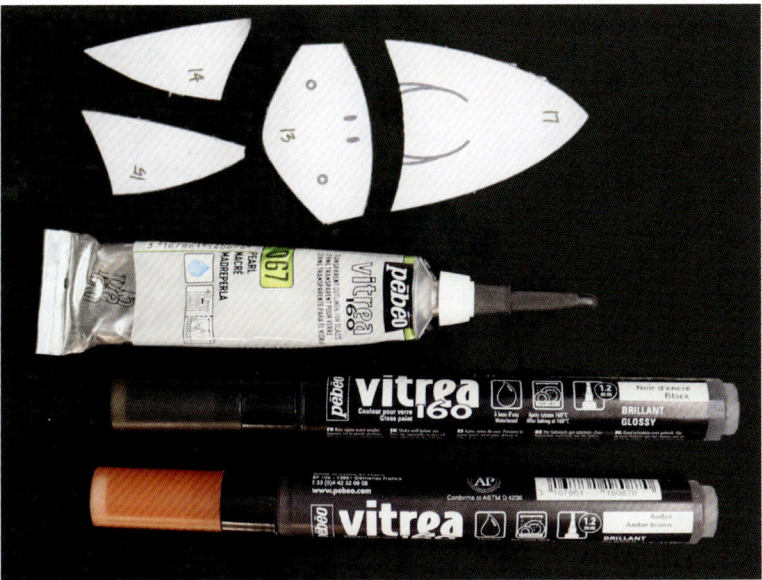

Pattern

3 copies of the Havisham Bat pattern on page 191, enlarged to 120%

Instructions

1 Cut paper templates from one pattern. For the long straight edge, use a straightedge and craft knife. Cut the curved perimeter lines using regular scissors, then use pattern shears to cut the interior lines.

2 Select your glass and glue the templates to the glass.

3 Cut, grind, clean, and number all the pieces (a).

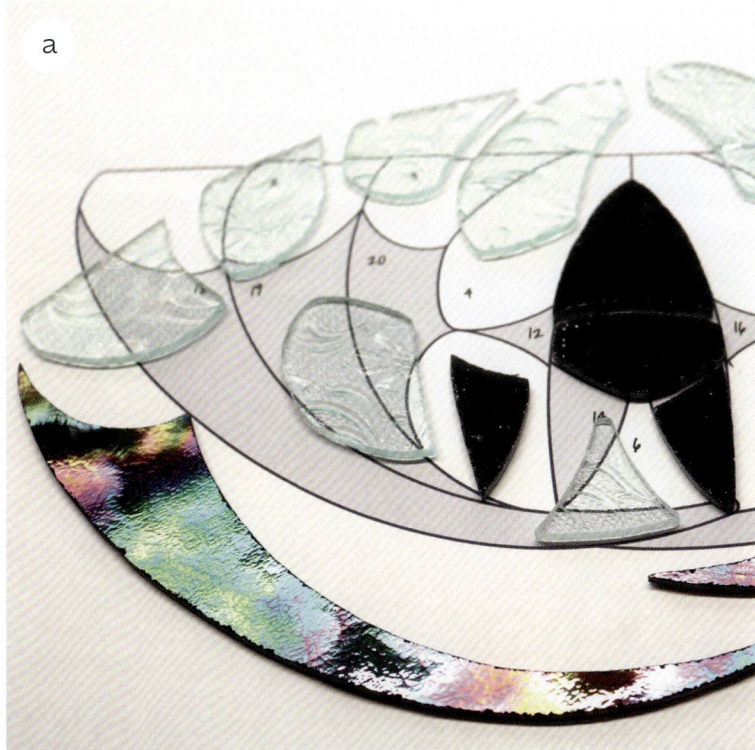

4 Paint the glass. Draw eyes and nose onto the head piece and fangs onto the body piece (b). Bake them and let cool (see the Painting Glass instructions on page 55).

5 Foil, using foil with a backing color that matches your chosen patina, and burnish.

6 Pin a straightedge or layout strip at the top edge of the pattern.

7 Lay the foiled pieces on the pattern, making sure that the top edges are perfectly snug against the straightedge. Pin the bottom perimeter in place with horseshoe nails or pushpins (c).

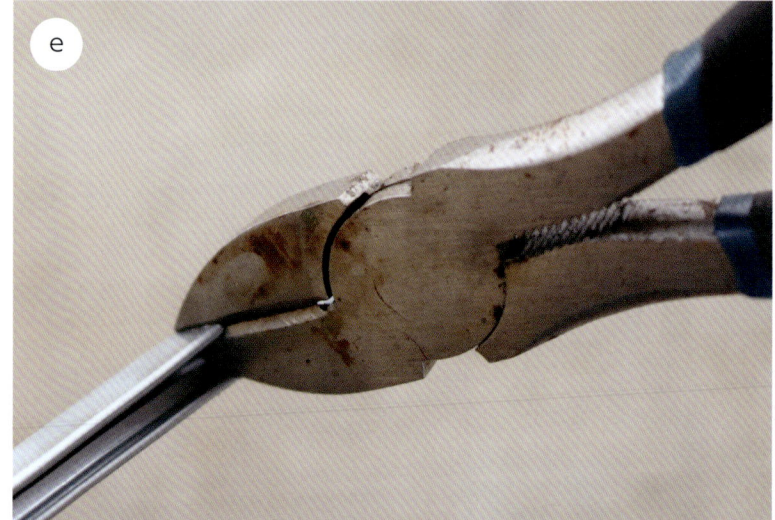

8 Flux and solder the front and back interior lines. End the interior lines just short of the perimeter to leave room for the lead and zinc came, and leave the perimeter unsoldered.

9 Cut the zinc came to the length and angle indicated on the pattern. First, draw the cut line onto the zinc with a marker, then cut with a chop saw (d) or wire cutters. To avoid crushing the U-channel with wire cutters, cut through each flange of the U separately, then bend a few times so that the back snaps (e, f, g). File smooth any burrs or jagged edges (g).

10 Insert the project into the zinc channel and push it up against the layout strip.

11 Flux and solder at every intersection between zinc and an interior line, using just a neat little touch of solder on the zinc.

12 Use wire cutters to cut a piece of stretched U-channel lead came to roughly the length of the bottom perimeter.

13 Butt the leading end of the lead came up against the bottom edge of the zinc came (h). Press the lead firmly onto the perimeter so that the glass fills the U-shaped channel, working around the bottom perimeter. Then mark and cut the trailing end of the came with wire cutters.

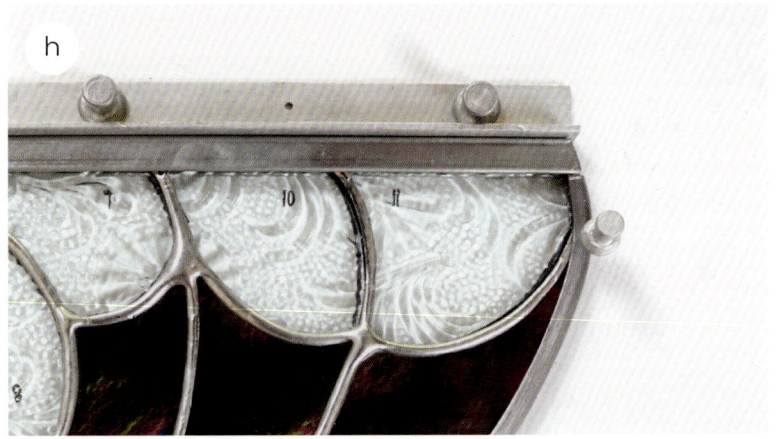

14 Pin the lead came in place on your work surface using horseshoe nails. If you see any foil peeking out from under the came, trim it off with a craft knife.

15 Extend all interior solder lines so that they connect neatly to the lead came. Turn down your heat a little to avoid melting the lead. Fill in the gaps on the cut ends of the zinc came with solder and create a smooth junction with the lead came (i, j).

HAVISHAM BAT   **115**

16 Make the hanging rings: Coil 6" (15 cm) of 12 gauge copper wire around the barrel of a felt tip marker so that a little more than two full circles are formed. Remove from the marker and cut two "C" shaped rings (about three-quarters of a circle) from the coil using wire cutters (k, l).

17 Solder the rings to the top edge of the zinc. Be sure to hold the rings with pliers – the copper wire will heat up. First, flux and tin each ring with a thin coat of solder so that the copper is entirely covered. Next, flux the top edge of the zinc at the locations indicated on the pattern, hold the ring in place and tack the front (m). Flip the project and solder the other side fully, creating a neat join all around the wire. Let cool, then return to the tacked side of the ring and solder fully (n). Repeat with the second hanging ring.

18 Clean, patina, and polish.

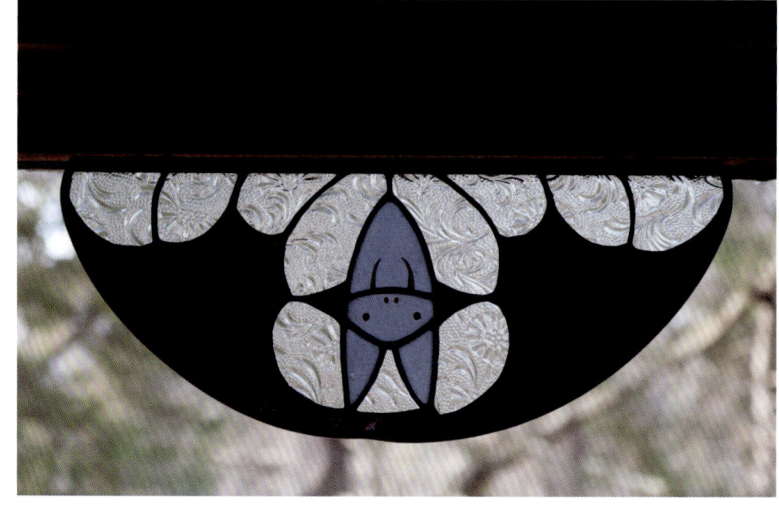

8
FOREST TREASURES MINI SHELVES

Difficulty: Advanced

Create a cute place to display all of your special foraged finds. We'll construct a three-dimensional box and then add shelves to the interior.

Opaque or opalescent glass is suggested for the side walls of the box, so the shelf edges don't distract from the branch design. For this tutorial, I've used Oceanside System 96 Medium Amber/White. It is quite a unique glass with a streaky wood-like grain on one side and mostly white on the reverse. The little pieces that make up the mushrooms and honeycomb are a great way to use up some scrap glass.

One way to personalize this project is to design your own adornments. Notice that each of my mushrooms is small and has two anchor points, assuring that it will attach securely. Keep these guidelines in mind as you create your own, and go for it!

Supplies

- All standard stained glass tools and supplies (see page 15)
- Straightedges
- Layout strips and pushpins
- 16 or 18 gauge tinned copper wire for hanging loops

Pattern

3 copies of the Forest Treasures Mini Shelves patterns on page 192

Instructions

1 Cut the paper templates from one pattern. For the straight perimeter lines, use a straightedge and craft knife. Cut the curved perimeter lines using regular scissors, then use pattern shears to cut the interior lines.

2 Select your glass and glue the templates to the glass.

3 Cut the glass, using a straightedge for all straight cuts.

4 Grind all pieces, taking extra care to keep the lines and angles of the rectangular pieces straight and square.

5 Clean, dry, and number all the pieces.

6 Foil, using foil with a backing color that matches your chosen patina. On the long side pieces, start and end the foil in an area that will be on an interior solder line, not on an outer straight edge. Burnish all pieces.

7 Lay out the pieces for the left and right side walls upon the pattern, using layout strips to ensure that the perimeter is straight and square and matches the dimensions of the pattern (a).

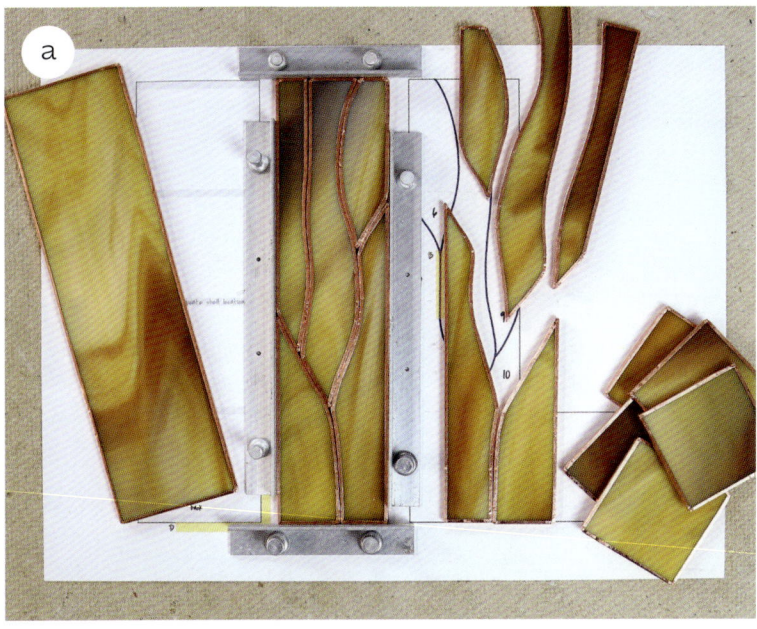

FOREST TREASURES MINI SHELVES

8 Flux, then solder only the front face (which will be the outside of the project) (b), leaving unsoldered the lengths indicated in yellow on the pattern (where the mushrooms will attach). The back face must remain free of solder so that the shelves will butt flush up to the back face of the side.

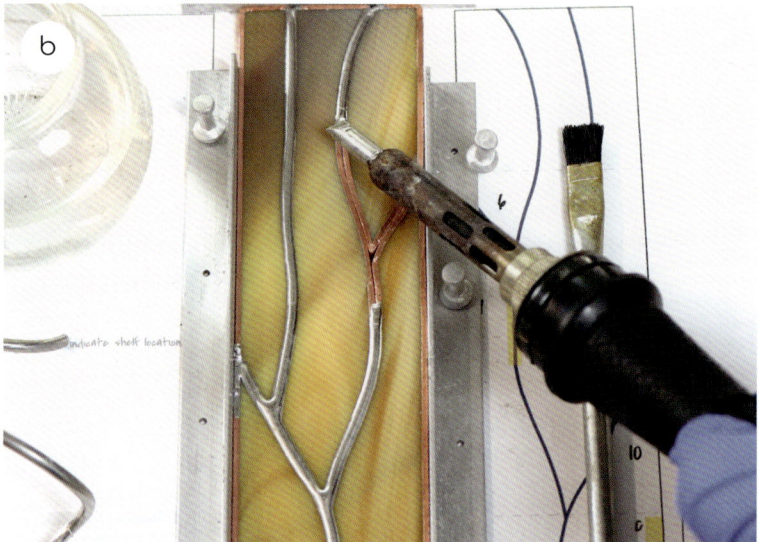

9 Flip these soldered side walls over onto the pattern with their back (interior) unsoldered faces oriented up. Use a marker on the glass face to trace the locations where the shelves will attach (indicated by gray lines on the pattern) (c). Do the same on the rectangular piece that will become the project's back wall.

10 Now assemble the exterior box (the two long side pieces, the back piece, and two of the five smaller square pieces as the top and bottom) (d). Hold a wide wall piece perpendicular to your work surface. Butt the edge of one of the narrow square walls up against the face of the wide wall piece (e). Check that they form a right angle, then flux and tack solder the pieces together on the top edge and then again halfway down.

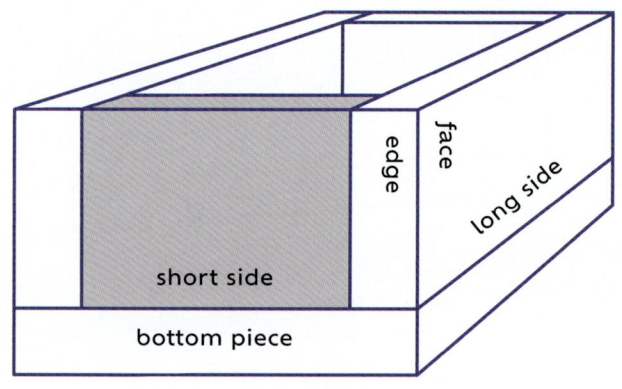

▲ An overview of the box construction

11 Next, place the other wide wall piece in position, checking that the design is oriented properly relative to the other side, and tack in place with the square wall butting up against its face (f).

12 Finally, tack the fourth wall in place, being sure that the square piece is butted between the wide walls (g).

13 Now position this assemblage atop the base piece. Double-check that the design on the long side is oriented properly (so that the front of the design is facing up from the work surface) (h). Check that everything is square and flush, then tack the sides to the base (i).

FOREST TREASURES MINI SHELVES

14 Slide a shelf piece into the box, making sure that the location of the overlapping foil end is facing the back of the box (j). Align the shelf with the marks you previously made, and secure in place by tacking it to the front (top) edge of the sides (k), the interior lines of the side walls, and the little bit of foil visible on the back face. Repeat with the other two shelves.

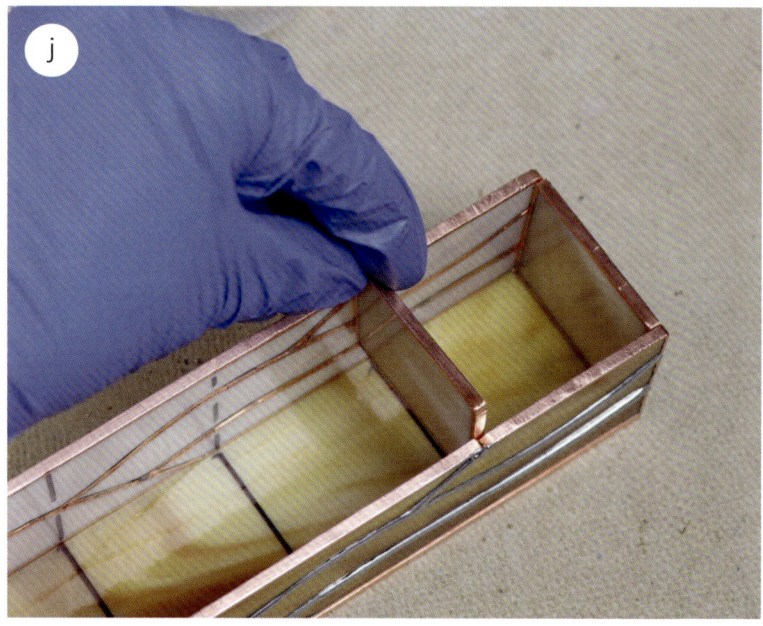

15 Flux and tin all of the visible foil in the interior and run a neat bead on the interior design lines of the sides. These interior design solder lines should meld neatly with the bit of tinned foil on each shelf (l).

16 Flux and solder all of the exterior box seams, except the lengths indicated in yellow on the pattern (where the honeycombs and hanging wires will attach). If you get any drip-through, try turning down your heat, or holding a damp rag against the reverse side of the spot you're soldering.

17 Make a neat, sturdy edge bead along the front edges of the shelves and sides, using enough solder that the junctions blend together nicely.

18 Create the hanging loops. With tinned copper wire, fashion two P-shaped loops, as indicated by the dashed lines in the pattern (you can bend the wire around a thin paintbrush handle). Use pliers to hold each loop in the proper position on the project, then solder it into the seam at the rear top, nearly flush with the back surface, encompassing the wire neatly with solder (m).

▲ Hanging loops on the finished piece

19 Flux and solder the front and back of each mushroom and honeycomb adornment piece, leaving unsoldered the lengths indicated in yellow on the pattern (n). Create an edge bead on the perimeter of each adornment, again leaving the yellow lengths unsoldered.

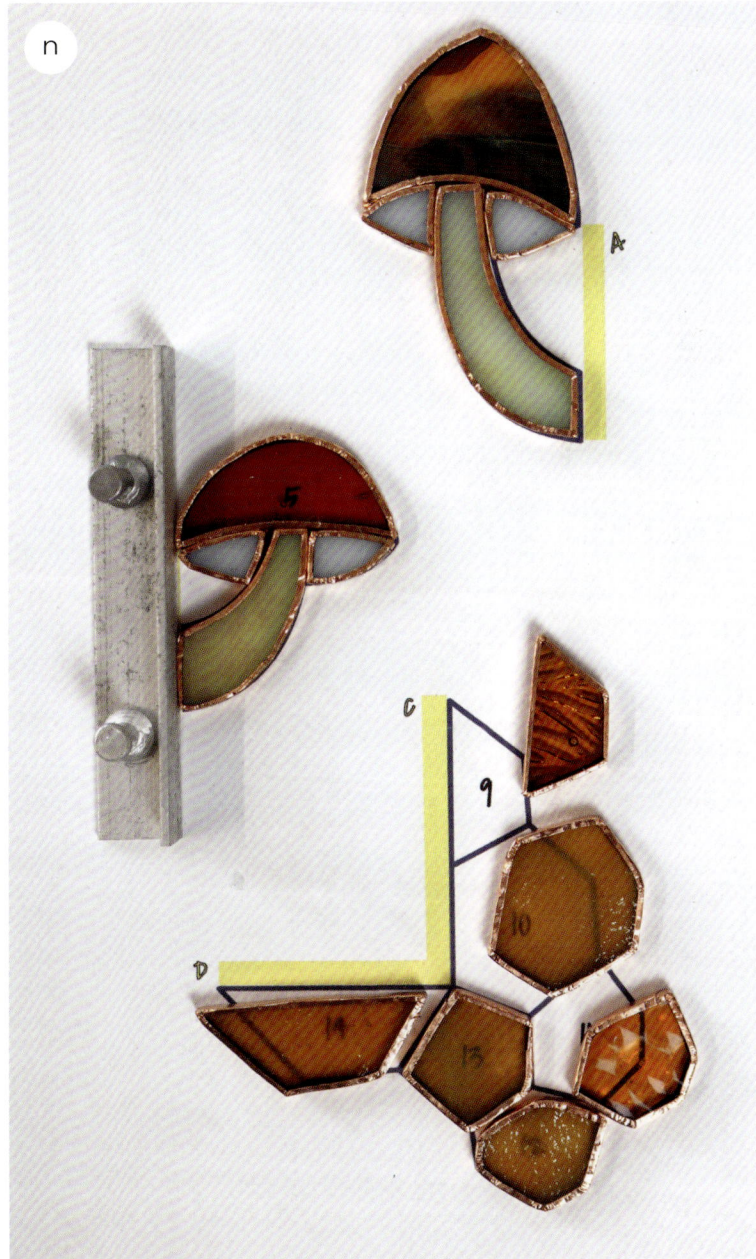

20 Using pliers, hold each adornment to the box at the location indicated (by a yellow line and letter) on the pattern, and then solder neatly into position (o). Blend each adornment's edge soldering into the solder line on the box side (p, q).

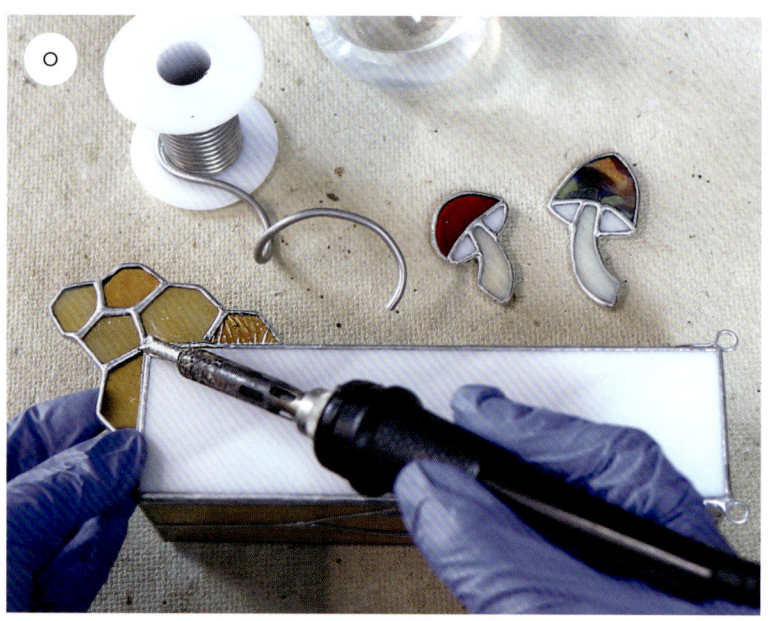

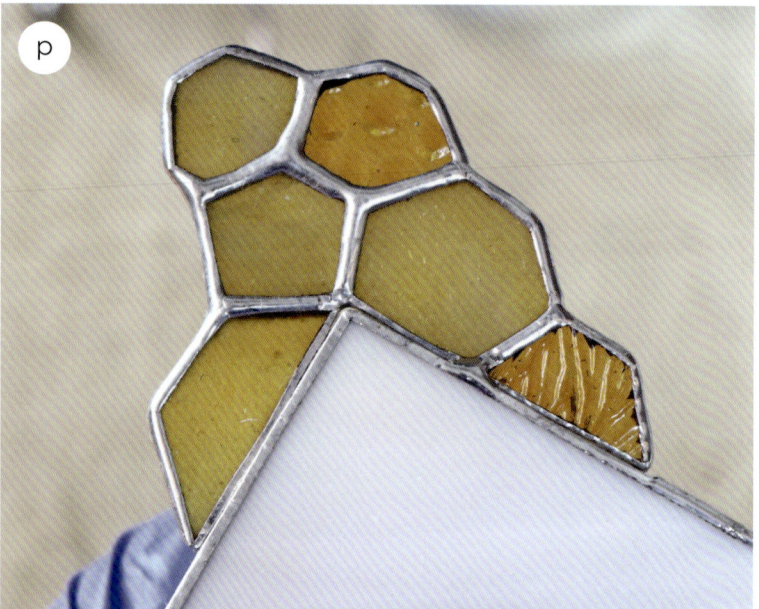

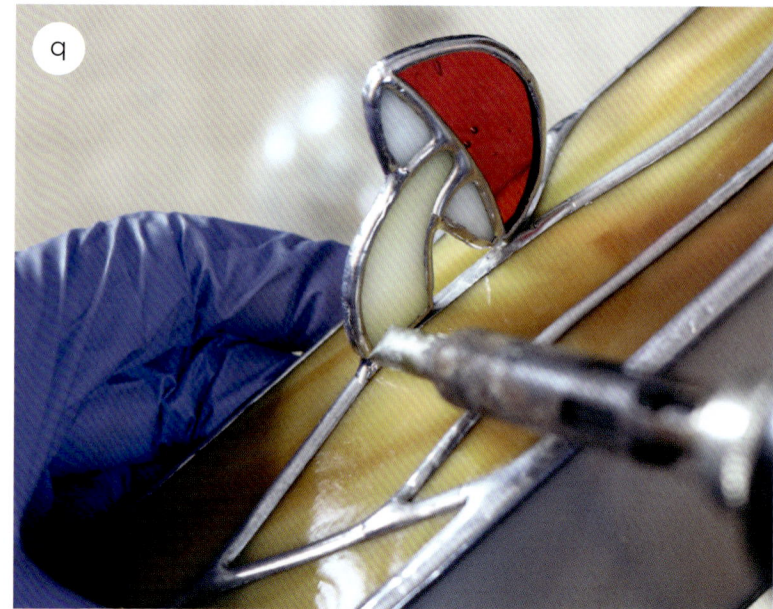

21 Clean, patina, and polish (r). Take great care with the adornments, and use a cotton swab to get into each of the interior shelf corners.

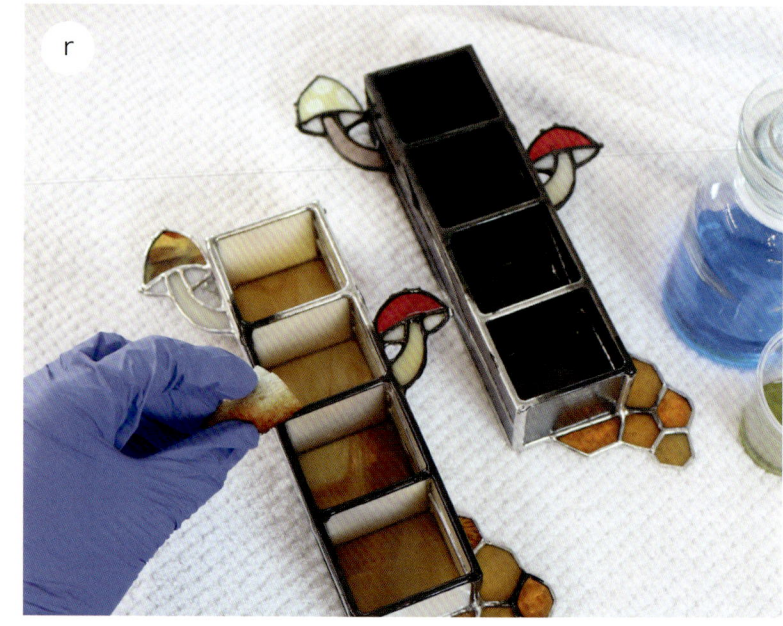

9
POETS SOCIETY DESK SET

The art you create matters. Honor your commitment to your artistic practice by setting aside a dedicated space laid out with this vintage-style desk set – a pencil box and Moleskine slipcase – as a perfect place to preserve your memories, sketches, or poems. Or make the set as a lovely meaningful gift for the poet in your life.

PENCIL BOX

Difficulty: Advanced

This gorgeous pencil box is perfect for storing all your favorite, most inspiring drawing and writing tools. Opaque or opalescent glass is recommended for a neat appearance; I used Bullseye's French Vanilla Opalescent as the main glass, and assorted scrap glass for the leaves and berries. The brass hinge tubing can be found at stained glass supply shops (see Suppliers, page 206).

Note: A box lid always requires a design with interior lines because the hinges need "anchor points" that attach them firmly to the lid.

Supplies

- All standard stained glass tools and supplies (see page 15)
- Straightedge
- Lead-free solder
- Layout strips and pushpins
- Brass hinge tubing (usually 3/32"/2 mm)
- 16 gauge tinned copper wire for inner hinge pin
- Wooden toothpick

Tip

Be sure to use lead-free solder because these items are intended to be frequently touched by hand.

Pattern

3 copies of the Pencil Box pattern on page 193

Straight lines

For three-dimensional constructions like these, it is imperative that the edge lines are cut perfectly straight and square, as accuracy will aid in assembling and soldering the box. See Cutting Straight Lines on page 29 for tips.

Instructions

1 Cut the paper templates from one pattern. For the straight perimeter line, use a straightedge and craft knife. Use pattern shears to cut the interior lines.

2 Select your glass and glue the templates to the glass.

3 Cut the pieces. For straight lines, use a straightedge with your glass cutter.

4 Grind the glass, keeping all box corners square and clean, and all straight edges straight.

5 Clean, dry, and number all the pieces.

6 Foil, using foil with a backing color that matches your chosen patina. On the top lid pieces, start and end the foil in an area that will be an interior solder line, not an outer (straight) edge, so that the final edge bead soldering will be neat. Likewise, on the rectangular walls, position the foil breaks on one of the bottom edges that will be enclosed in a box seam, not on a top edge, where the foil could possibly separate as you solder the top edge bead.

7 To construct the walls, hold one wide wall piece and one narrow wall piece upright on the work surface, and butt the edge of the narrow wall up to the face of the wide wall at a right angle (b). Flux and tack solder at the top of the junction and then again halfway down (c). Now take the other wide wall piece and place it into the proper position in your assemblage, with its face up against the edge of the narrow wall, hold at 90 degrees, and tack solder. Position the final narrow wall piece between the two wide walls, and tack solder.

8 Place the wall assemblage atop the base piece. The walls should line up to the base perfectly. If the walls are not quite square, gently wiggle them into the proper position. Tack the walls to the base at all four corners (d).

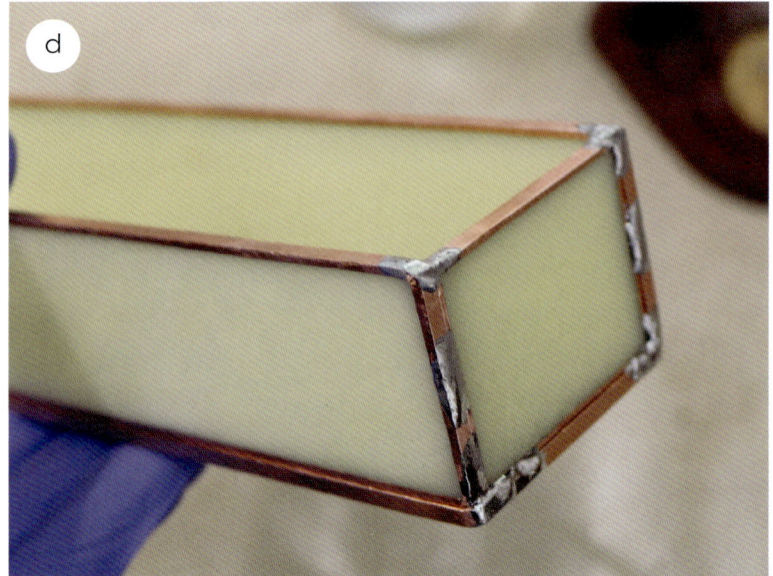

9 Flux and solder the outside of the box, except at the top of the two rear wall junctions where the hinge wire will later be embedded (see pattern). At these locations, leave the top 1/2" (1 cm) unsoldered (e). As you work, be sure to keep the seam that you're soldering horizontal, so that gravity will not cause the molten solder to run off. If you get any drip-through, try turning down your heat or holding a damp rag against the reverse side of the spot you're soldering.

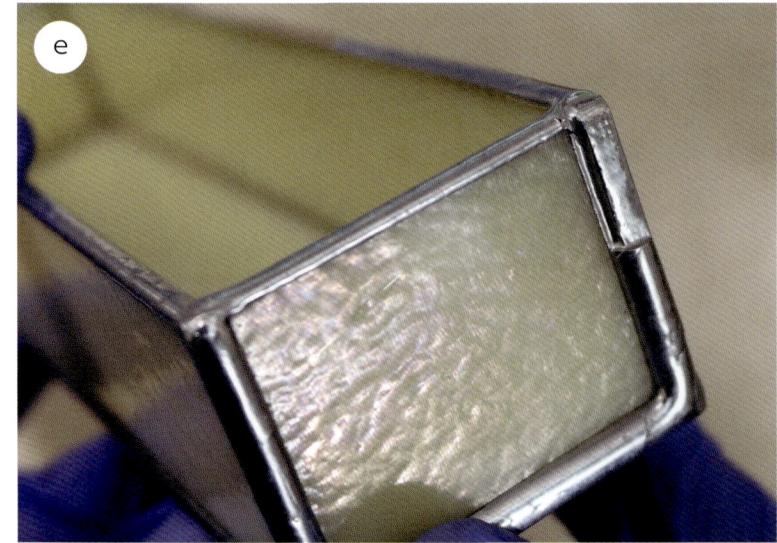

10 Create a round, thick edge bead along the top perimeter (where the cover will lie) to prevent the foil from pulling away from the glass (f).

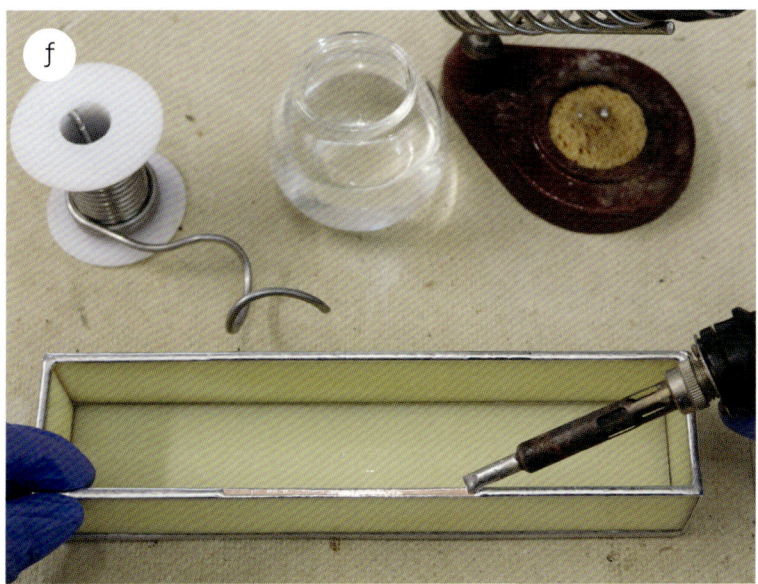

11 Lay out the cover pieces. Use layout strips pinned to your work surface to create a perfectly straight perimeter (g). It will be difficult to attach the hinge neatly if you have an uneven edge.

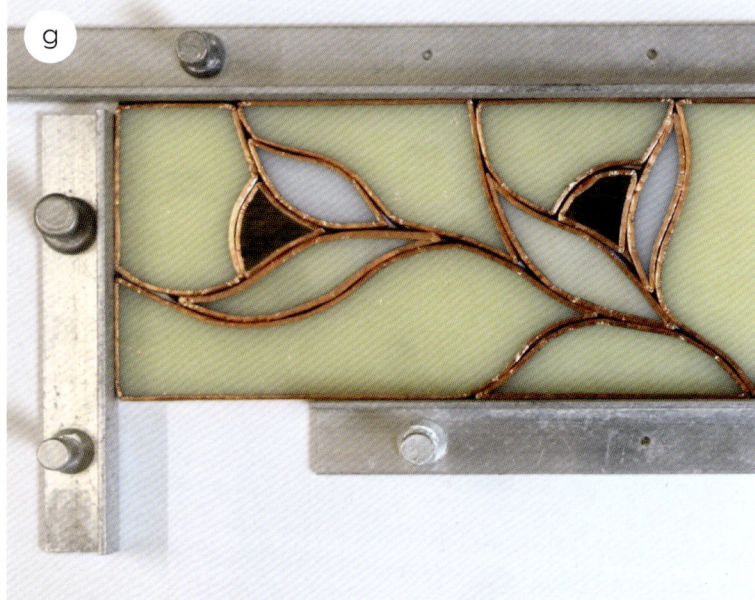

12 Flux and solder the interior lines of the cover but leave the hinge edge unsoldered. Flip, then solder the back interior lines. Finish the cover with a nice edge bead on three sides, again leaving the hinge edge unsoldered.

13 Cut the brass hinge tubing to the length indicated on the pattern. To cut the tube, lay it on your work surface, place a craft knife at the cutting location, and roll the tube back and forth with the blade, pressing down with moderate pressure so that the tube is scored (h). Keep rolling the tube until there is a deep score, then pick up the tube and snap the pieces apart. You cannot use wire cutters to cut the hinge, as you will crush the tube.

14 Clean the brass tube with steel wool until shiny, removing oxidation so that solder will bond with the clean surface. Then insert a toothpick into each end of the tube to prevent any solder from entering it (i).

PENCIL BOX 131

15 Flux the tube and the back edge of the box cover, then tack the tube into position (j).

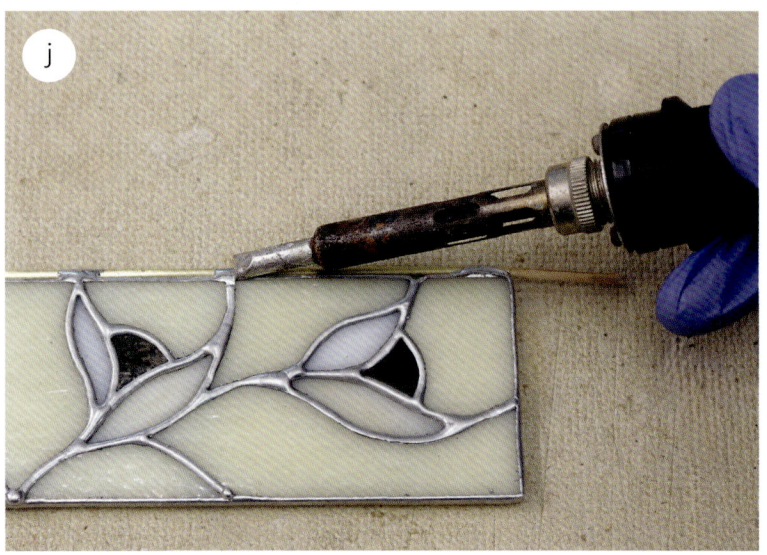

16 Solder a strong bead along the hinge joint. Work slowly and patiently, a short length at a time, and let the joint cool periodically.

17 Remove the toothpicks and insert 16 gauge tinned copper wire through the hinge tube. At each end, just past the end of the tube, bend the wire to a right angle and trim to about 1/2" (1 cm) (k).

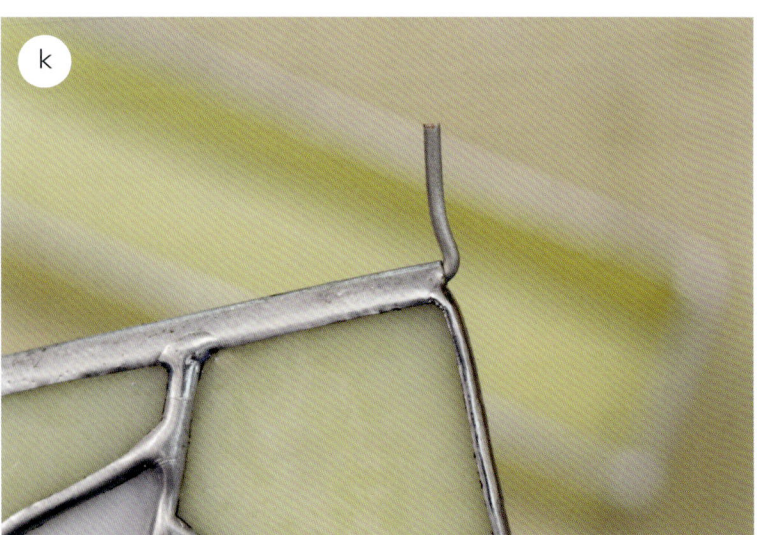

18 Align the cover carefully on top of the box. Holding the cover firmly in place, align the wire to sit in the seams left unsoldered on the back of the box (l).

19 Flux and solder the wire into the seam. Blend the whole seam into a smooth bead. Be careful not to solder the cover to the box, and avoid getting solder in the hinge tube. Check that the cover opens and closes properly.

20 Clean, patina, and polish.

21 Fill with your favorite, most inspiring drawing and writing tools.

MOLESKINE SLIPCASE

Difficulty: Advanced

To complete the desk set, here I've used the same glass as the pencil box – Bullseye's French Vanilla Opalescent as the main glass, and assorted scrap glass for the leaves and berries. If a simpler appearance is desired, the slipcase can be made with two blank sides – perfect to showcase an especially beautiful sheet of glass.

Note: This pattern is designed specifically to fit the medium hardcover Moleskine® Classic Notebook. If your own favorite sketchbook is a different type, you will need to adjust the pattern to suit its measurements.

Supplies

- All standard stained glass tools and supplies (see page 15)
- Lead-free solder
- Layout strips
- Straightedge
- Medium Moleskine® Hardcover Classic Notebook (4.5 x 7"/11.5 x 18 cm, 208 pages)
- Felt: 8 x 10" (20 x 25 cm), approximately 1.5 mm thickness, in a color complementary to your glass
- Spray adhesive

Pattern

3 copies of the Moleskine Slipcase patterns on pages 194–196

Instructions

1 Cut the paper templates from one pattern. For the straight perimeter lines, use a straightedge and craft knife. Use pattern shears to cut the interior lines.

2 Select your glass and glue the templates to the glass.

3 Cut the pieces. For straight lines, use a straightedge with your glass cutter. Accuracy will aid in assembling and soldering the sleeve.

4 Grind the glass, keeping all box corners square and clean, and all straight edges straight.

5 Clean, dry, and number all the pieces.

6 Foil, using foil with a backing color that matches your chosen patina. On the top cover pieces, start and end the foil in an area that will be an interior solder line, not an outer (straight) edge, so that the final edge bead soldering will be neat.

7 Lay out the top cover pieces on the pattern and pin down straightedges to keep them in place.

8 Flux and solder the interior lines of the top face neatly (a). Do not solder the perimeter. Flip and solder the interior lines of the back (inside) face. Here, use a flat solder bead so that the notepad will be able to slide in easily. You should always strive for a neat appearance, but since this side won't be visible, don't obsess over it.

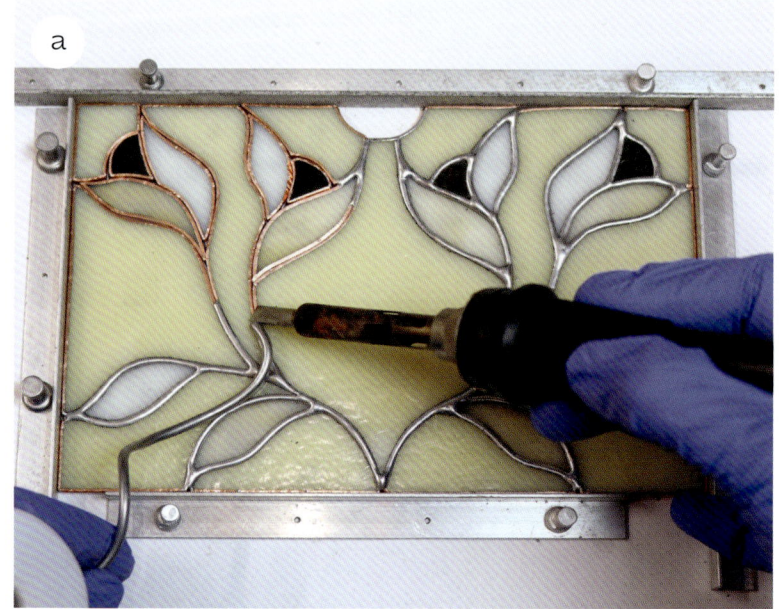

134 RAISE YOUR GLASS

9 Assemble the walls. Hold a long wall piece perpendicular upon your work surface. Butt a short wall piece's edge up to the face of the long wall, creating a right angle. Flux and tack along the vertical junction and at the top (b). Be sure that this top tack is flat and smooth so that the top cover will rest flush atop the walls when placed in position. Butt the other short wall piece up against the face of the long wall, and tack into place.

▲ Narrow side butted up against the face of the wide side

10 Carefully lift this assemblage of three walls and set it upon the base piece, lining up the edges. Gently wiggle the walls into right angles, if necessary. Tack the walls to the base piece (c).

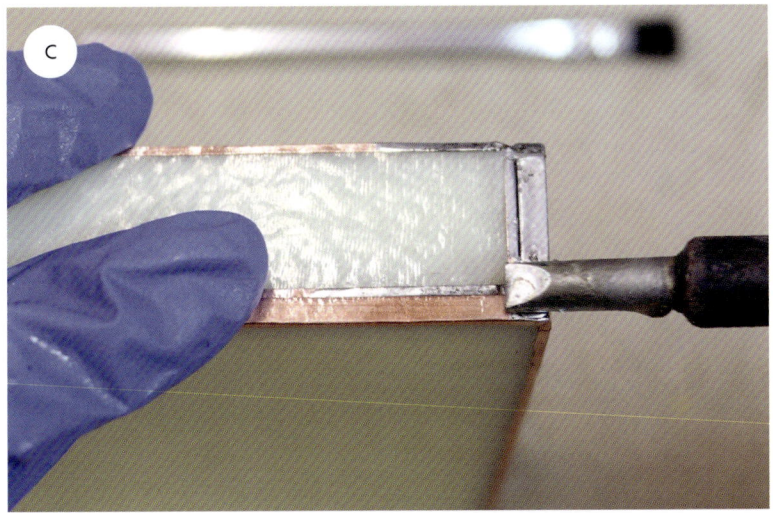

▲ Sides placed atop base

11 Set the top cover in place and check that it rests flat upon the walls and that all junctions square up (d). If not, check that your corner tacking is flat with the top edges of the walls, and that there are no gaps where the walls are tacked to the base. Make any necessary adjustments before moving on.

12 Before tacking the cover onto the walls, thoroughly clean all interior surfaces of the slipcase – you will not be able to clean this again easily once the cover is tacked in place.

13 Tack the cover in several spots along each wall (e).

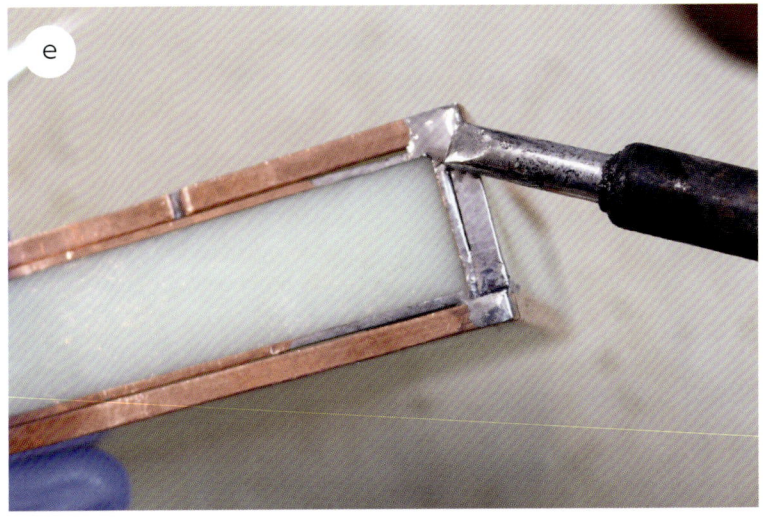

MOLESKINE SLIPCASE

14 Now solder all seams, being careful to avoid drip-through – your iron will no longer fit inside the slipcase for cleanup, and a solder blob inside could interfere with the fit of the notebook. If you are not confident with this type of soldering, try running an inch long (2.5 cm) long bead, every inch or so, and let everything cool. Then go back and fill in the spaces, neatly connecting to the earlier soldering (f). An alternative technique to prevent drip-through is to stuff the slipcase with damp paper towels.

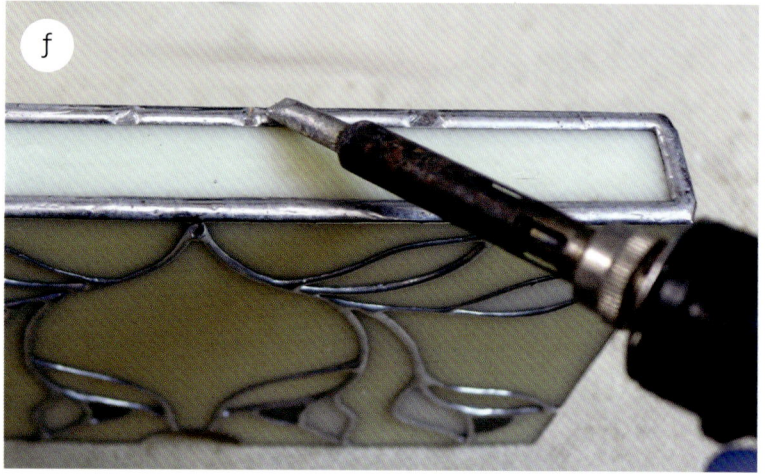

15 Create an edge bead around the perimeter of the opening. You'll want a heavier bead that will stand up to the notebook being slid in and out of the sleeve (g).

16 Clean, patina, and polish (h).

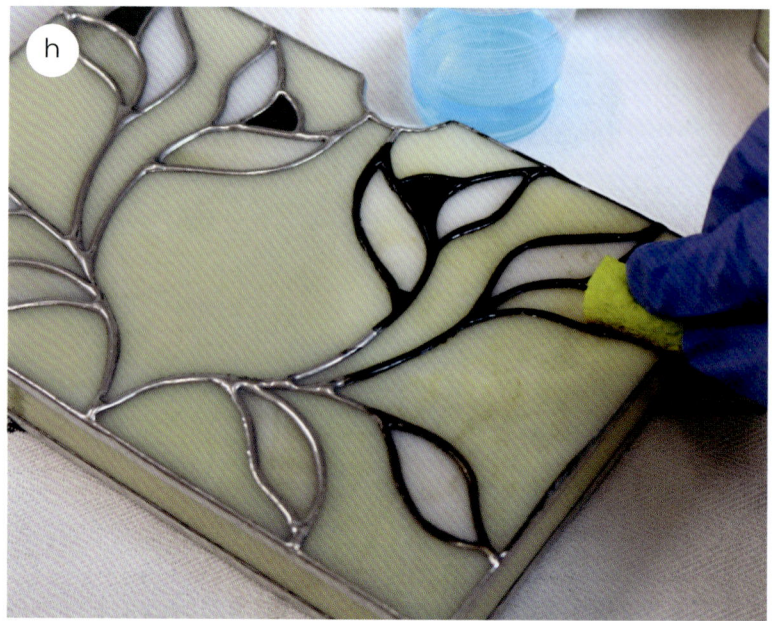

17 Line the interior with felt. Cut the felt using the template provided on page 195 (i). Apply spray adhesive to one side of the felt, then wrap the clean side around a properly sized notebook and insert everything into the slipcase. Remove the book and use a chopstick, ruler, or similar tool to press the felt into place firmly against the glass (j).

j

18 Compose a sonnet in the notebook as you are waiting for the glue to dry, then finally insert the notebook into its slipcase of honor.

REBEKAH MARXEN

Sparta, New Jersey, USA | www.rebekahmarxen.com @rebekahmarxen.art

Rebekah's sculptural works – assemblages of found material peppered with personal pop culture references – feel so autobiographical. She mixes stained glass techniques with items collected while mudlarking near her New Jersey home and studio and in travels around New England.

What inspires your unique style?
I love juxtaposing objects of seemingly unrelated time periods, materials, techniques, and subject matter. One of my favorite recent creations is a "portrait" of Princess Leia from Star Wars. She's this wild mash-up of acrylic portraiture and found objects featuring little bits of sea pottery that I found while beachcombing in Massachusetts. Her white robe is a grouping of old plate rim scraps with time-worn crackles in the glaze; likely, the result of tumbling in the Atlantic Ocean for nearly two centuries! Her iconic "cinnamon bun" hair is made of stoneware shards that date from the early to mid 1800s. The brown glazed stoneware has visible texture left by the potters' hands. I often remind myself that each recovered fragment was once part of a utilitarian object, crafted by an artist who took pride in their work and made a living as a potter or glassblower. I always wish I knew just who made these artifacts from what seems "a long time ago, in a galaxy far, far away."

What's your evolution as an artist?
I'd always considered myself a painter, but as a high school art educator, I had the opportunity to learn traditional stained glass techniques. I experimented with varnished magazine cut-outs sandwiched between two pieces of clear glass and soldered into mixed-media compositions. But soon I began painting my own images – small historical and pop portraits – on glass, and I grouped these with found objects and sea pottery fragments to create modern mixed-media works using traditional stained glass techniques.
   Incorporating sea pottery grew out of my "@lo_tide_archaeology"

project – a visual diary that documents and identifies all of the sea pottery fragments I've collected over the years. I've been picking up rocks, fossils, and artifacts for as long as I can remember. My parents were always taking me and my brother on local adventures to farm fields to see what the tractors churned up, and to explore the tide pools on our annual vacations to coastal Massachusetts. On one particular trip, my mother, who has an encyclopedic knowledge of antiques and historical collectibles, identified some broken bits of pottery that had washed ashore, and I was hooked on researching and documenting my finds. I soon amassed an expansive collection of yellowware, Rockingham ware, stoneware, transferware, and clay pipe fragments.

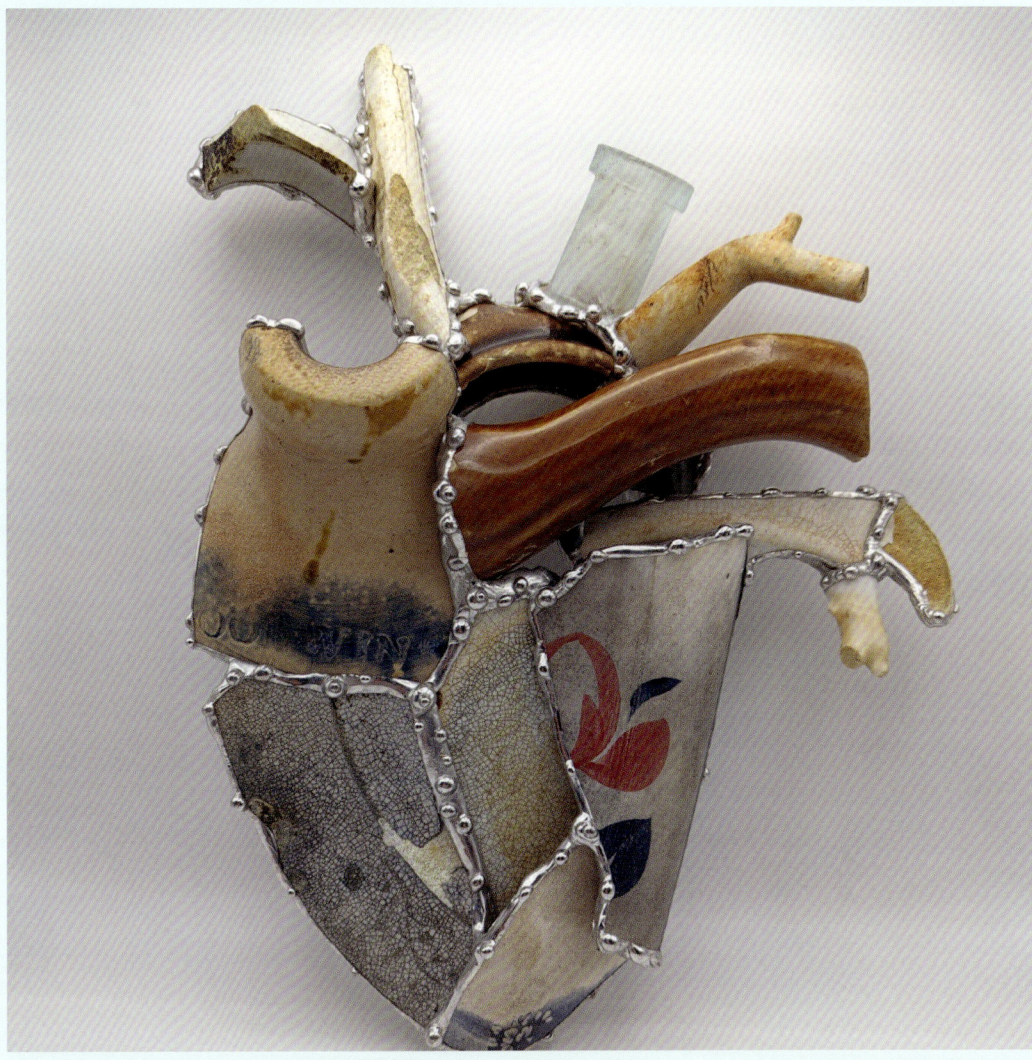

What's your process for the sea pottery pieces?

Originally, the random finds themselves would guide my process. I'd sit at my workspace, dump out a bunch of fragments and rearrange them until I'd see an object begin to form. I've never made traditional patterns or thumbnail sketches for my work, though I do look at reference photos for my portrait paintings and for general inspiration.

Recently, however, the tides have turned (pun intended). While working on a series of anatomical heart sculptures (using an old medical illustration for reference), I found that I could settle into a formula of sorts: 1 jug mouth + 1 glass bottle neck + 1 jug handle, etc = 1 heart. So now I'm a bit more focused on actively seeking out stoneware jug handles on my next beachcombing adventure!

I don't grind or break my sea pottery fragments as I feel it's important to leave them in their found state. This makes foiling pretty frustrating! The pieces all have really different surface textures: some are quite smooth, and the foil slides on with ease, while other pieces are more porous or jagged and always seem to want to reject the foil. I use crumpled aluminum foil as an armature for my sculptures. It allows me to visualize what the final three-dimensional form will look like prior to soldering.

REBEKAH MARXEN

10
PENDANT LIGHTS

These projects are inspired by the charming vintage enamel and milk glass pendant lights found in the decor of Parisian cafés of the early twentieth century – a classic look that's totally on trend right now. Your choice of glass allows for lots of opportunity for variations in mood: colorful scallops for a carnival vibe in a child's room, clear textured glass for a classy bistro spirit, even glow-in-the-dark greens and yellows for a fantasy firefly that continues to luminesce when the light is turned off.

Because these projects are three-dimensional, they are more advanced and require some extra skill and care. Precision is very important for a good final fit and overall symmetry. The straight lines must be cut straight, then ground carefully to retain the straight edges. A little extra patience is required for a smooth assembly, so take your time and enjoy the process. The Hélène pattern is the simplest; St. Judie and Mara are based upon this construction but have more complicated designs.

Special supplies for pendant lights

◎ Pendant light fixture
The circular openings in these patterns are sized to fit light fixtures that accommodate uno-style lampshades ("uno" specifies the dimensions of the ring that secures the lampshade to the fixture). You can source these common light fixtures at many hardware stores, online retailers, lighting suppliers, or on Etsy. Use keywords such as "vintage shade-ready pendant light fixture with plug-in cord" to find appropriate options: you'll find many variations of cord color and covering, switch placement, and fixture material. It must have a "medium", "standard", "e26" size bulb receptacle (those three terms are interchangeable).

As well as a pendant light fixture, you will need:
◎ A fun round Edison bulb
◎ 10 gauge copper wire for the fixture ring (page 142)
◎ A handful of rags for propping up the pieces as you solder

PENDANT LIGHTS   **141**

MAKING THE FIXTURE RING

The "fixture ring" lines the central opening of the glass shade. It will fit around the threaded part of the light fixture, held in place by the fixture nut.

1 Coil a length of 10 gauge copper wire around the threaded part of the lamp fixture so that a little more than one complete circle of wire is formed around the fixture (you'll have excess wire on each end). There should be just enough wiggle room that the ring can slide on and off the fixture.

2 Mark a cutline across the overlapping ends, defining one complete circle, and slide the wire off the fixture.

3 Cut with strong wire cutters and bend the ends toward each other gently, easing the coil into a perfect ring.

4 Check this ring on the fixture for fit – it should slide on easily but should be held securely in place between the fixture flange and the threaded nut/ring. The ring will measure approximately 11 1/16" (4.3 cm) inside.

5 Clean to a pure copper sheen by rubbing with a nylon scouring pad, fine steel wool, or sandpaper.

HÉLÈNE

Difficulty: Advanced

This is the simple, classic version of our three pendant light projects. It looks great with a black or pewter black patina.

Supplies

- All standard stained glass tools and supplies (see page 15)
- Straightedge
- Layout strips and pushpins
- All special supplies for pendant lights (see page 141)

Pattern

15 copies of the Hélène pattern on page 197

> **Important:** we'll call each piece cut from template A, a **"wedge."** Groups of five wedges will be assembled into three larger **"sections,"** then the three sections will be assembled into a single unit. Pieces cut from template B can be set aside until step 13.

Instructions

1 Make the center fixture ring (see Making the Fixture Ring on page 142).

2 Cut fifteen copies of each of the two (A and B) templates. For template A pieces, use a straightedge and craft knife to make sure the straight lines are perfect. Use regular scissors to cut curved lines.

3 Select the glass and glue the templates to the glass, taking care that the grain of the glass is oriented as you desire (a).

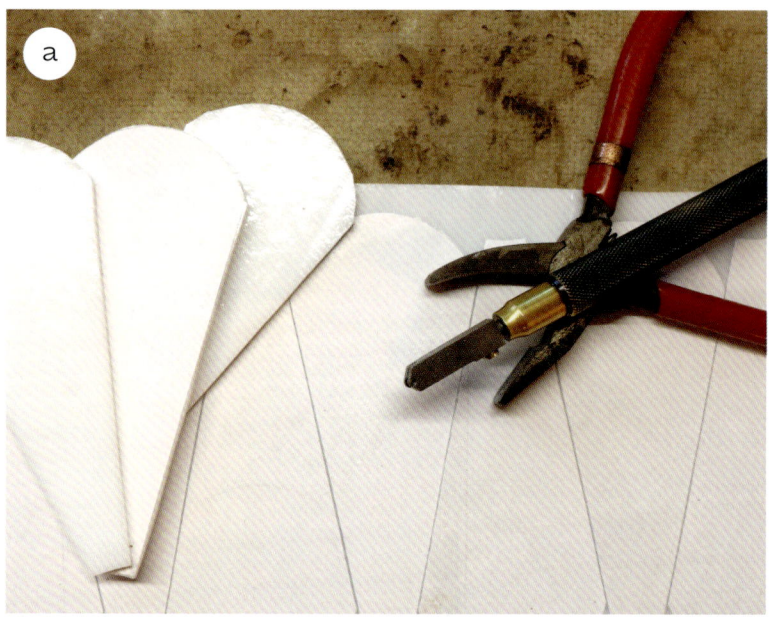

4 Cut the glass, using a straightedge for straight lines.

5 Grind carefully to maintain your straight edges. Be sure that each piece is precisely the size of the template. Clean and dry all pieces.

6 Foil, using foil with a backing color that matches your chosen patina, and burnish.

7 Now we'll tack the **wedges** into **sections**, cradling the pieces into their three-dimensional shape using rags to support. Lay out one group of wedge pieces back side (lamp interior side) up (b). Place two wedges together with their long edges abutting, with the short edges exactly aligned (c). Lift one wedge off the surface at a slight angle and tack solder the seam twice, about an inch (2.5 cm) from either end. Don't use too much solder, just a light tack so the glass can hinge a little on the foil. Handle gently, using caution to avoid pulling the foil away from the glass. Place another wedge next to this assemblage, using rags to support the raised pieces, and again tack at an angle (d). Continue tacking pieces until you have assembled a full section, put this **section** aside, and start over on another group of **wedges**.

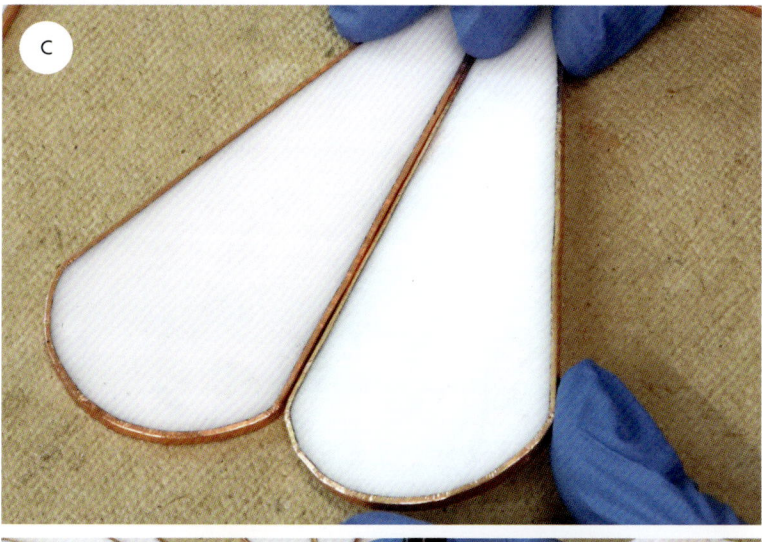

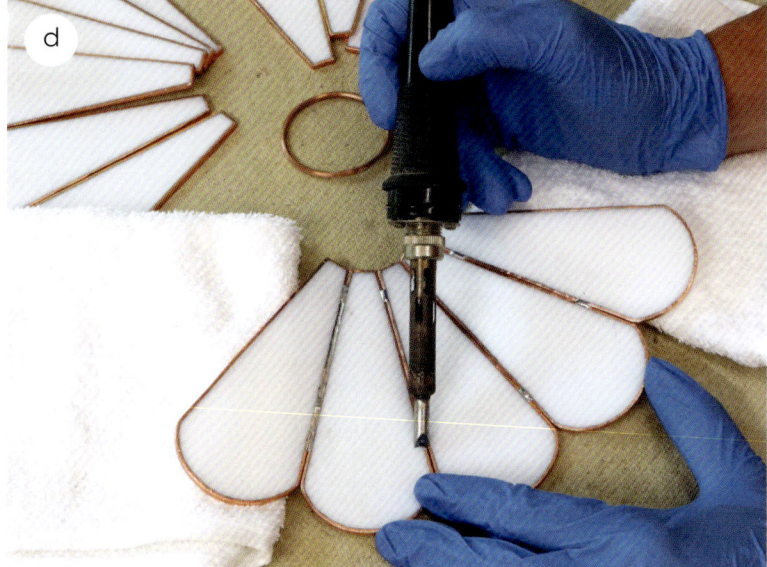

8 Now we'll assemble the **sections** to complete the full shade. Gently arrange the sections into their final positions, using folded rags to support them and the copper ring as a guide (e). The short edges of the pieces should form a ring touching the work surface, while the opposite curved ends should be propped up so that they align. Tack the long sides of the sections together, in the same way as the other pieces, making sure that the short ends are aligned perfectly and that the faces of the long sides are flush (f). Now that all of the sections are tacked together, adjust the angles between each pair of wedges gently so they are symmetrical. Tack at more places along the long seams to add strength to the entire project.

HÉLÈNE   145

9 Place the center fixture ring into the center and tack into place (g). Be careful, this wire will get hot as you solder and will stay hot longer than you're used to from more typical constructions.

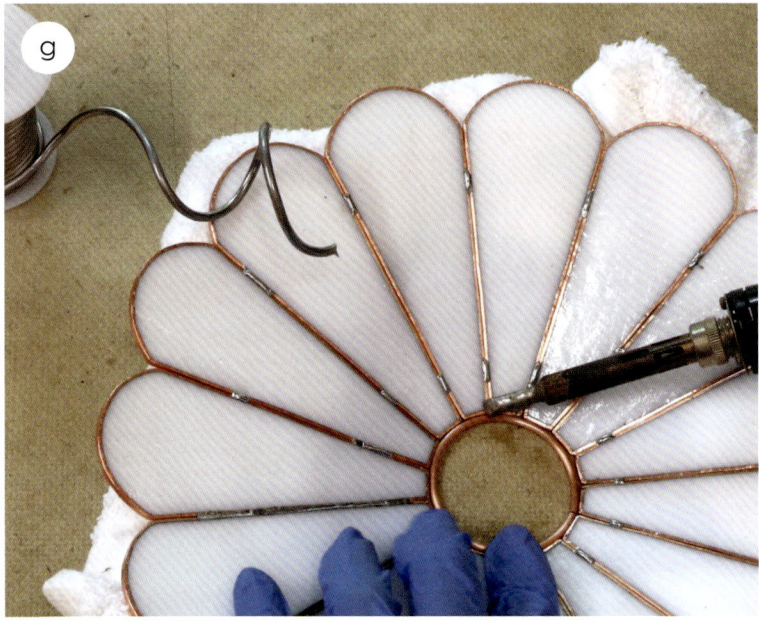

10 Apply more tack soldering all around the project, finessing it into a symmetrical shape, until the assemblage is rigid and strong.

11 Create nice bead solder lines all along the long seams on the interior of the shade, then repeat on the outside. Run each long solder bead right up to the wire ring in the center (h). Do not solder the outer perimeter, where the B pieces will be attached. This step can be frustrating because of drip-through, so use patience. Try holding a damp rag against the reverse side of the spot you're soldering.

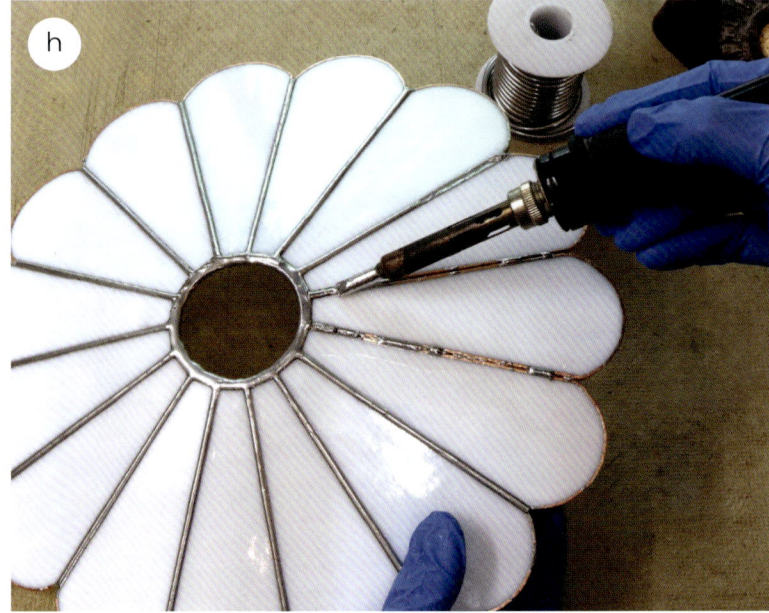

12 Fully encompass the wire ring in solder along the short edges. You may need to go over the center ring several times to create a smooth bead and junctions. If solder builds up on the interior of the ring, lift the piece off of the work surface and run your iron around the inner circumference, allowing excess solder to melt and drip off.

13 (Skip this step if you're making St. Judie.) Tack each B piece in place around the outer edge (i), then bead solder both sides.

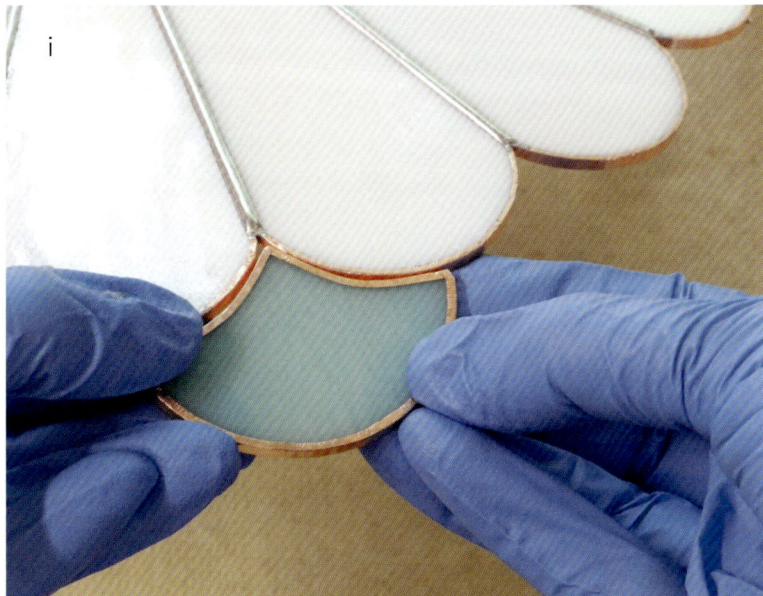

14 Create a clean, heavy edge bead all around the perimeter (j).

15 Clean, patina, and polish.

16 Place the shade onto the fixture and secure it with the nut, twist in a pretty lightbulb, hang the project, and be charmed!

ST. JUDIE

Difficulty: Advanced

If ever there were a perfect excuse to indulge in the fabulous glow-in-the-dark glass made by Fremont, this firefly pendant light is it! I picture this lamp hanging bedside, so that when the light is turned off you can bask in the gentle firefly glow as you drift off to sleep. A bright green or yellow glass would be perfect too, catching the eye even when the light is off.

Supplies

- All standard stained glass tools and supplies (see page 15)
- Straightedge
- Layout strips and pushpins
- All special supplies for pendant lights (see page 141)

Pattern

4 copies of the St. Judie pattern on page 198

Instructions

1 Make the center fixture ring (see Making the Fixture Ring on page 142).

2 Prepare three copies of the paper templates. Use a straightedge and craft knife to cut the six straight lines (indicated by thin black lines) radiating from the center. Use pattern shears to cut the curved interior lines.

3 Select glass and glue the templates to the glass.

4 Cut the glass pieces, using a straightedge for straight lines.

5 Grind, clean, and number all the pieces.

6 Foil, using foil with a backing color that matches your chosen patina, and burnish (a).

7 Pin down the layout strips upon the guide provided on the pattern to use as a jig for soldering. The project consists of three identical **sections** (all fourteen pieces on one copy of the pattern), each of which consists of five **wedges** (each group of pieces between straight lines). The jig will help to make each **wedge** the same overall size and shape (b).

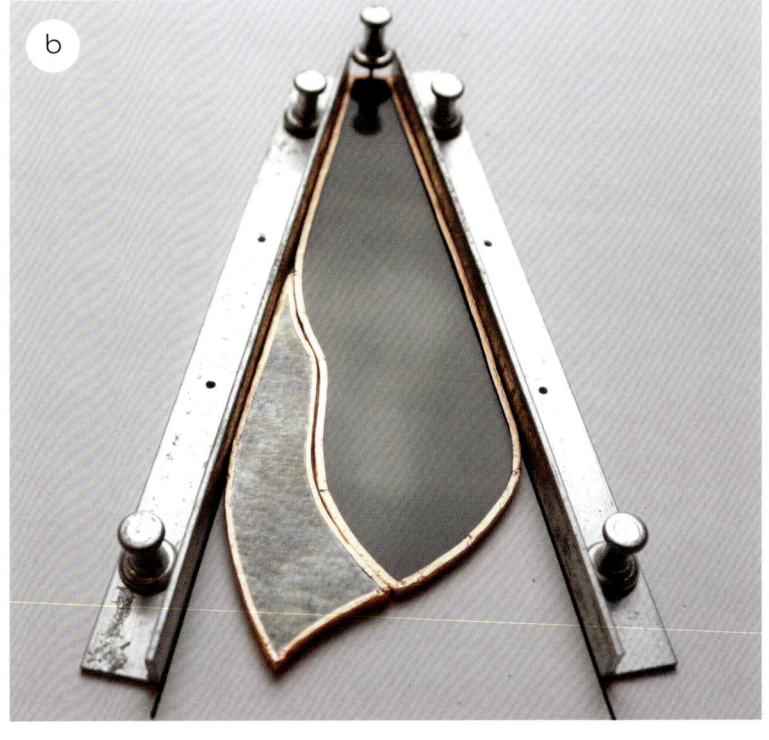

8 Flux and solder the front of a wedge, remove from the jig, and do the same for the back (c). Do not solder the perimeter of the wedge. You do not need to be too precious about perfect soldering at this point, as any perfect beads that you make now might get a bit messed up as you proceed with the three-dimensional assembly.

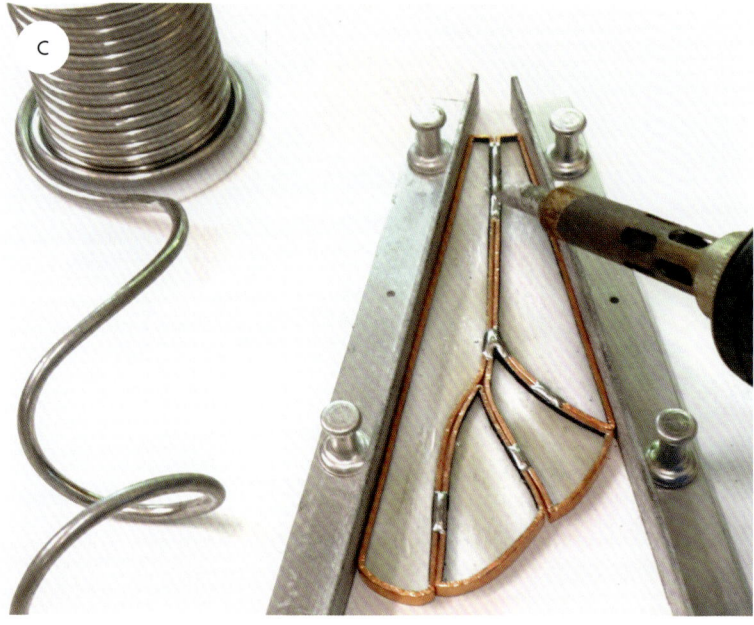

Important: You now have fifteen soldered **wedges**. Groups of five **wedges** will next be assembled into three larger **sections** (d). Then the three **sections** will be assembled into the single shade.

9 Follow instructions from the Hélène lampshade from Step 7 (pages 144–147).

MARA

Difficulty: Advanced

For this variation, we'll feature a favorite Art Nouveau motif on our café light. This peacock design will look stunning if you go literal with the colors – teal, turquoise, emerald – in your glass selection, but you can also go more playful with pinks and purples or more subdued with whites.

Supplies

- All standard stained glass tools and supplies (see page 15)
- Straightedge
- Layout strips and pushpins
- All special supplies for pendant lights (see page 141)

Pattern
8 copies of the Mara pattern on page 199

Instructions

1 Make the center fixture ring (see Making the Fixture Ring on page 142).

2 Cut paper templates from eight copies of the pattern. Use a straightedge and craft knife to cut the straight edges (indicated by thin black lines). Use pattern shears to cut the curved interior lines.

3 Select your glass and glue the templates to the glass.

4 Cut the glass pieces, using a straightedge for perfect straight lines when necessary. A few pieces (numbers 3 and 8) are good practice for cutting inside curves. If necessary, try cutting in two scores: first cut a gentle, shallow curve, then remove the glass, and finally cut a deeper curve that matches the template.

5 Grind, clean, and number all the pieces.

6 Foil, using foil with a backing color that matches your chosen patina, and burnish.

7 Pin down layout strips upon the guide provided on the pattern to use as a jig (a). Each grouping of five glass pieces is called a **wedge**, and each needs to be exactly the same overall size and shape.

8 Flux and solder the front of each wedge, remove from the jig, and do the same for the back. Do not solder the perimeter of the wedge. You don't need to be too precious about perfect soldering at this point. Do not attach any B pieces at this time, just set them aside for later.

Important: You now have sixteen soldered **wedges**. Next, groups of four **wedges** will be assembled into four larger **sections**. Then, the four **sections** will be assembled into a single unit.

9 Follow instructions from the Hélène lampshade from Step 7 (pages 144–147).

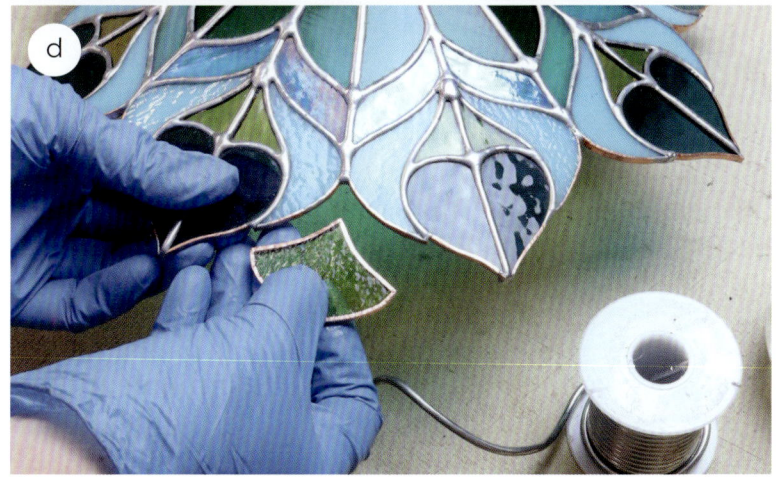

GERTRUDE DUFEUDEDIEU

Bretagne, France | **Instagram:** @gertrude_dufeudedieu

French artist Gertrude Dufeudedieu creates figures that participate in the long tradition of portraiture in stained glass, while presenting these badass women in a bold new refreshing style, informed by the artist's work as a tattoo artist. "Don't worry, girls will save the world!"

What inspires your work in stained glass?
My inspiration comes from the people who I encounter throughout my day: my tattoo clients, people who I meet on the street, and even the characters whose faces I imagine as I read. I muse upon their lives and their personalities. I'm inspired every day when I tattoo a woman — by her physique, by her personal story.

Music is also a source of inspiration: I visualize characters with the words I hear. I love art in all its forms (illustration, painting, sculpture), so I'm influenced by these media too. After several other artistic approaches (pastel painting, ceramics), I became interested in working with glass. For me, stained glass is very inspiring because of the choice of textures, colors, and transparencies that glass provides. I have always admired the stained glass windows in churches, as well as the work of artists who I've discovered on the internet.

What's your process?
I'll invent characters based on people that I've met, or sometimes I'll work from a photo. Once I've discovered their theme, I'll create

the faces and background. I sketch my own faces on a tablet in a "tattoo style," focusing on creating powerful facial expressions using simple lines. I create my templates on paper with Procreate. The lines get painted onto the glass, but I don't want to share too much about my painting technique because it's what makes me unique! I use the Tiffany technique to assemble the glass pieces. I once tried using leaded glass, but I found it too crude for the details that I desired.

What's your workspace like?
I have a workshop in a *longère* (a Breton stone house). It contains a presentation space whose walls are covered with my drawings. Another room is for cutting and storing my glasses, which are arranged by color and texture. The third room holds the fusing furnace and is where I do torch work.

What's a difficult aspect of being a glass artist?
As a self-taught artist, I've suffered from impostor syndrome, but I was able to overcome this fear thanks to the positive and benevolent feedback I received from people in the art world and from my followers on social networks. I continually find confidence thanks to the people around me, my family in particular—because they're the ones who pushed me to share my art and my vision of women!

How do you hope that your work will exist in the world?
In the beginning, I was inspired by my favorite painters like Klimt and Modigliani—I love how they represent women in their simplicity and strength. Through my creations, I'd like to represent women from all over the world, so that they can assume themselves as they are, with their qualities and faults, their physiques, their strengths, and weaknesses!

GERTRUDE DUFEUDEDIEU

11
PROPAGATION STATIONS

These propagation stations are designed to hang in a window and allow light to reach a plant clipping from both sides, with a test tube set within the stained glass. The test tube can be easily removed for cleaning. You can also use this pretty suncatcher as a bud vase for that single perfect bloom when you're not propagating new plant babies.

ROOT DOWN

Difficulty: Advanced

Propagating in a test tube allows you to watch nature's vitality close up. It won't be long before you see your plant baby develop a root system that can be planted in soil, leaving your propagation station ready for a new cutting!

Supplies

- All standard stained glass tools and supplies (see page 15)
- Test tube: 50 ml (2.5 cm diameter, 15 cm height)
- 10 gauge copper wire for the rings to hold the test tube
- 18 gauge copper or tinned copper wire for hanging loops
- Optional for finishing perimeter: U-channel lead came, 3/16" size

Pattern

3 copies of the Root Down pattern on page 200

Instructions

1 Cut the paper templates from one pattern. For the straight perimeter lines, use a straightedge and craft knife. Cut the curved perimeter lines using regular scissors, then use pattern shears to cut the interior lines.

2 Select the glass, glue the templates to the glass, and cut.

3 Grind the glass. Note: Pieces 3 and 7 contain tight curves. When grinding, swapping out your normal grinder bit to a smaller 3/4" bit will make it easier.

4 Clean, dry, and number all the pieces.

5 Foil, using foil with a backing color that matches your chosen patina, and burnish.

6 Prepare the test tube for shaping wire rings. Just below the rim of the test tube, wrap masking tape three turns around to act as a temporary spacer – when you wrap wire here, this spacer will create rings that are slightly wider than the test tube. You should also wrap some tape in a spiral down the length of the tube as a safety measure to hold things together if the glass cracks (a).

7 Make two test tube rings. Use wire cutters to cut an approximately 12" (30 cm) length of 10 gauge copper wire. Use steel wool, sandpaper, or a scouring pad to clean until it shines. Wearing safety gloves for protection, coil the wire around the test tube several times, making a little more than two complete rings (b). Mark cutting locations on the wire with a thin-tip marker. Remove the test tube from the loops, then cut at the marks to create two separate circles (c). Use pliers to bend the cut wire lengths into perfect circular rings. Check for proper size on the test tube: the rings should fit loosely, though tightly enough that the test tube rim does not slip through (d).

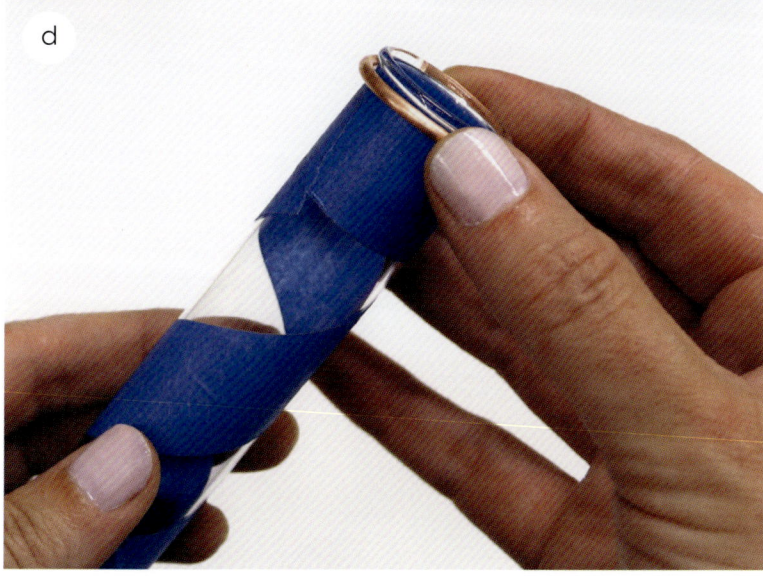

8 Tack layout strips to the straight lines on the pattern where the test tube will fit, so that you will have perfectly straight edges on each side (e). Lay your foiled pieces out on the pattern. At the top edge where the rim of the test tube will be, check that the pieces create a notch where the upper wire ring will sit.

9 Flux and solder the project as one piece, front and back, without flooding the ring notches indicated by yellow circles on the pattern.

10 Attach hanging loops. Cut two 2" (5 cm) lengths of 18 gauge wire, and leave them straight. Solder each wire into the proper position in the interior line on the front of the project (indicated by a dashed line on the pattern). Bend the hanging wire around a flux brush or pencil toward the back so that it forms a loop. Trim wire to the proper length and solder into position on the back.

11 If you like, you may finish the perimeter of the project with U-channel lead came, but do not apply it to the interior edges where the test tube will fit. Otherwise, finish the perimeter with a nice edge bead. In either case, finish the interior test tube gap edges with an edge bead, but leave unsoldered the notches where the rings will fit.

ROOT DOWN   159

12 Tin both copper rings, fully covering each with a thin layer of solder. The metal will get very hot, so use pliers or a third hand clamp to hold.

13 Lay the project back on the pattern. Slide the project to the edge of your work surface, with the top edge overhanging slightly so that the upper ring can be fit in place. Stand the test tube upright on its mouth between pieces 10 and 14 to act as a spacer between the halves.

14 Use the third hand clamp or pliers to hold the upper ring in place within the top notch between pieces 1 and 5, centered front to back and perpendicular to the glass. Tack the ring in place, then remove the clamp and lift the project from the work surface so that you can add solder to create a strong joint that fully encompasses the wire and incorporates into your neat edge beading (f).

15 Add the lower ring in the same manner at the gray dots between pieces 22 and 28 (g, h).

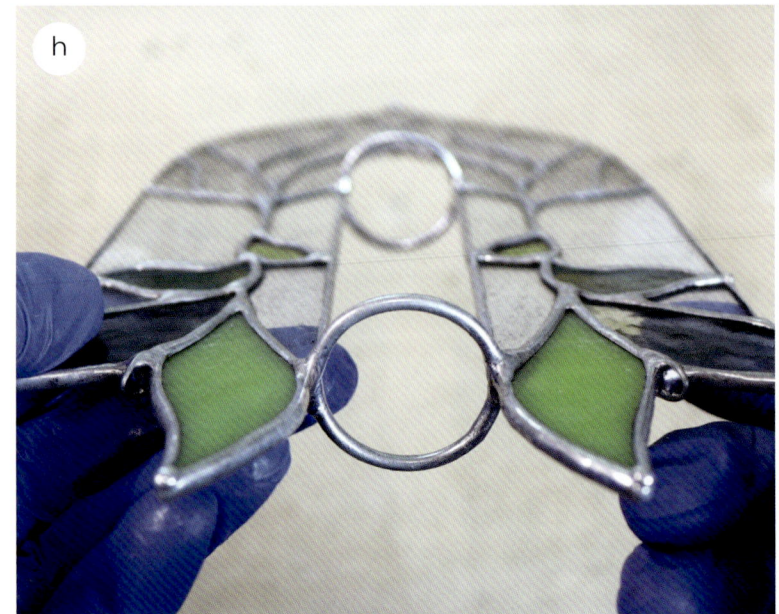

16 Clean, patina, and polish.

17 Hang in a window, add a clipping, and enjoy watching those roots grow!

FRIENDSHIP

Difficulty: Advanced

I love the idea of sharing clippings of your favorite houseplants with your friends, starting the life of a whole new plant. It reminds me of the lovely tradition of sharing an Amish friendship bread starter. I thought this cheerful summery butterfly would be a great symbol to celebrate that "rebirth."

Supplies

- All standard stained glass tools and supplies (see page 15)
- Test tube: 50 ml (2.5 cm diameter, 15 cm height)
- 10 gauge copper wire for the rings to hold the test tube
- 18 gauge copper or tinned copper wire for the hanging loops

Pattern

3 copies of the Friendship pattern on page 201, enlarged to 110%

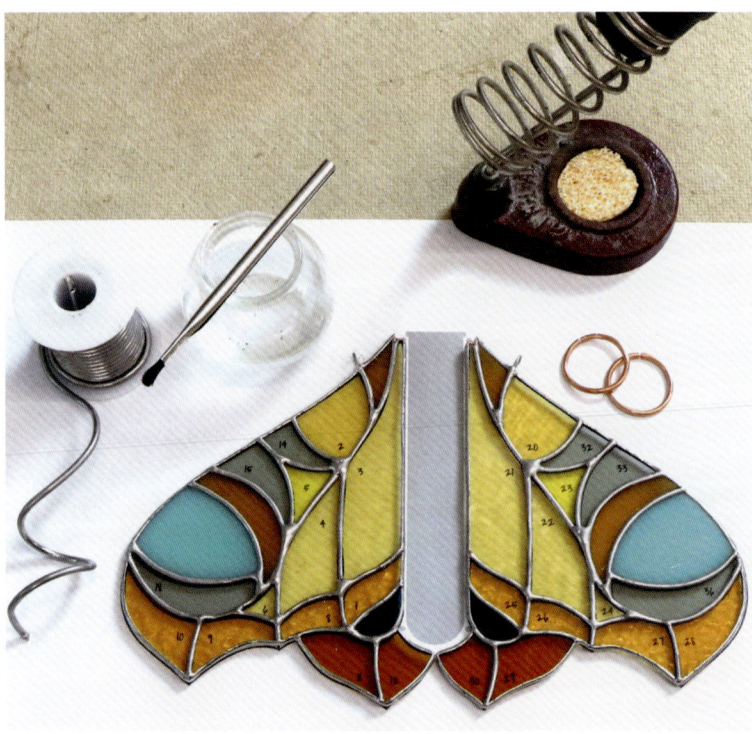

Instructions

1 Cut the paper templates from one pattern. For the straight lines, use a straightedge and craft knife. Cut the curved perimeter lines using regular scissors, then use pattern shears to cut the interior lines.

2 Select your glass and glue the templates to the glass.

3 Cut, grind, clean, and number all the pieces.

4 Foil, using foil with a backing color that matches your chosen patina, and burnish.

5 Prepare the test tube for shaping wire rings and make two test tube rings, following Steps 5–6 for the Root Down Propagation Station (see page 158).

6 Tack layout strips to the straight lines on the pattern where the test tube will fit, so that you will have perfectly straight edges on each side (a). Lay your foiled pieces out on the pattern. At the top edge where the rim of the test tube will be, check that the pieces create a notch where the upper wire ring will sit (b).

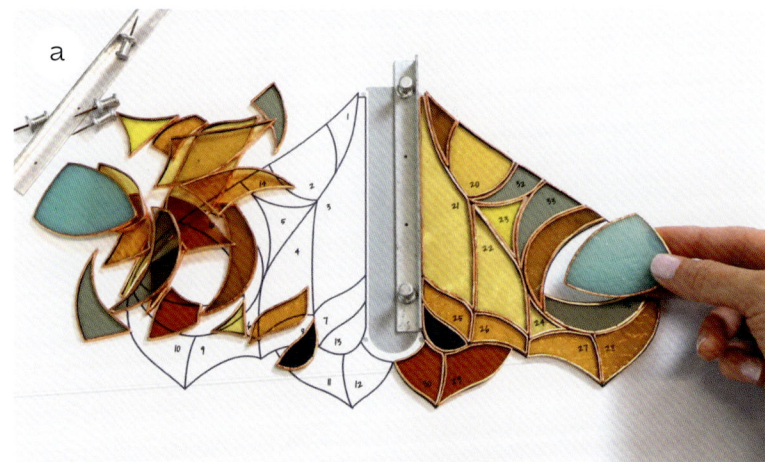

7 Flux and solder the front and back of each side, leaving the halves separate for now. Do not solder the bottom-center pieces (12 and 30) together.

8 Attach hanging loops. Cut two 2" (5 cm) lengths of wire, and leave them straight. Solder each wire into the proper position (indicated by a dashed line on the pattern) in the interior line on the front of the project. Bend the hanging wire around a flux brush or pencil toward the back so that it forms a loop. Trim wire to the proper length and solder into position on the back.

9 Make a neat edge bead all around each wing, except for the areas near the gray dots where the rings will fit – leave these areas clear of solder (c).

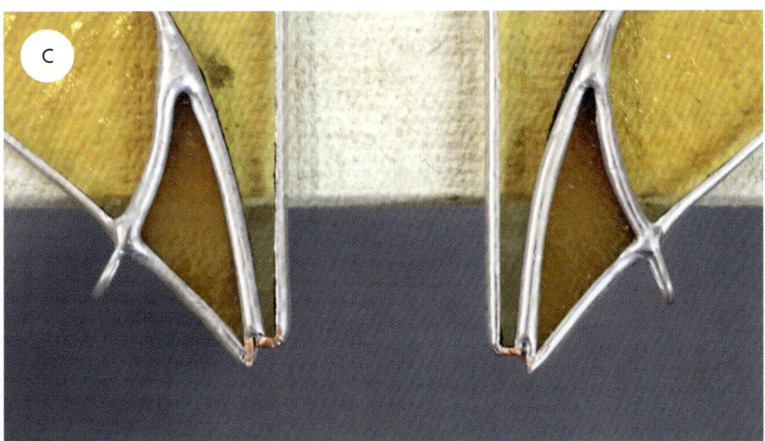

10 Tin both copper rings, fully covering each with a thin layer of solder. The metal will get very hot, so use pliers or a third hand clamp to hold.

11 Lay both soldered wings back on the pattern, and tack solder the halves together at pieces 12 and 30, using enough solder for a sturdy connection (d).

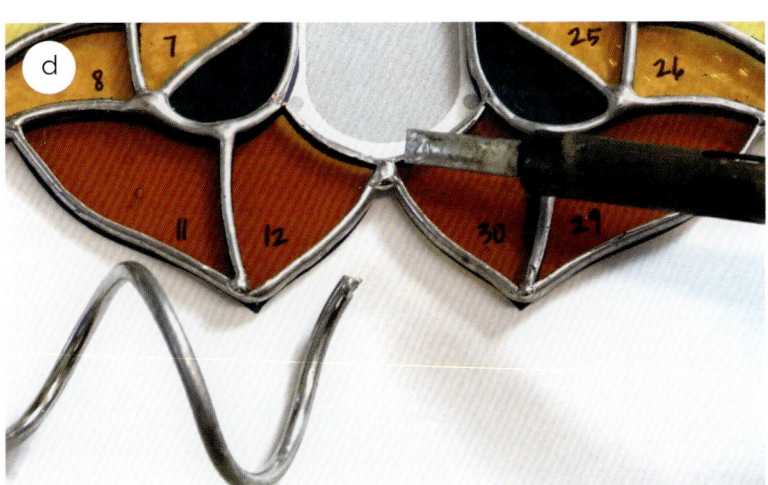

12 Slide the project to the edge of your work surface, with the top edge overhanging slightly so that the upper ring can be fit in place. Stand the test tube upright on its mouth between pieces 3 and 21 to act as a spacer between the wings (e). Use the third hand clamp or pliers to hold the upper ring in place within the top notch between pieces 1 and 19, centered front to back and perpendicular to the glass (f).

FRIENDSHIP

13 Tack the ring in place, then remove the clamp and lift the project from the work surface so that you can add solder to create a strong joint that fully encompasses the wire and incorporates into your neat edge beading (g).

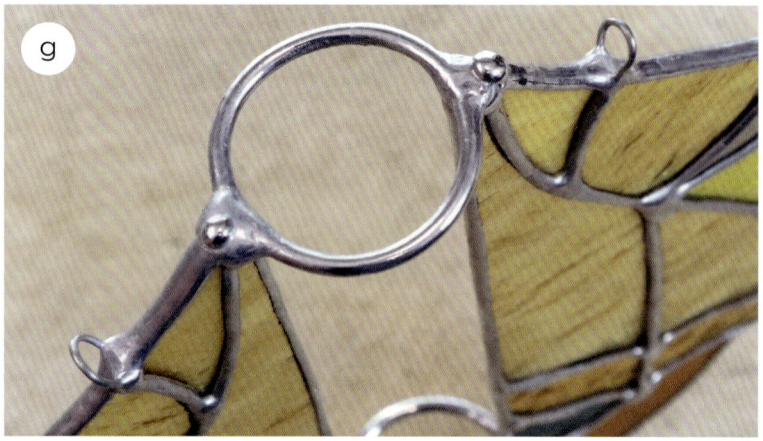

14 Add the lower ring in the same manner at the gray dots between pieces 13 and 31 (h, i).

15 Clean, patina, and polish.

16 Hit up your plant momma friends for clippings to place in the test tube, hang in a sunny spot, and start your new houseplants off in style!

12
BUILDING ON A 3D FORM

This project demonstrates a technique rather than a specific object. We'll use a three-dimensional form to create a sculptural stained glass light – a playful adaptation of a Tiffany-style lampshade.

I first experimented with this technique when I was approached by the wonderful people at Maker's Mark Distillery to design a trophy for the annual Maker's Mile horse race at Keeneland Race Course in Kentucky. They gave me complete creative freedom, and I challenged myself to create a Maker's bottle in the manner of a Tiffany lampshade. I covered an actual bourbon bottle with a tacky wax, and onto this I pressed an infinitude of tiny (cut, ground, foiled, and ultimately soldered) glass pieces of vivid color – red for the brand-signifying wax on each bottle, and amber for the gorgeous bourbon inside.

▶ Initial experimentation

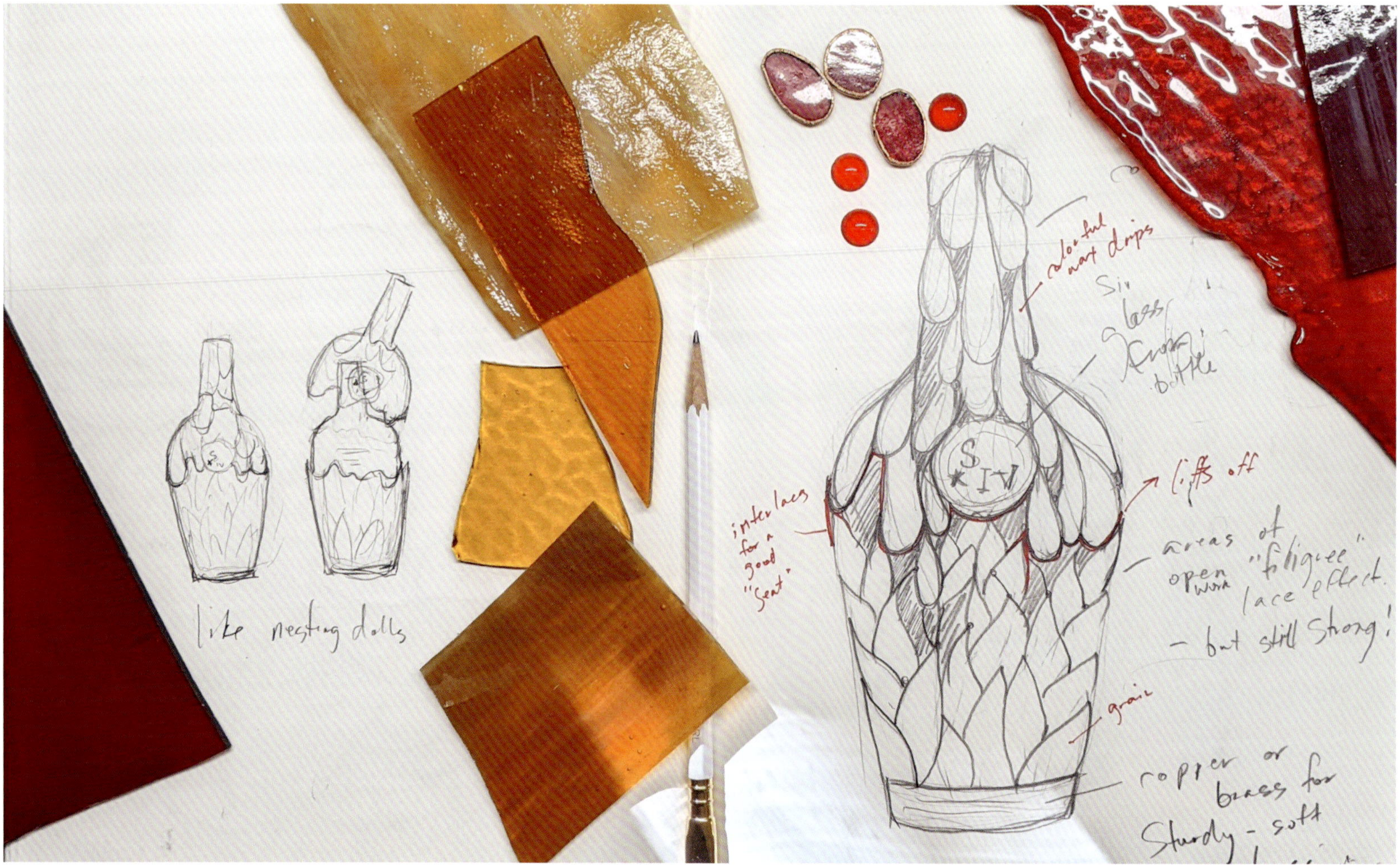

I've returned to this technique several times, creating several of my favorite projects! I made a free-form commemorative sculpture for a wonderful family. I also created another piece for Maker's Mark – a sculpture to house and display a very special reserve select bottle of their bourbon. Such unique commissions inspired this three-dimensional glass mosaic project.

Below, you'll find templates and steps for making the Weeping Willow Lampshade, but I hope you'll consider this as a demonstration of a fun technique that you can riff on to make your own creations. You can use so many things as forms: bowls, bottles, even a shape that you execute in papier-mâché. At first, keep your shapes relatively simple, and always remember that too many curves and ins-and-outs can make it more difficult to remove the glass from your form for final assembly. The technique described here will work for a fairly small project (let's say, keep it smaller than your head). Larger projects will require some reinforcement, such as Strong Line or wire hidden in the seams.

For a more traditional Tiffany-style project...

This process deviates significantly from the traditional Tiffany lampshade technique. If you are interested in making a more traditional Tiffany-style project, search for "Odyssey Lamp Molds" in reseller marketplaces. They're becoming harder to find, but up until recently Odyssey provided all of the forms, patterns, and hardware necessary for making a vast variety of Tiffany shades, including direct replications.

BUILDING ON A 3D FORM

WAX

Wax is a useful tool for holding glass in place on your form, especially if the form is made of a hard material. For softer forms, such as the Styrofoam ball we use in the Weeping Willow Lampshade, you can opt to use sewing pins instead.

Odyssey sells Tacky Wax specifically for stained glass. Homemade wax is an easy alternative: simply mix two parts beeswax with one part petroleum jelly; I used 1 cup of wax to 1/2 cup of jelly (250:125 ml) here. For either wax, set up a double boiler – a small pot to melt the wax, set inside a larger pot containing simmering water – and stir until completely melted. If the wax isn't sticky as you apply glass to it, move to a warmer room or work near a space heater.

SOLDERING ON A 3D FORM

For some shapes, such as our egg, you'll need to tack solder the glass into two separate halves and then remove the form before joining the halves. If you're constructing atop a hemisphere form, you can just solder the whole top as one piece and lift it off the form.

Soldering requires some special considerations when creating a three-dimensional shape with small glass pieces. You'll want to use the thinnest foil possible so that your solder lines remain delicate. I suggest using 50/50 solder when initially soldering the pieces together, then use 60/40 to finish up all lines. The higher melting point of the 50/50 will help to prevent drip-through as you focus on creating a perfect raised bead with the 60/40. If you prefer, you can use 60/40 throughout.

GLASS CHOICES

Some Tiffany style purists use only Youghiogheny glass for their lampshades, but I've been more freewheeling here. Yes, Youghiogheny opalescent glass is perfect for lampshades, as it beautifully filters and disperses the bright light of the bulb, so I've used some mottled for this project. I've complemented it with assorted opalescent green and gold glass, Bullseye Avocado, and hints of yellow and pink as highlights. I also think this design would look stunning in all one glass – but I just don't have it in me to be so minimalist!

WEEPING WILLOW LAMPSHADE

Difficulty: Advanced

For this lampshade, we'll use an egg-shaped form and simple leaf-shaped glass pieces. I've provided templates for a few shapes, but it's not necessary to follow them exactly. You can skip the templates, cutting and grinding your own freehand shapes, but you should keep the pieces to about the size of my templates.

There's no overall pattern – you'll improvise as you apply the foiled pieces to the form. You can futz around with glass placement – considering color, shape, and fit – until you finally tack solder the pieces into sections, remove them from the form, and cleanly finish soldering inside and out.

Supplies

- All standard stained glass tools and supplies (see page 15)
- Pendant light fixture: see note opposite
- A light bulb sized to fit through the lampshade opening; I suggest a small traditional LED bulb or candelabra bulb
- 8" (20 cm) Styrofoam egg
- Sewing pins
- Masking tape
- Odyssey Tacky Wax, or homemade wax (see page 168)
- Disposable application brush: 1–2" (2.5–5 cm) size
- 50/50 solder (optional: helps with drip-through)
- Rag towels
- Double boiler (a pot and a bowl that fits inside it)
- About 8" (20 cm) of 10 gauge copper wire
- A good TV series to binge, because we have a lot of foiling ahead of us!

Pattern

Weeping Willow Lampshade templates on page 197. You can supplement or replace my shapes with your own, but keep them to a similar size for easy construction.

Light fixtures

The circular opening in this pattern is sized to fit light fixtures that accommodate uno-style lampshades ("uno" specifies the dimensions of the ring that secures the lampshade to the fixture). You can source these common light fixtures at many hardware stores, online retailers, lighting suppliers, or on Etsy. Use keywords such as "vintage shade-ready pendant light fixture with plug-in cord" to find appropriate options: you'll find many variations of cord color and covering, switch placement, and fixture material. It must have a "medium", "standard", "e26" size bulb receptacle (those three terms are interchangeable).

Instructions

1 Cut the glass (a). As you will be cutting so many pieces (my finished lamp contains about 235), the cutting process will go a lot faster if you are willing to freehand it. You can cut narrow, straight strips from your glass sheets, then freehand cut leaf shapes to the approximate sizes and shapes of the templates. Alternately, you can repeatedly trace the templates onto glass with a marker, then cut. A variety of shapes will create a natural feel.

WEEPING WILLOW LAMPSHADE **171**

2 Cut fifteen or so pieces so that they have a straight edge (see the template). These will form the top row that abuts the copper ring.

3 Grind all pieces fully (b). Don't worry too much about accuracy to the template (that's the only time I'll say that in this book!).

4 Clean, dry, and foil, using foil with a backing color that matches your chosen patina (c). Use the narrowest foil that still covers around the front and back surface of the glass. Burnish well and trim off any sloppy foil with a craft knife.

5 Make the center fixture ring (see Making the Fixture Ring on page 142).

6 Locate the center of the top of the narrow end of the egg form and mark it with a pin.

7 Cover the Styrofoam form completely with masking tape so the solder won't melt it (d).

8 Melt the wax in a double boiler and paint it onto the form with a disposable brush (e).

172 RAISE YOUR GLASS

9 Place the copper fixture ring so that its center aligns with the pin at the center of the egg form. Secure the ring in place with pins if the wax doesn't hold it.

10 Apply a straight-sided glass piece into position touching the copper ring, and press into the wax. Repeat this with all the straight-sided pieces, all the way around the ring (f).

f

11 Apply leaf-shaped pieces all around the form, varying the colors in a pleasing array. You can make little clusters of leaves, then fill in surrounding spaces more randomly. Pieces should abut each other loosely (g). There will be gaps – try to keep them small, but don't obsess. The pieces are flat, and the form is curved, so the glass edges will be raised from the surface; you'll need to "split the difference" of what is raised on each piece. The tacky wax should allow you to reposition pieces as needed. If necessary, use pins and tape to help secure pieces to the form.

g

12 Continue adding pieces down toward the bottom, leaving an opening wide enough to get your hand inside to install the light fixture nut and the light bulb.

13 When all pieces are applied, mark a vertical division that creates two halves which won't be soldered together until the form is removed from between them. I used a row of pins to make a barrier (h), but you can use thin masking tape or a marker instead.

h

WEEPING WILLOW LAMPSHADE   173

14 Flux and tack with 50/50 solder all around (i) (except for the division line and copper ring).

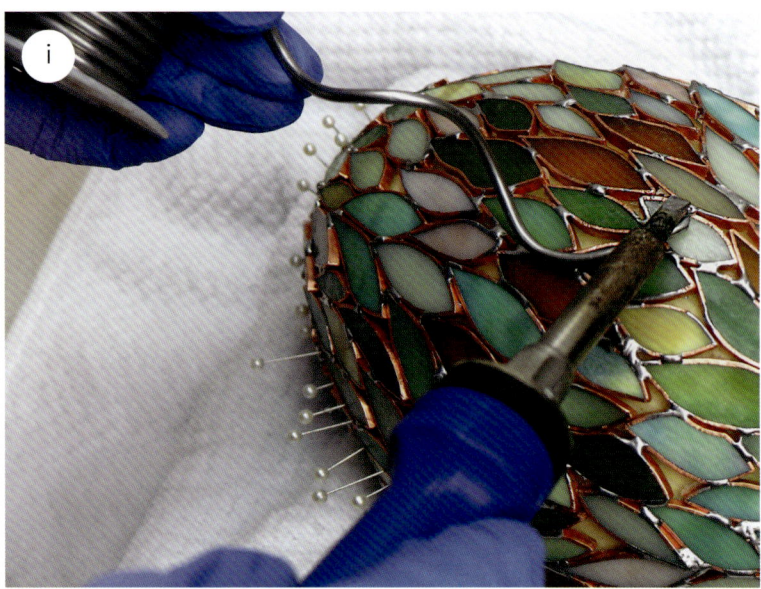

15 Lightly solder along all interior lines of each half, but don't worry about making a neat bead – you'll tidy up later. Prop the project up on towels, repositioning it as you go, so that the area you're soldering is always horizontal.

16 To create a prettier profile along the bottom edge, hold the final pieces away from the form as you tack them on (j).

17 Tack the copper ring to ONE of the halves, but not the other.

18 Make alignment marks so that when you remove the halves from the form, you'll know exactly how they fit back together (k). Remove the halves from the form (l, m). If you have difficulty, try warming the project with a blow-dryer, and gently prying with a plastic fid all around. Wipe off any leftover wax.

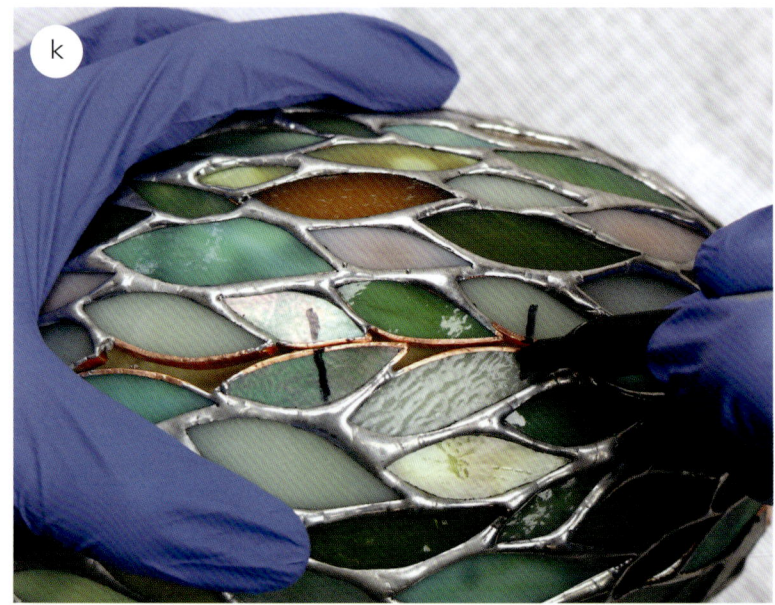

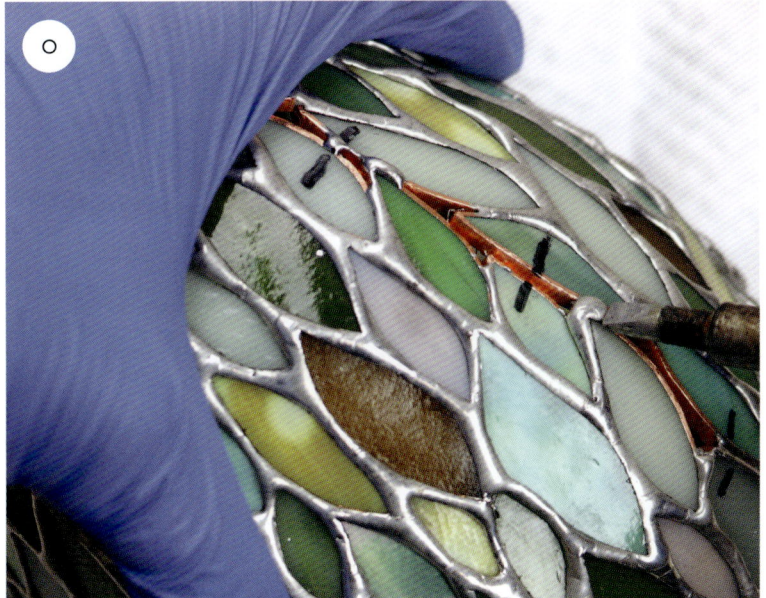

19 Fully solder the inside of each half with 50/50 solder (n), holding the outside with a damp cloth. Avoid deforming the shape as you go.

20 Align the two halves, using the alignment marks (o), and tack solder together on the outside.

21 Fully solder the inside junction line.

22 Use 60/40 solder to create a neat solder bead over the entire exterior of the lampshade.

23 Blend the copper ring into the project nicely (p).

WEEPING WILLOW LAMPSHADE **175**

24 Consider the bottom opening of the lampshade. If necessary, add some additional leaves to perfect your elegant shape, but be sure to leave enough space to install the light fixture nut and the light bulb. Patiently create a nice, raised edge bead along the bottom perimeter of the opening (q).

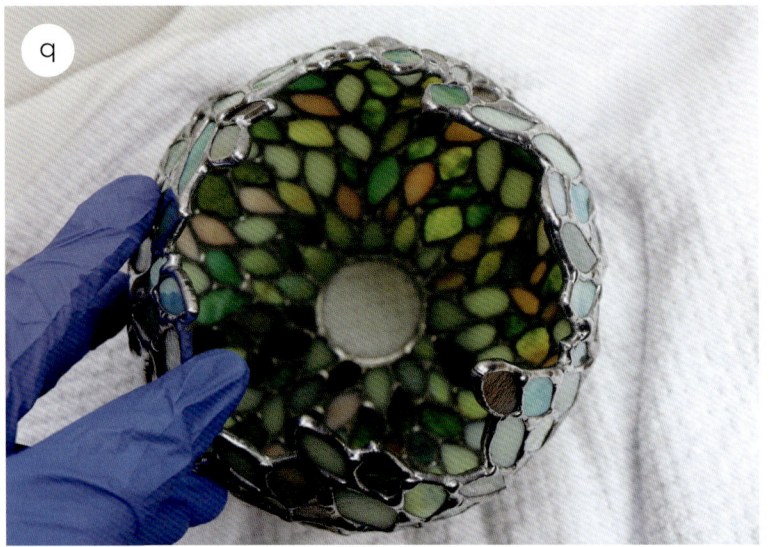

25 Clean, patina, and polish (r).

26 Place the light fixture into the lampshade and secure it with the nut, install the lightbulb, and hang.

PATTERNS

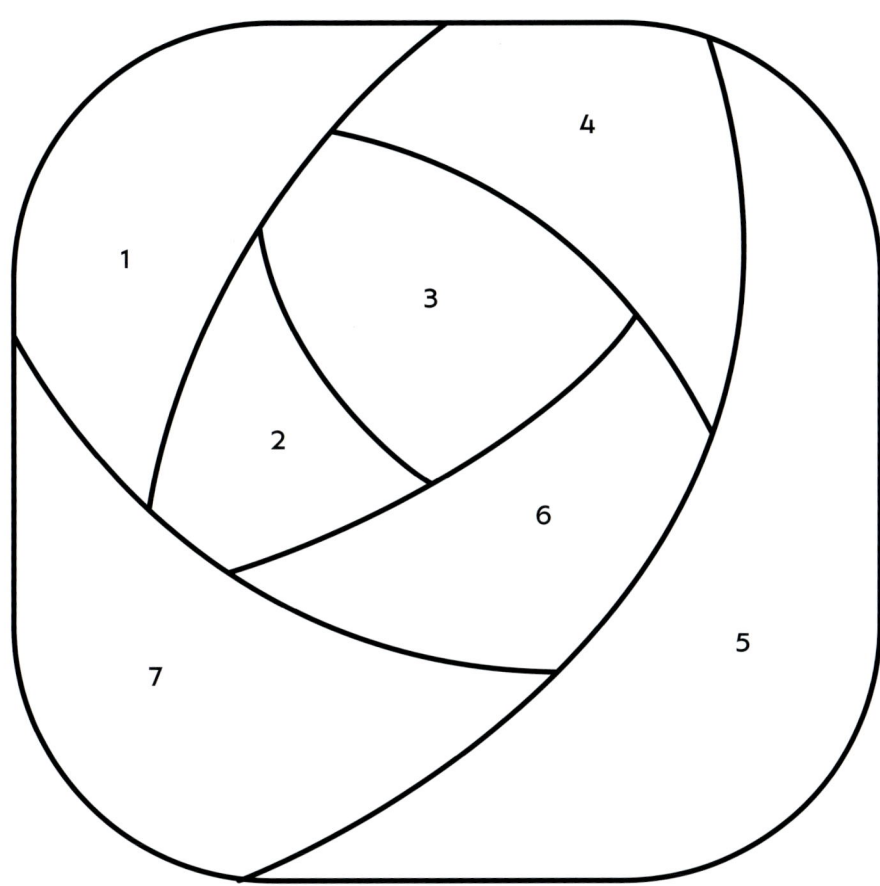

MACKINTOSH ROSE
SUNCATCHER p. 23

Calibration lines should each measure 1" (25.4 mm)

Copyright information

The patterns in this book may be reproduced by the purchaser to create handcrafted stained glass pieces for personal use or for (non-mass-produced) sale, with design credit given to Neile Cooper. The patterns may not otherwise be reproduced, digitized, shared, posted online, nor resold. Copyright, design credit, and all other rights are retained by © Neile Cooper.

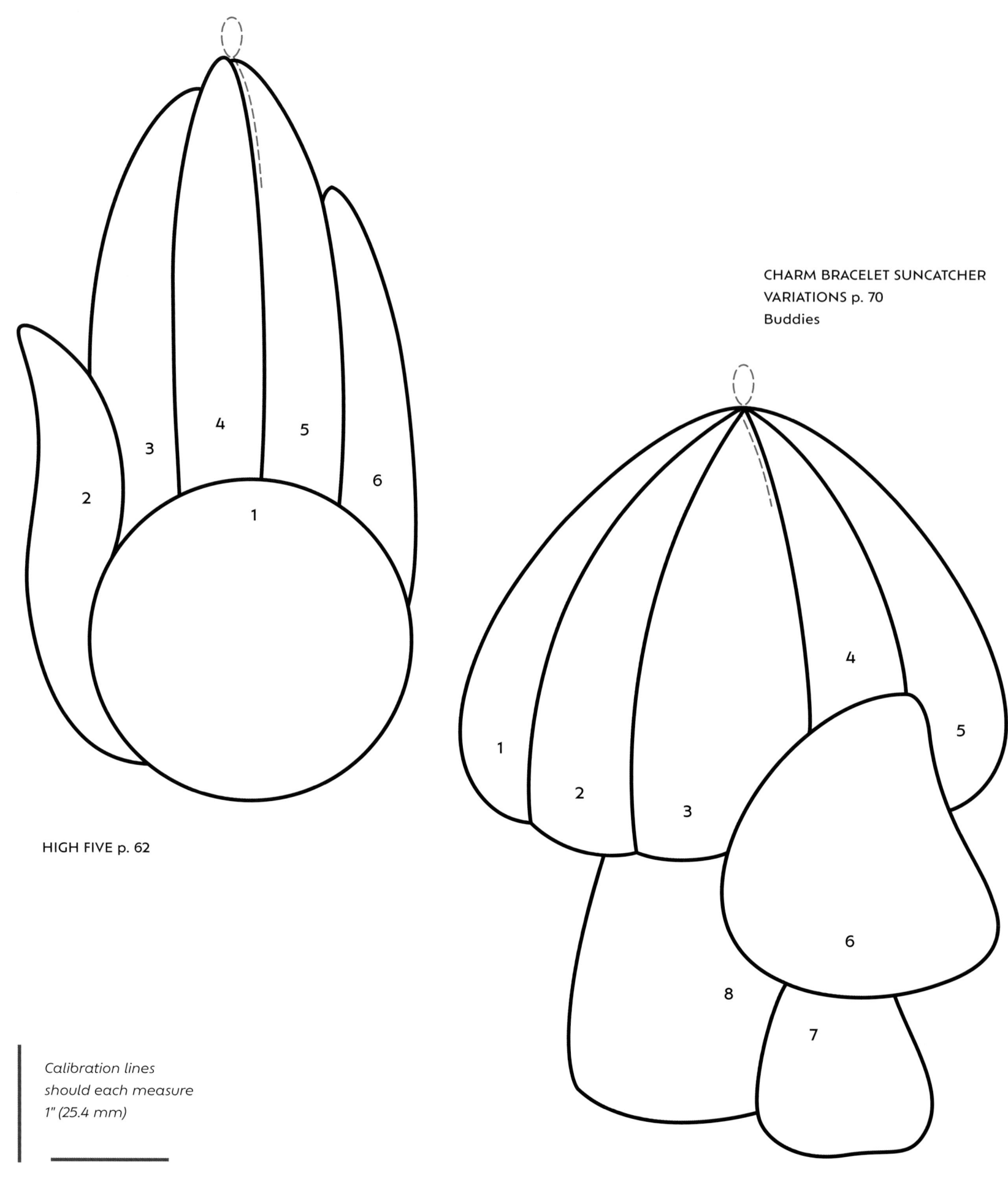

CHARM BRACELET SUNCATCHER
VARIATIONS p. 70
Buddies

HIGH FIVE p. 62

Calibration lines should each measure 1" (25.4 mm)

178 RAISE YOUR GLASS

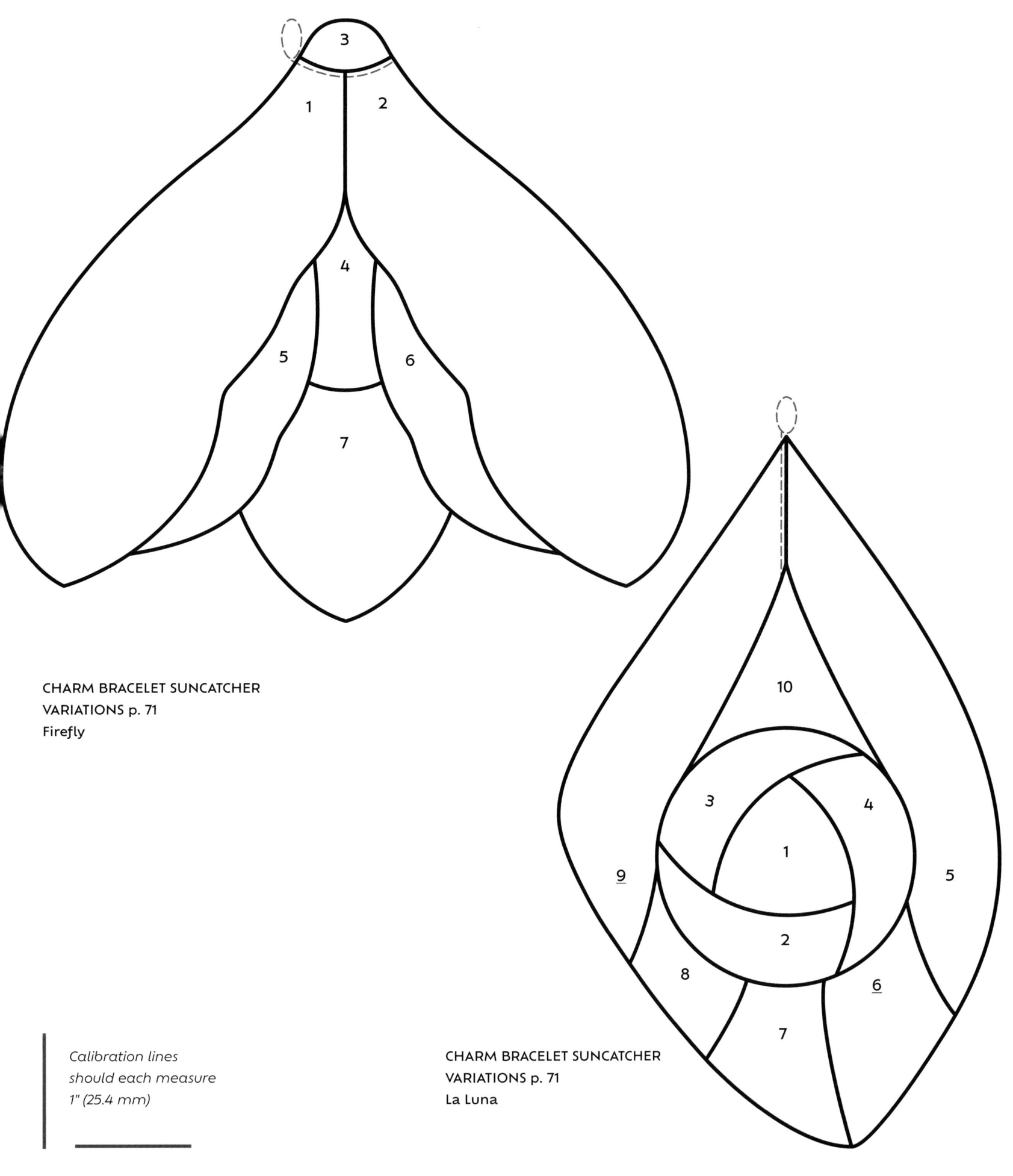

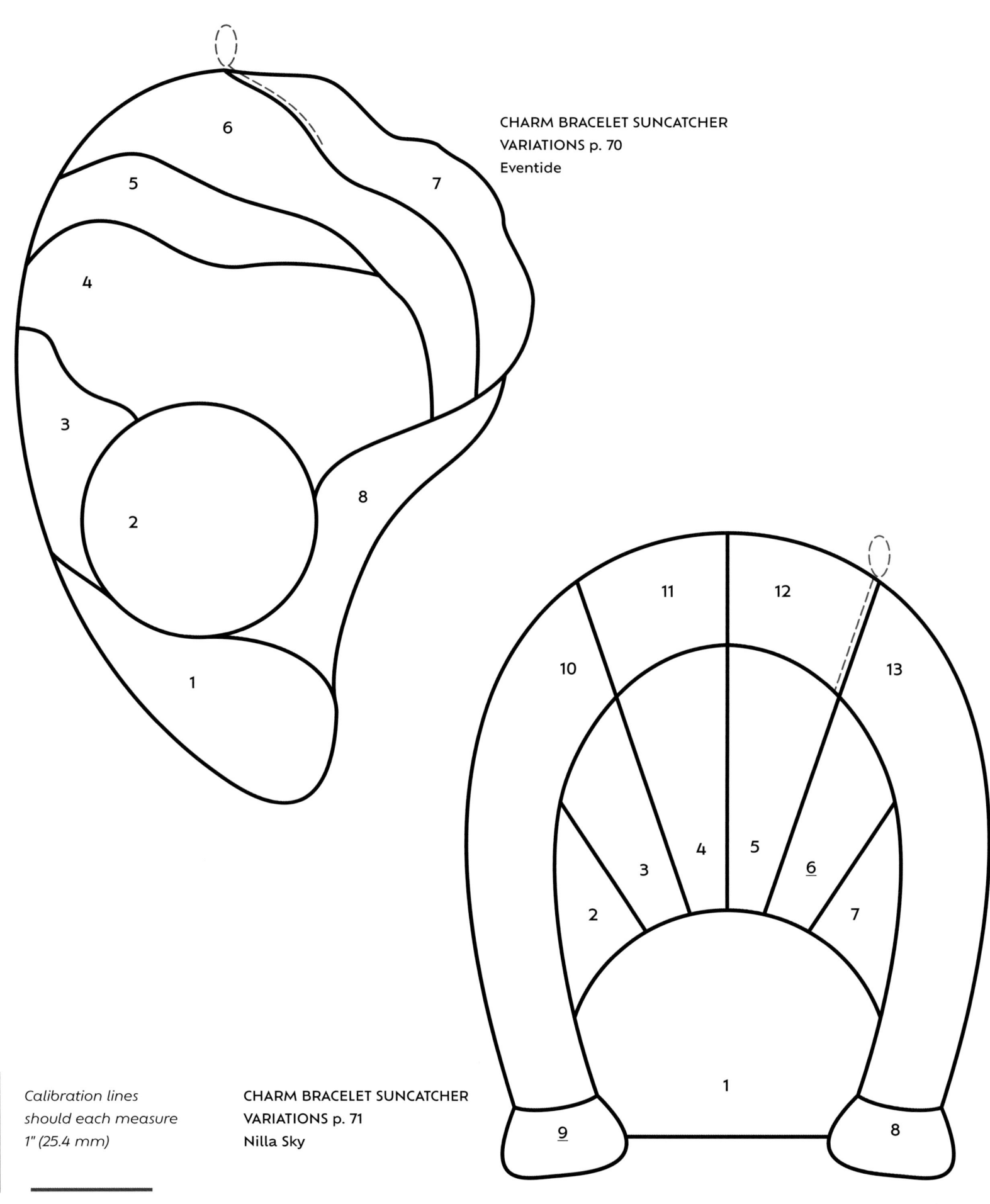

CHARM BRACELET SUNCATCHER
VARIATIONS p. 70
Eventide

CHARM BRACELET SUNCATCHER
VARIATIONS p. 71
Nilla Sky

Calibration lines should each measure 1" (25.4 mm)

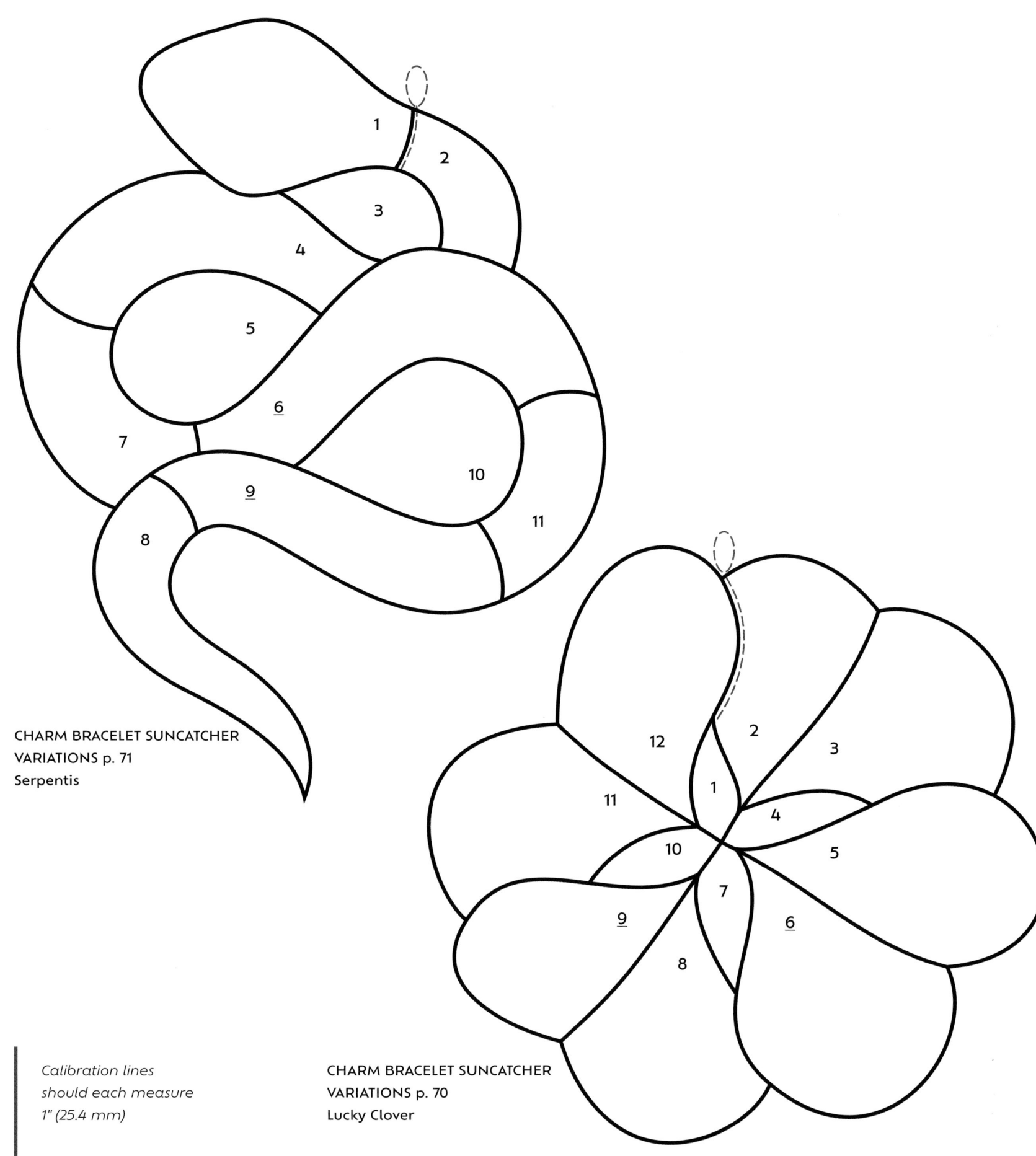

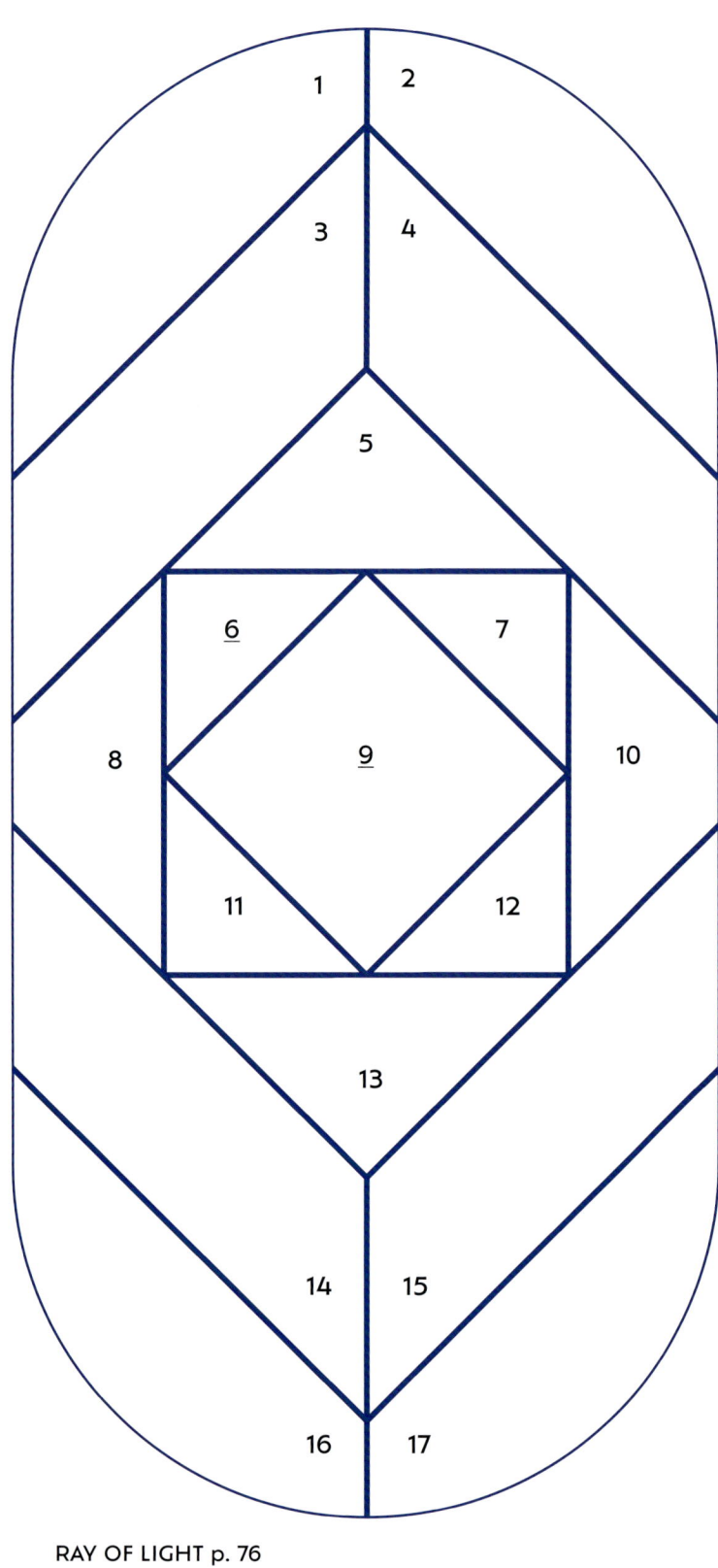

OCULUS p. 82

RAY OF LIGHT p. 76

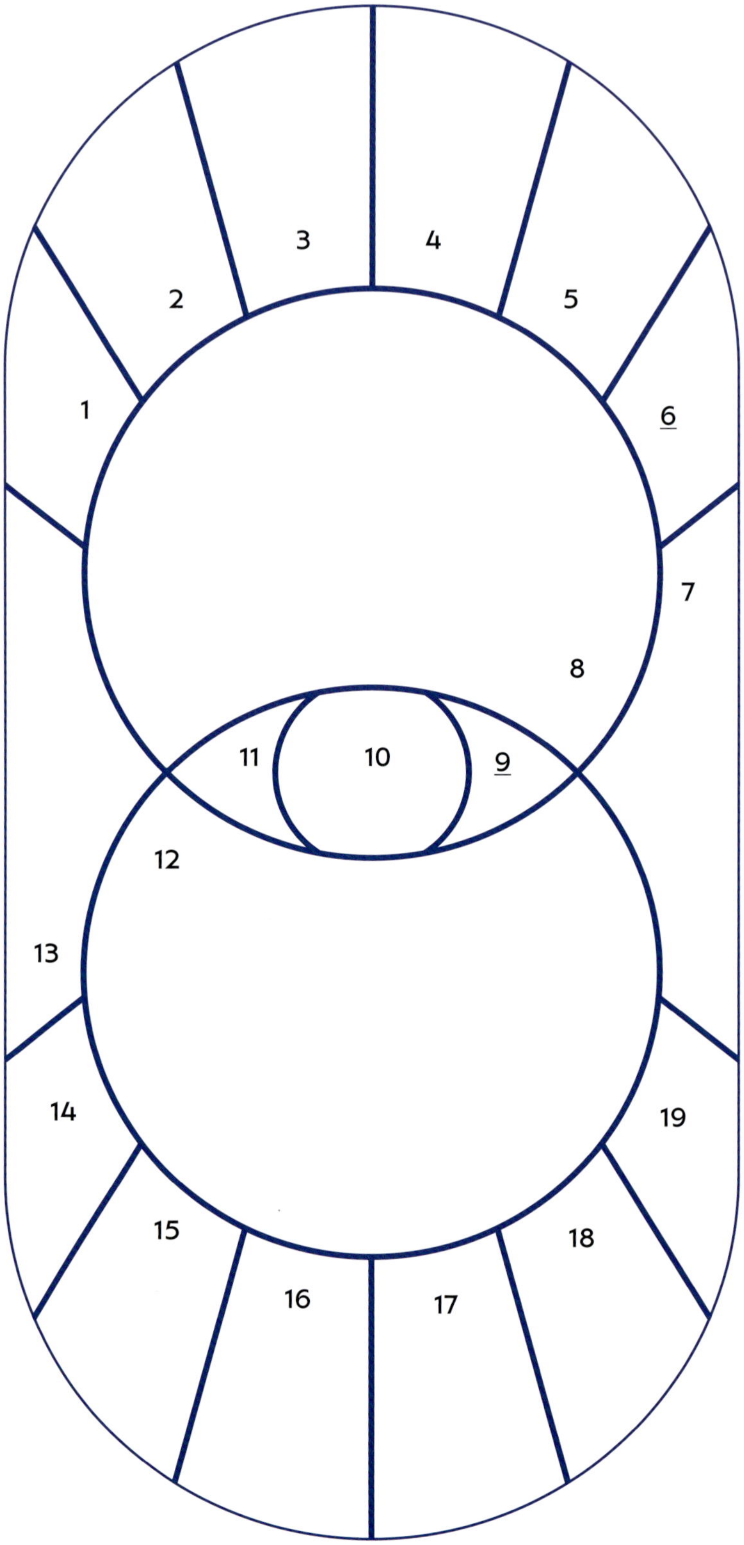

Calibration lines should each measure 1" (25.4 mm)

182 RAISE YOUR GLASS

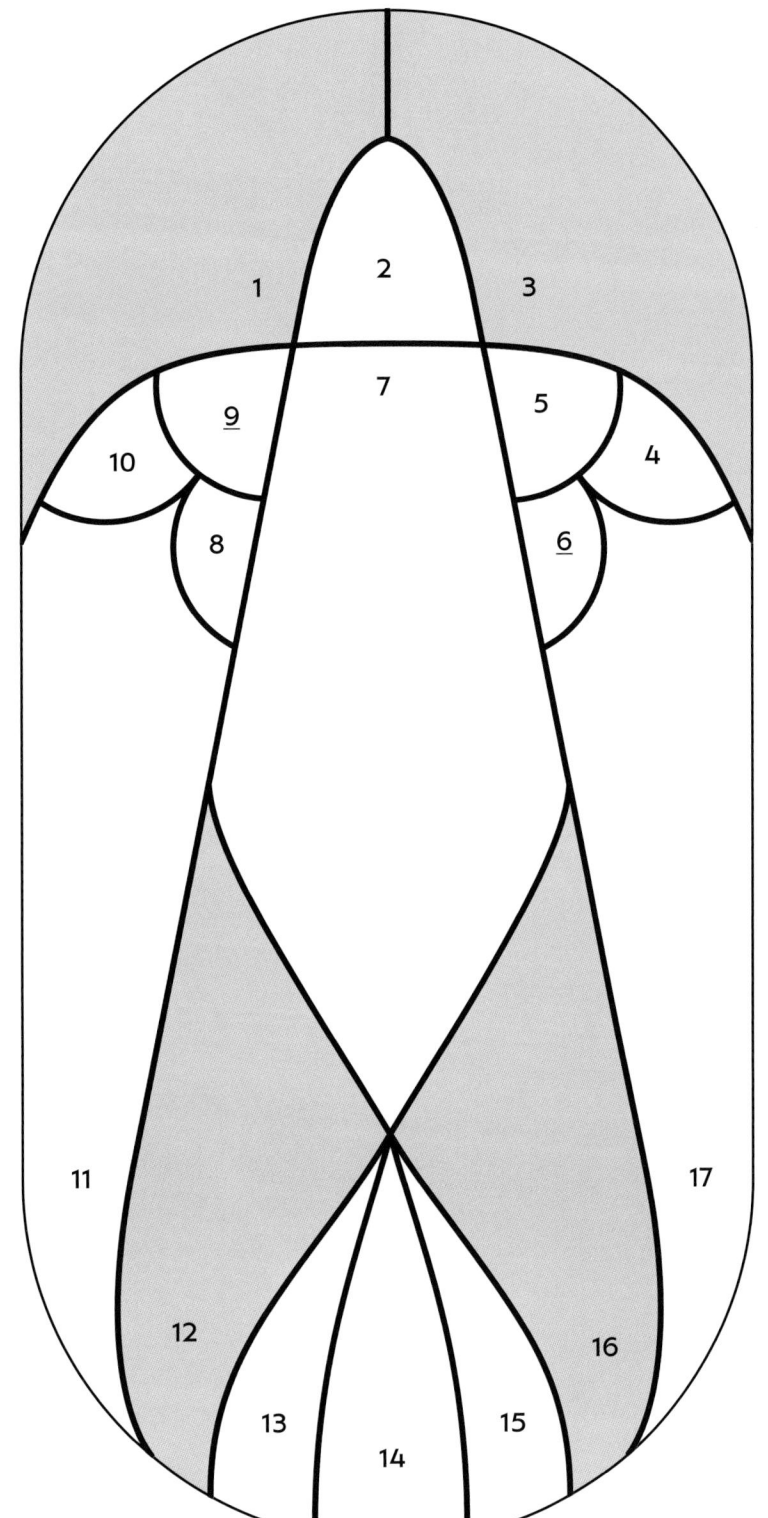

PALOMA p. 82

Calibration lines should each measure 1" (25.4 mm)

PATTERNS **183**

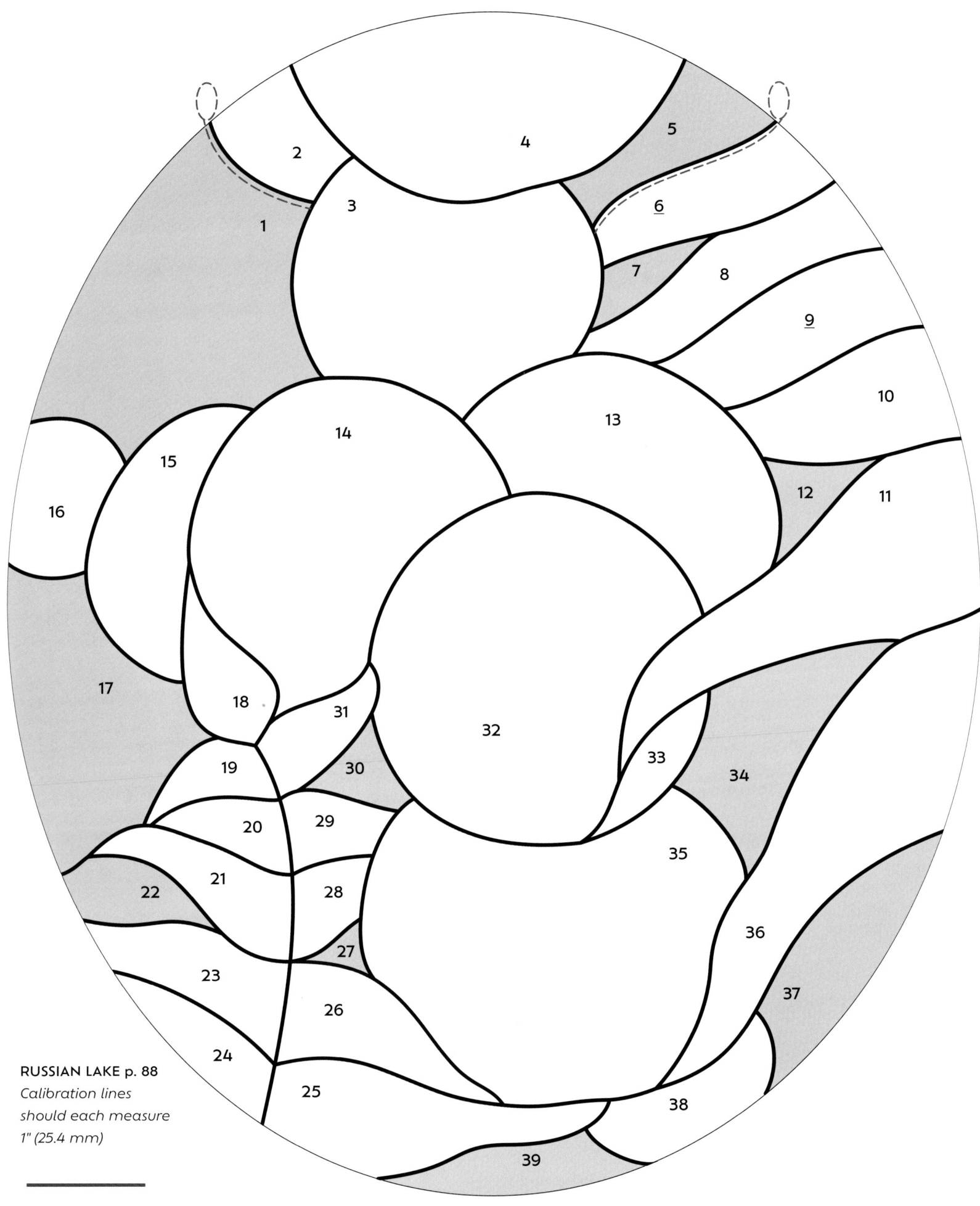

RUSSIAN LAKE p. 88
Calibration lines should each measure 1" (25.4 mm)

184 RAISE YOUR GLASS

EAST BAY p. 88
Calibration lines should each measure 1" (25.4 mm)

WOODLAND MIRROR p. 98
*Enlarge to 110%
Calibration lines should each measure 1" (25.4 mm)*

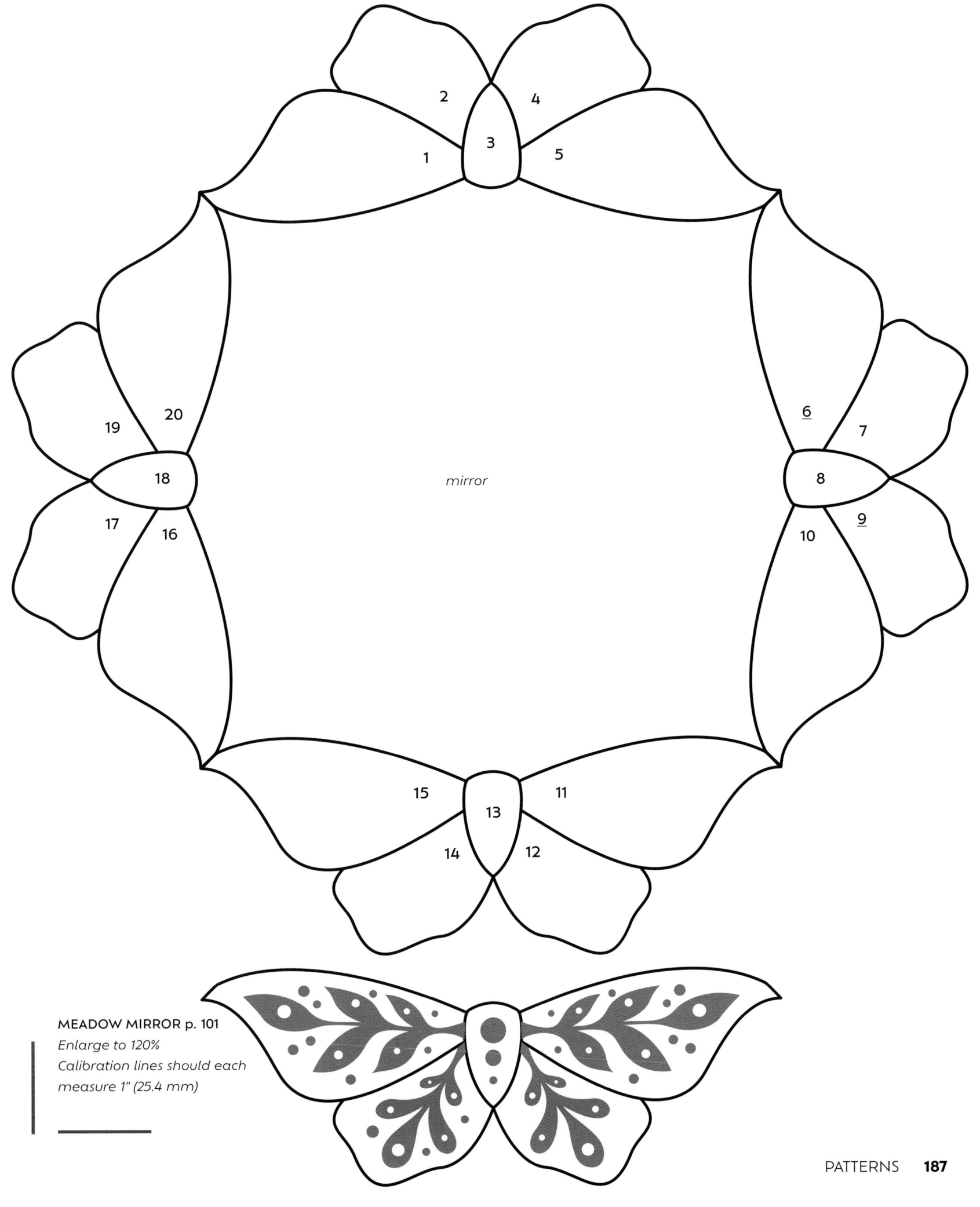

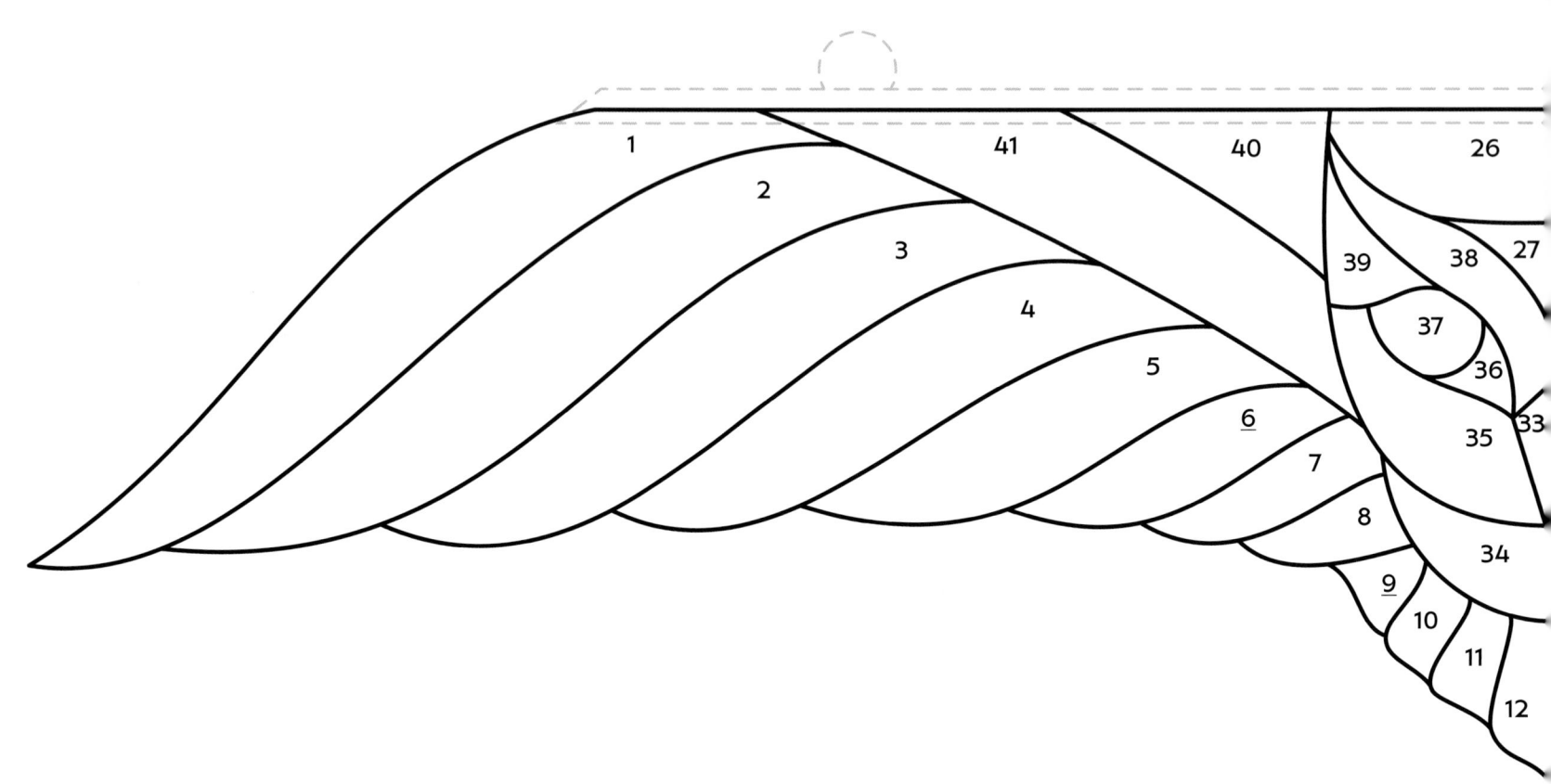

ARCHIMEDES OWL p. 106

Enlarge to 130%
Calibration lines should each measure 1" (25.4 mm)

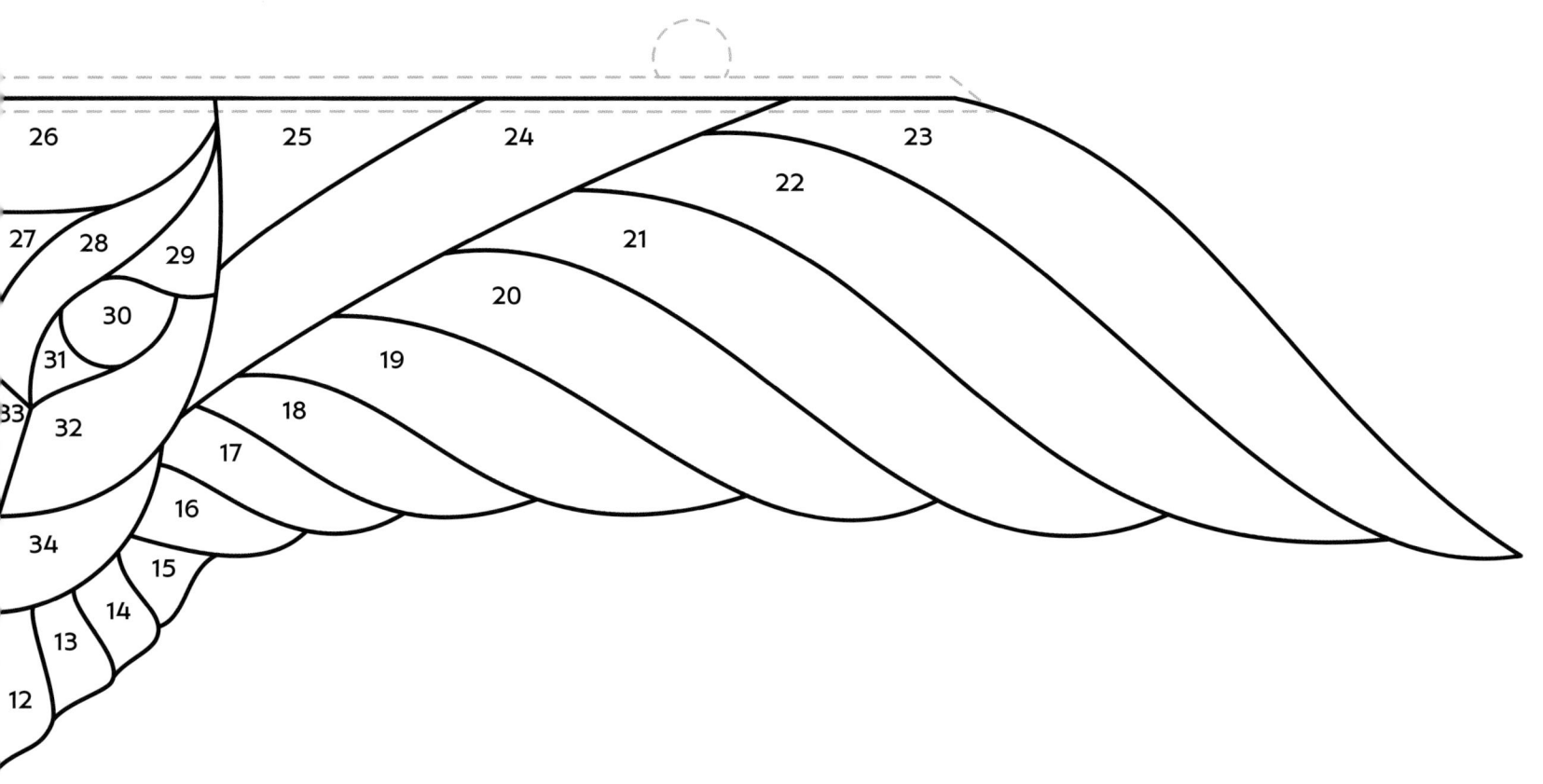

PATTERNS

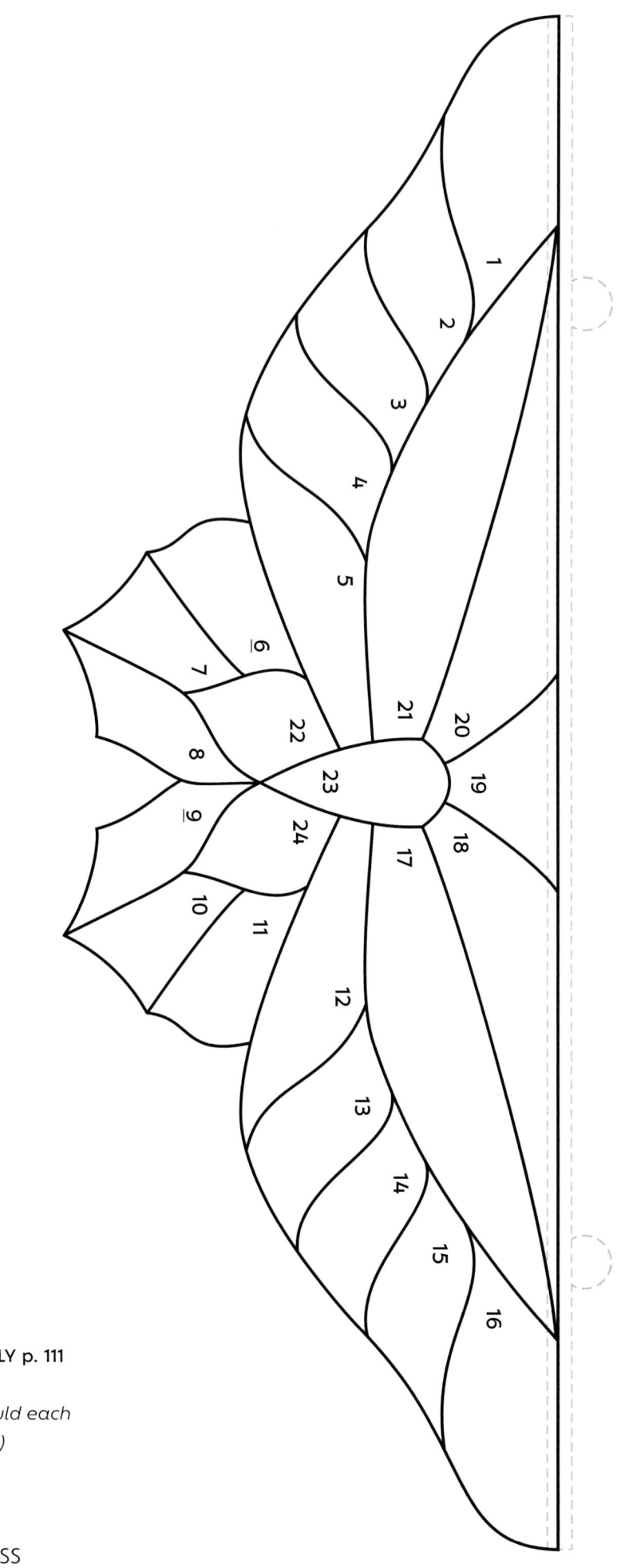

BIRDWING BUTTERFLY p. 111
Enlarge to 160%
Calibration lines should each measure 1" (25.4 mm)

190 RAISE YOUR GLASS

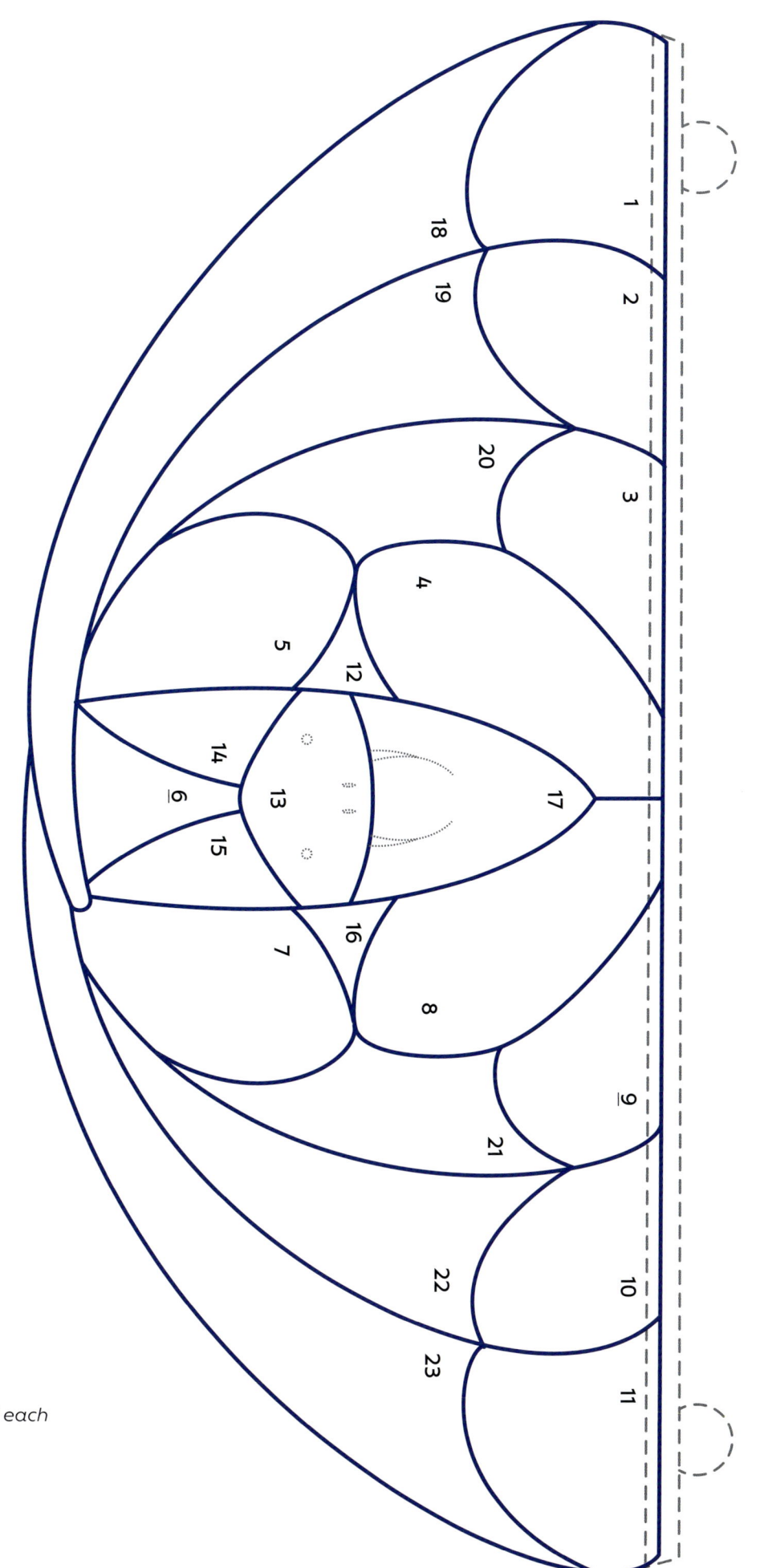

HAVISHAM BAT p. 112
*Enlarge to 120%
Calibration lines should each measure 1" (25.4 mm)*

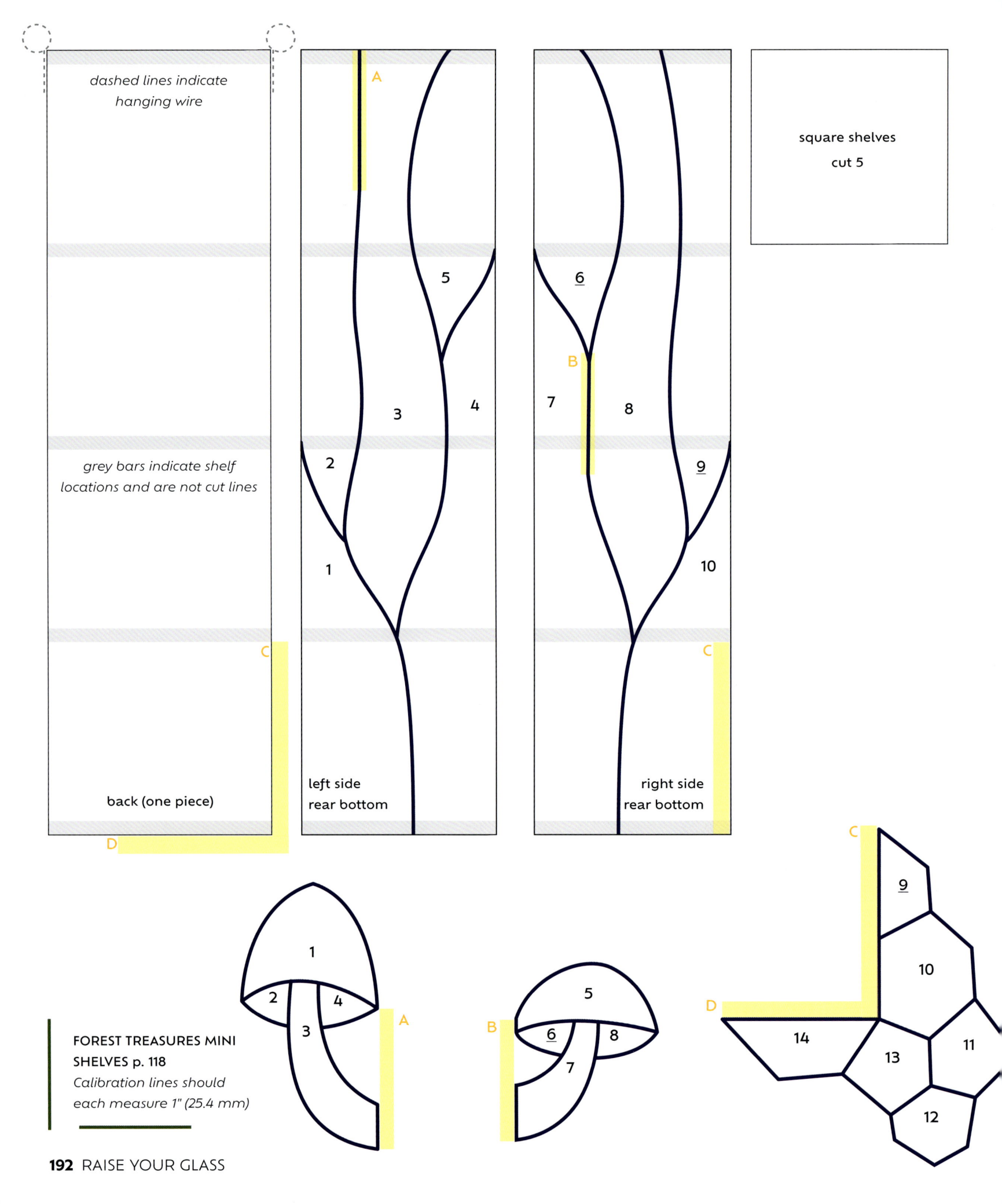

*leave yellow areas unsoldered
until installing hinge wire*

back

front

*grey areas show where left and right
sides butt up inside front and back*

dashed line is hinge location - leave edge unsoldered until installing hinge tube

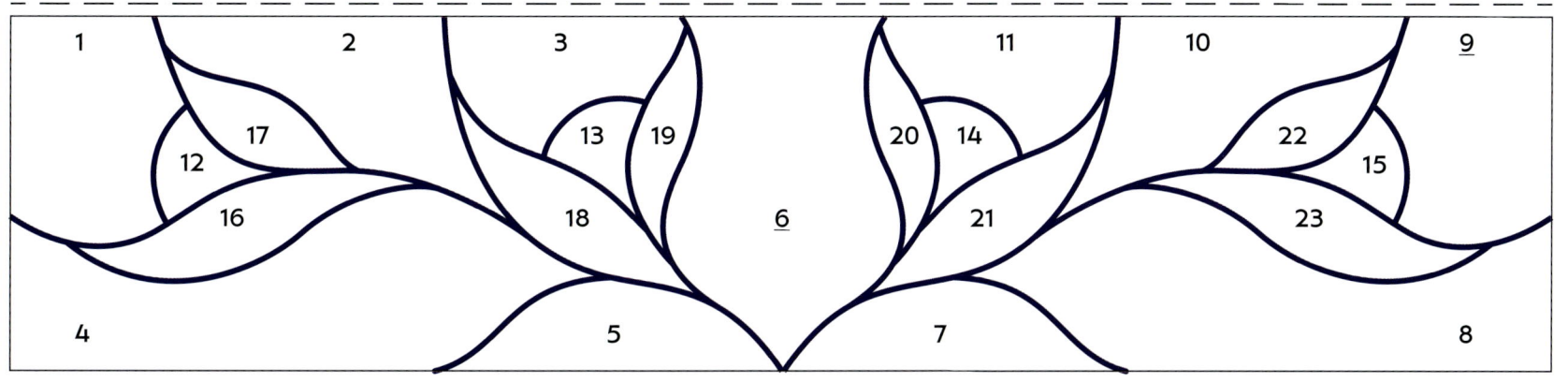

bottom

PENCIL BOX p. 128
*Calibration lines should
each measure 1" (25.4 mm)*

left side
outside face

right side
outside face

MOLESKINE SLIPCASE p. 133
Slipcase
Calibration lines should each measure 1" (25.4 mm)

felt template

MOLESKINE
SLIPCASE p. 133
Felt

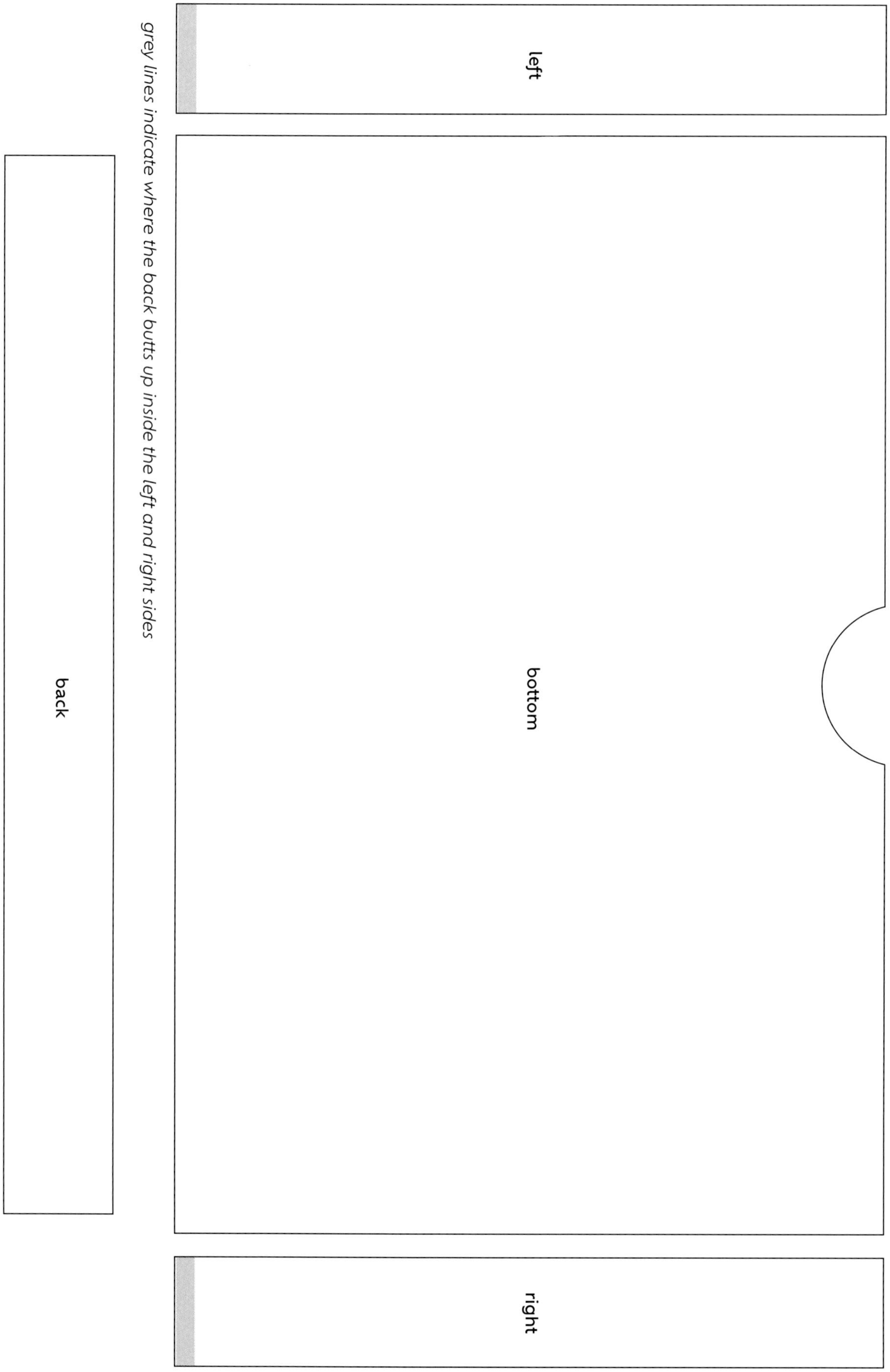

left

grey lines indicate where the back butts up inside the left and right sides

bottom

back

right

MOLESKINE SLIPCASE p. 133
Slipcase
Calibration lines should each measure 1" (25.4 mm)

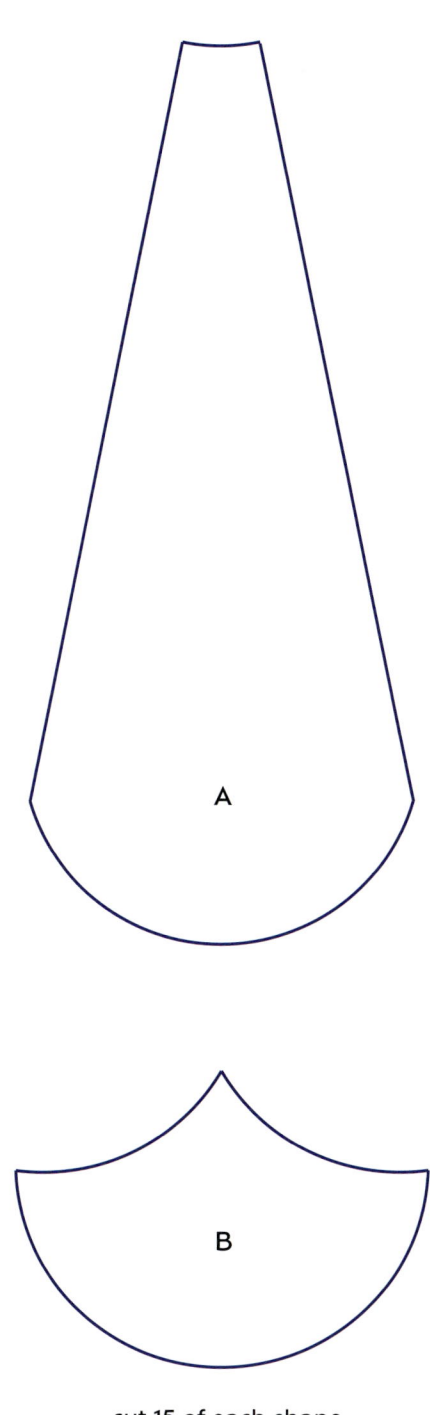

A

B

cut 15 of each shape

HÉLÈNE p. 143

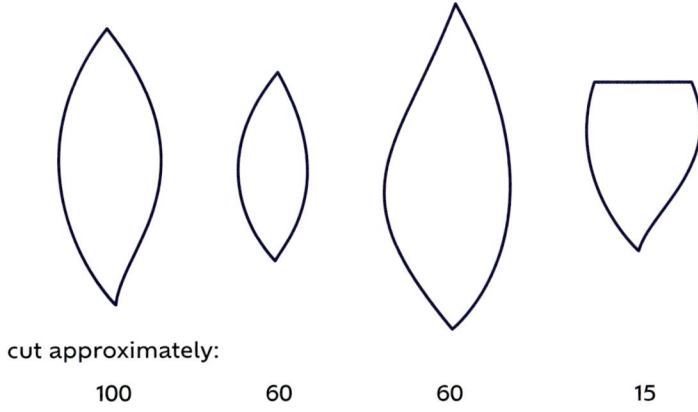

cut approximately:

100　　　60　　　60　　　15

WEEPING WILLOW LAMPSHADE
p. 170

PATTERNS **197**

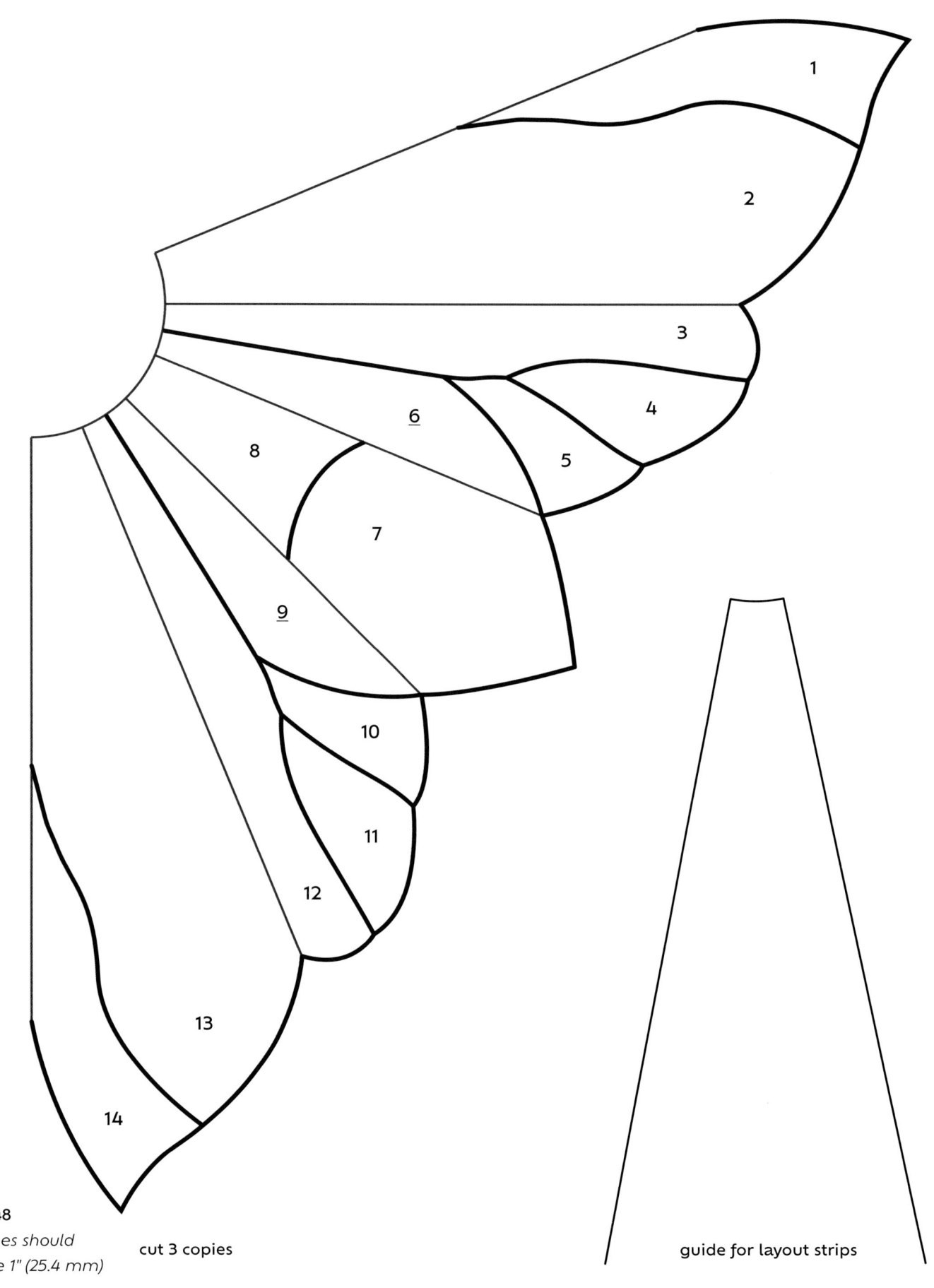

ST. JUDIE p. 148
Calibration lines should each measure 1" (25.4 mm)

cut 3 copies

guide for layout strips

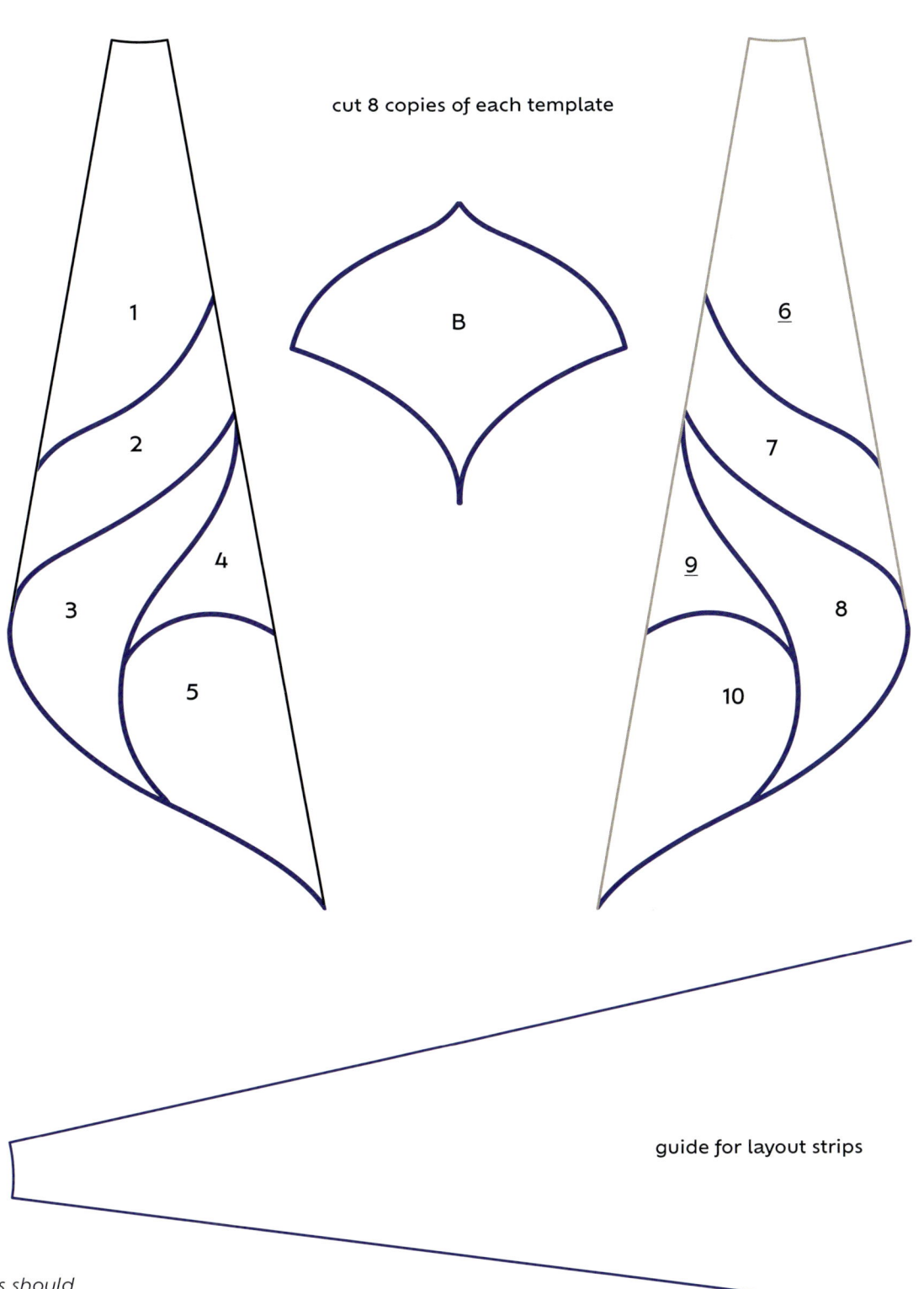

cut 8 copies of each template

guide for layout strips

MARA p. 151
Calibration lines should each measure 1" (25.4 mm)

PATTERNS

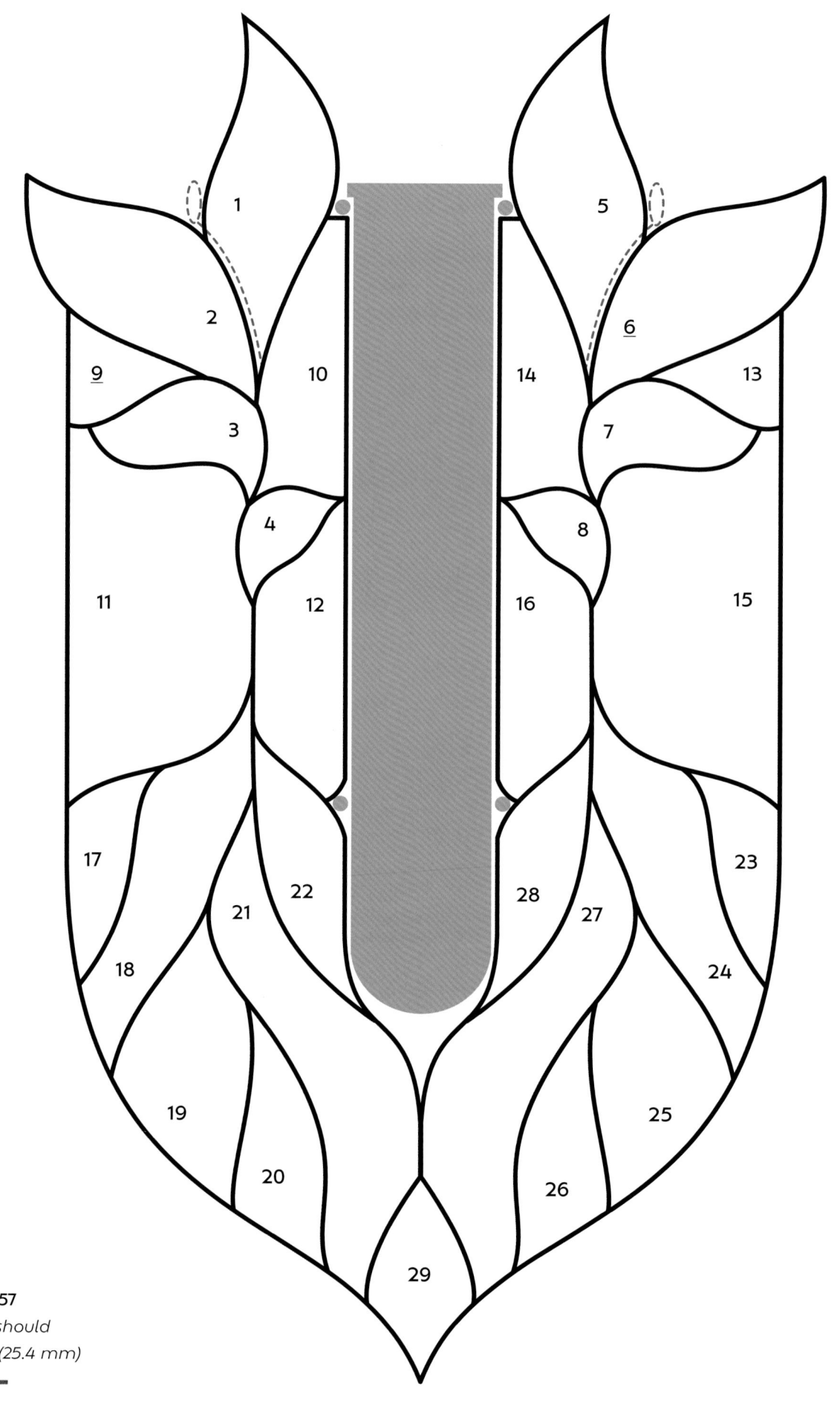

ROOT DOWN p. 157
Calibration lines should each measure 1" (25.4 mm)

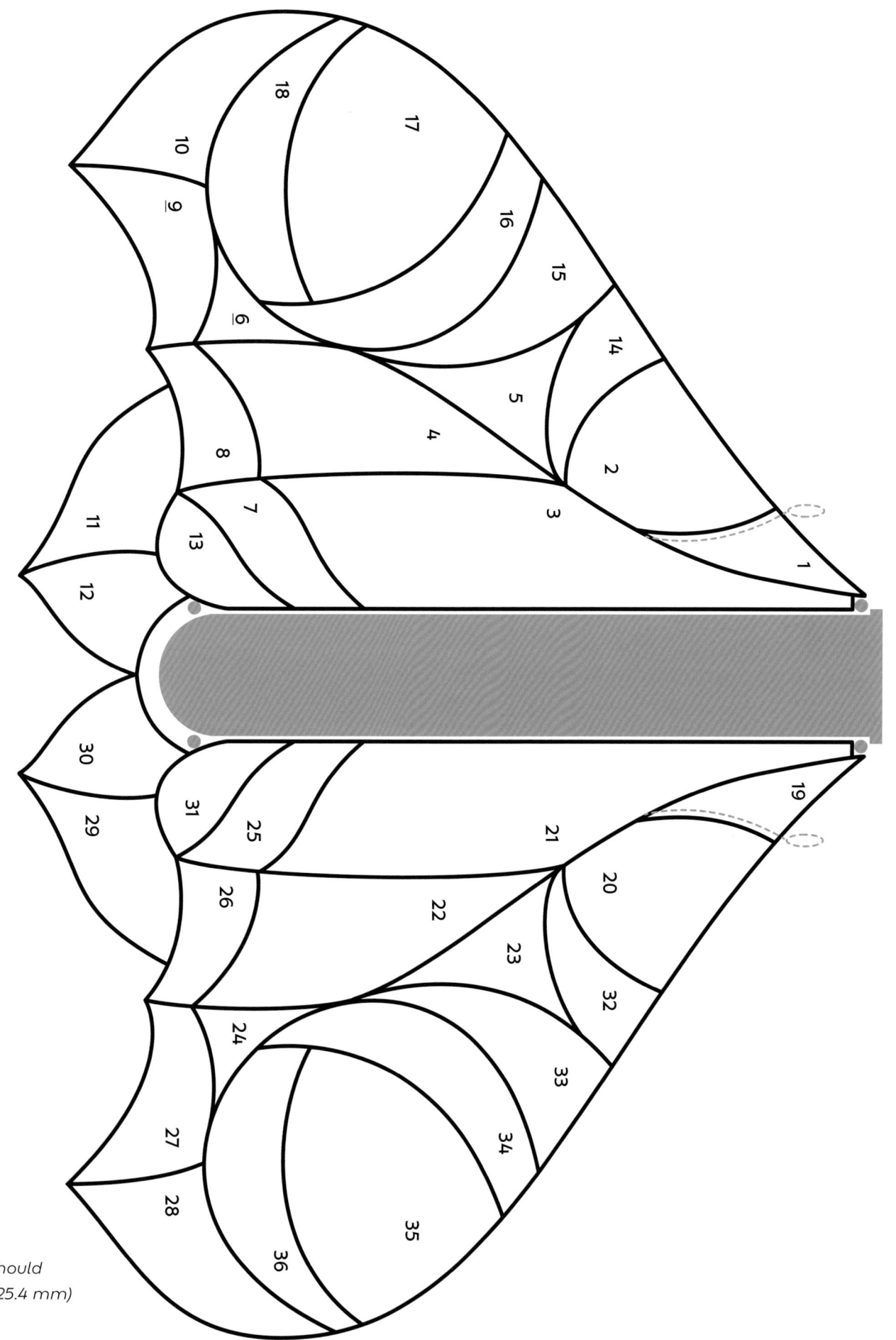

FRIENDSHIP p. 161
Enlarge to 110%
Calibration lines should each measure 1" (25.4 mm)

GLOSSARY

The following words are defined as used in *this* book for our specific purposes.

Assemblage: A group of glass pieces joined in a three-dimensional arrangement.

Back side: Generally, the side of a project that is soldered second, after the front side.

Bead: A smooth, rounded surface of solder; the goal of most stained glass soldering. (See also Edge bead.)

Breaking: Running the score so that the glass separates into two pieces

Burnishing: The act of smoothing copper foil onto the edges and faces of a piece of glass using a fid.

Butting: Placing the edge of one piece of glass against the face of another when constructing three-dimensional projects.

Concave: A curve like the inside of a crescent. These can be somewhat difficult to cut (and foil).

Convex: A curve like the outside of a circle.

Cut/cutting (glass): Breaking glass into multiple pieces by scoring it and then running the score.

Curing: Using heat to cause paint to adhere permanently to the glass surface.

Drip-through: When molten solder drips between glass pieces rather than forming a bead. Some techniques to control drip-through include allowing the area to cool, using a cooler soldering iron temperature, and/or using a damp rag on the back side of the project.

Edge: The thin cross-section of glass, as opposed to the face; the surface that is ground and foiled.

Edge bead: Used as both a noun and a verb to indicate the creation of a neat, smooth, strong, arched line of solder along the perimeter of a project. A strong edge bead resists the pulling away of foil from the glass perimeter, where adherence is weakest. A neat edge bead is visually appealing and shows meticulous craftsmanship. (Full description on page 46.)

202 RAISE YOUR GLASS

Face: The wide surface of a piece of glass, as opposed to the edge.

Fid: A simple tool that burnishes copper foil by rubbing.

Form: A three-dimensional shape used as a structure for assembling sculptural stained glass.

Front side: The side of a project that is normally soldered first. Usually, the side that will be viewed most closely when the project is installed.

Grain: The overall direction of any details (i.e. bubbles, streaks) in the glass.

Hanging loop: A wire loop soldered to a sturdy section of a project. (See also Wire.)

Hinge: A brass tube and wire used to attach a lid to a box (not to be confused with Hinge point).

Hinge point: A straight, unbroken line extending across the design from one side of the perimeter to the other. These are to be avoided because they are structurally very weak.

Interior lines: Any lines that occur between multiple pieces of glass, as opposed to perimeter lines.

Layout strip: A straight strip that is pinned down to a work surface and is used to ensure a straight line for the perimeter of a project.

Lead came: See U-channel lead came.

Leading/trailing end: For foil and lead came, the leading end is the cut end that is first applied to the project; the trailing end eventually touches or overlaps the leading end.

Mirror edge sealant: A liquid used to coat the edge of mirror glass so that the silvering of the glass does not deteriorate over time.

Miter: Cutting across a strip of zinc or lead at an angle.

Opaque: Not translucent; preventing the passage of light.

Oxidize: The tendency of copper foil, solder, and other metals to form a layer of "tarnish" that interferes with soldering and usually creates a dull look.

Panel: A flat portion or subsection of a project.

Pattern: A drawing that is cut apart to create templates or used as a guide for laying out glass pieces. You'll usually need two copies of a pattern – one for each of these uses – though it's nice to have extras to use for fixing mistakes.

Perimeter: The outside edge of an assembled project, where exposed solder lines exist. When referring to a pattern, it means the outline of a whole shape.

Piece: A piece of cut glass that will be ground, foiled, and soldered to create the final project.

Project: The stained glass piece as a whole, i.e. a suncatcher, panel, or box.

Run/running: Causing a break to run along the line created by scoring glass with a cutter. (Full description on page 28.)

GLOSSARY 203

Score/scoring: Using a glass cutter to create a break in the surface tension of the glass along which the glass can be broken. (Full description on page 26.)

Sheet: An uncut area of raw glass from which a piece will be cut.

Stretched lead came: See U-channel lead came.

Strong Line: A coppered steel strip that provides reinforcement when embedded in a solder line. This is a Morton branded item available at most stained glass supply shops.

Tacking: Placing just a dab of solder between two pieces to preliminarily hold them together while assembling. Tacking is eventually blended into a final solder line.

Template: A paper shape that is cut from a pattern and is used to represent the shape of a glass piece. It is glued to (or drawn on) the glass for cutting and grinding.

Third hand clamp: A relatively cheap but often overlooked tool that makes working with three-dimensional constructions much easier. It holds a piece of glass in a stable position so that your hand is freed up to hold something else (or avoid the risk of getting burned in tight spaces). The simplest versions are a roach clip at the end of a flexible arm, attached to a sturdy base or clamp.

Tinning: Applying a thin coat of solder to copper foil or copper wire so that the color changes to silver.

U-channel lead came: A U-shaped length of lead that is often used to finish the perimeter of a stained glass project. It should be stretched before use. The "leaded glass" technique uses H-channel and U-channel lead came to hold pieces together, rather than copper foil and solder. It comes in a variety of sizes; we use 3/16" (5 mm) in this book. Also called "U lead came" and "U profile lead came".

U-channel zinc came: A rigid U-shaped length of zinc that can be used to finish straight perimeters. It provides some strength and reinforcement. It comes in a variety of sizes; we use 1/4" (6 mm) in this book. Also called "U zinc came" and "U profile zinc came".

Wire: The projects in this book use thicker 10 gauge copper wire for several projects, and thinner 16–18 gauge copper, tinned copper, or brass wire (interchangeable) for others.

Zinc came: See U-channel zinc came.

RESOURCES & SUPPLIERS

Visiting a local stained glass retailer is the best way to buy glass and supplies – you'll be surrounded by so many beautiful raw materials, and you'll have a chance to forge relationships with local crafters. Tools and supplies can easily be found online as well. Here are some of the retailers that I use, as well as recommendations from the artists featured in the book, and the names of some of my favorite glass manufacturers.

USA

Anything in Stained Glass
Frederick, MD
anythinginstainedglass.com

Colorado Glass Works
This shop hosts frequent classes – what a great place to learn the craft, surrounded by the foothills of the Colorado Rocky Mountains!
Boulder, CO
coglassworks.com

Delphi Glass
Lansing, MI
delphiglass.com

Ed Hoy's International
Warrenville, IL
edhoy.com

Erin Glassworks
Erin is the supplier of the layout frames used in several projects in this book.
Online
eringlassworks.com

Franklin Art Glass
Columbus, OH
franklinartglass.com

Pasadena Stained Glass
Owned by Janel Foo, one of the amazing artists featured in Kicking Glass.
Pasadena, CA
pasadenastainedglass.com

SW Art Glass
Phoenix, AZ
swartglass.com

Warner Art Glass
My local shop – fully stocked and run by awesome people!
Whitehall, PA
warnerartglass.com

Canada

Lucent Glass and Art
Guelph, ON
lucentglassandart.com

Stained Glass Stuff
Ottawa, ON
stainedglassstuff.com

UK and Europe

Creative Glass Guild
Bristol, UK
creativeglassguild.co.uk

Foka Glas-in-lood Tiffany
Sint-Oedenrode, The Netherlands
fokaglasinlood.nl

Lead and Light
Camden, London, UK
leadandlight.co.uk

Tempsford Stained Glass
Bedford, UK
tempsfordstainedglass.co.uk

Silent Art
Spankeren, The Netherlands
silentartshop.nl

TGK Gmbh
Schloss Holte, Germany
tgk.de

Warm Glass
Online
warm-glass.co.uk

Australia

Australia Stained Glass Supplies
Sydney
asgs.com.au

Perth Art Glass
Perth
perthartglass.com.au

The Lead Light Workshop
Kempsey
theleadlightworkshop.com.au

Japan

Merry Go Round Glass
Hyogo
merrygoroundglass.com

Jujo Glass
Nagoya
jujo.net

Favorite Glass Manufacturers

Bullseye Glass
Alameda, CA; South Pasadena, CA; Portland, OR; Santa Fe, NM; Mamaroneck, NY
bullseyeglass.com

English Antique Glass
Oxfordshire, England
englishantiqueglass.co.uk

Fremont Antique Glass
Seattle, WA
fremontantiqueglass.com

Kokomo Opalescent Glass
Kokomo, IN
kog.com

Lamberts Glass
Waldsassen, Germany
lamberts.de

Monarch Glass Studio
Kansas City, MO
monarchglassstudio.com

Oceanside Glass
Vista, CA
oceansidecompatible.com

Tatra Glass
Loughborough
tatraglass.co.uk

Wissmach Glass
Paden City, WV
wissmachglass.com

Youghiogheny Opalescent Glass
Connellsville, PA
youghioghenyglass.com

Other Resources

Stained Glass Association of America
stainedglass.org

Simple conversion chart
1/4 in = 0.6 cm
1/2 in = 1.25 cm
1 in = 2.5 cm
5 in = 12.7 cm
1 yard = 0.9 m

RESOURCES & SUPPLIES

PHOTO CREDITS

Photographs by Neile Cooper, except as noted below

Illustrations and editing by Robert Giaquinta

Pages 5, 8 (top), 15, 17, 19 (both), 21 (bottom), 22, 32, 35 (bottom left), 40 (top), 44, 45, 207 (bottom): **Nicole Bedard Photo & Video**

Pages 6, 14, 203, 208: **Kim Edwards**

Pages 7 (bottom): **The Metropolitan Museum of Art, New York, Tiffany Studios**

Pages 9 (bottom left), 92, 93: **Laure Forêt**

Page 10 (bottom): **Saddie Kendall**

Pages 58, 59: **Carolyne Heppenstall**

Pages 72, 73: **Chevonne Ariss**

Page 84: **Masako Ozaki**

Pages 138, 139: **Rebekah Marxen**

Pages 154, 155: **Gertrude Dufeudedieu**